EXPERIENCING
GOD
AT HOME

EXPERIENCING
GOD
AT HOME

TOM & RICHARD
BLACKABY

B&H
PUBLISHING GROUP
Nashville, Tennessee

978-1-4336-7982-7

Published by B&H Publishing Group
Nashville, Tennessee

Tom Blackaby and Richard Blackaby are represented by the literary
agency of Wolgemuth & Associates, Inc.

Dewey Decimal Classification: 649
Subject Heading: PARENTING \ CHILD REARING \ GOD

Unless otherwise stated, all Scripture references are taken from the
New King James Version (NKJV), copyright © 1979, 1980, 1982,
Thomas Nelson, Inc., Publishers.

Also used: the Holman Christian Standard Bible® (HCSB), Copyright
© 1999, 2000, 2002, 2003, by Holman Bible Publishers. Used by
permission. Holman Christian Standard Bible®, Holman CSB® and
HCSB® are federally registered trademarks of Holman Bible Publishers.

Also used: New American Standard Bible (NASB), © the Lockman
Foundation, 1960, 1962, 1963, 1968, 1971, 1972, 1973, 1975, 1977,
used by permission.

1 2 3 4 5 6 7 8 • 17 16 15 14 13

Dedication

Richard

I'd like to dedicate this book to the many moms and dads I have met over the years who sincerely want their children to experience God's best for their lives. Don't give up on the children and family you know God wants you to have! Thanks also to my wife, Lisa, who has been such an amazing mom, and to Mike, Daniel, and Carrie, who make me proud and bring me joy every day.

Mike, Sarah, Richard, Lisa, Sarah, Daniel, Carrie, and Sam

Tom

I wish to thank my parents and grandparents who have gone before me to lay such a great foundation for me to follow as a parent. And thanks also to my wife, Kim, and three children—Erin, Matt, and Conor—for their patience with me as husband and dad and for being the family I always wanted to have.

Erin, Tom, Kim, Matt, and Conor

Contents

1. Introduction: Setting the Stage   1

2. Biblical Overview   8

3. Our Home   24

4. Richard's Family: A Study in Contrasts   32

5. Tom's Family: Leading by Example   41

6. The Seven Realities of Experiencing God   48

7. Roles Parents Play   62

8. God Is Always at Work around Us   75

9. God Calls Us into a Love Relationship   90

10. God Invites Us to Become Involved with Him
    in His Work   107

11. God Speaks by the Holy Spirit through the Bible, Prayer,
    Circumstances, and the Church to Reveal Himself,
    His Purposes, and His Ways   127

12. God's Invitation for You to Work with Him Always Leads
    You to a Crisis of Belief That Requires Faith and Action   142

13. You Must Make Major Adjustments in Your Life to Join
    God in What He Is Doing   157

14. You Come to Know God by Experience as You
    Obey Him and He Accomplishes His Purposes
    through You   172

15. Getting Your Family on the Right Track   187

16. Developing a Godly Legacy   203

17. Blessing Other Families   220

Conclusion: Helping Your Family Experience God Today   233

About the Authors   239

CHAPTER 1

Introduction: Setting the Stage

The fact that you are reading this book suggests you probably want to be a great parent or grandparent. You might also be concerned about whether each of your children will grow up to love and honor God. Unfortunately, today there is a lot to be concerned about! Parenting has never been an easy task. However, the world in which we are raising our children today contains ubiquitous temptations, pressures, and dangers unlike anything our parents could have dreamed of when they were raising us. We live in an age when we desperately need God's help if we are going to succeed in raising our children to become godly young adults.

Though this book is written from the context of modern American culture, the principles God uses when working with families are not limited to a particular era or cultural context. God's standards for the home remain the same, regardless of the generation or culture. The application of those principles will be unique to each home, but they have proven effective time and again as a means of building God-honoring homes and spiritually healthy families.

In this book we will apply the Seven Realities outlined in *Experiencing God: Knowing and Doing the Will of God* to the crucial task of raising children. To be honest, we have written numerous books before, but it has taken a long time for us to feel comfortable enough to write this particular one. There are several reasons. For one, while we have been leaders in numerous settings, being a parent has been one of the most challenging assignments we have ever undertaken. We have collected a bucketful of lessons on what not to do! However, we have always believed that if there was one thing we wanted to "get right," it was to be a good parent. To that end we have spent the last three decades learning everything we could on the subject, regardless of how painful some of those lessons were! We have finally come to the place where we believe we have gained some valuable lessons that need to be shared with other parents. Second, we wanted to wait until our own children had successfully "survived" our parenting failures before we ventured to put our thoughts on the subject down in writing! Both of us are married to our first wives and we each have three children (ages thirteen, nineteen, twenty, twenty-two, twenty-five, and twenty-seven). You'll hear more about them later, but as of today they are all walking with the Lord and doing great. We sincerely hope that the truths you learn in the following pages will result in a profound blessing for your family.

Throughout this book, we'll refer to our families. Often we do this not because we believe our families or our parenting skills ought to necessarily be emulated, but because we want to show how we have implemented biblical principles in our own homes. Our children provided the laboratory for our child-rearing research! (They may have wished we had used mice!) In this book, we'll relate to you some of our successes. Sometimes we got it right! But we'll also share some of our failures. The key is not so much what we did but the biblical principles we learned and experienced.

The Current Situation

As we begin, let's quickly review the context in which we are raising our children. The following statistics and summary statements are fairly current to the publication of this book. They were taken from a variety of research organizations, government sources, and Christian organizations that pertain to the family in North America. See if is anything surprises you.

Family Statistics

Marriage/Divorce

- Sixty-five percent of kids grow up in a home with two married parents, and 35 percent of all children in North America are affected by divorce.[1]
- Only 45 percent of children grow up in a home with both of their biological parents.[2]
- Divorce rate: in US 46 percent, in Canada 43 percent.[3]
- Living common-law increases the chance of a marital breakdown by 50 percent. Marriages preceded by a common-law union are distinctly less stable than those that began at the altar.[4]
- Religious belief decreases the chance of divorce. People who attend religious services during the year have between a 10 percent and 31 percent lower divorce rate.[5]
- In general, the predicted likelihood that a marriage will succeed is higher for people who marry in their thirties, did not live common-law before the wedding, have children, attend religious services, are university educated, and believe that marriage is important if they are to be happy.[6]
- Problems experienced by children of divorced couples:
  - Increased alcohol and marijuana use
  - Greater likelihood of problems with peers and authority figures
  - Less likely to marry and more likely to divorce
  - Twice as likely to experience anxiety, depression, and self-esteem issues

Bullying in Schools[7]

- One in four teens are bullied; one out of five kids admits to being a bully or doing some "bullying."
- As many as 160,000 kids stay home on any given day because of bullying. Fifteen percent of all school absenteeism is directly related to fears of being bullied at school.
- Forty-three percent of students fear harassment in the bathroom at school.

- Each month 282,000 students are physically attacked in secondary schools.
- Forty-three percent of kids have been bullied while online. Ninety-seven percent of middle-school students admit to being bullied while online.
- Every seven minutes a child is bullied. One out of every ten students who drops out of school does so because of repeated bullying.
- Every thirty minutes a teenager attempts suicide due to bullying. The leading cause of death among children under the age of fourteen is suicide. *Bullycide* is the new term for suicide as a result of being bullied.[8]

Rates of Obesity

- One out of three kids are considered overweight or obese.[9]

Internet Addiction

- Cybersex Addiction—compulsive use of Internet pornography, adult chat rooms, or adult fantasy role-play sites impacting negatively on real-life intimate relationships.
- Cyber-Relationship Addiction—addiction to social networking, chat rooms, and messaging to the point where virtual, online friends become more important than real-life relationships with family and friends.
- Net Compulsions—such as compulsive online gaming, gambling, stock trading, or compulsive use of online auction sites such as eBay often result in financial and job-related problems.
- Information Overload—compulsive web surfing or database searching, leading to lower work productivity and less social interaction with family and friends.
- Computer Addiction—obsessive playing of off-line computer games, such as Solitaire or Minesweeper, or obsessive computer programming.[10]
- Internet Porn Stats:
  - The largest consumer of Internet pornography is the twelve to seventeen age group.[11]

- ○ The average age of first Internet exposure to pornography is eleven years old.[12]
- ○ Twenty-one percent of teens say they have looked at something on the Internet that they wouldn't want their parents to know about.[13]
- ○ Seventy percent of sexual advances over the Internet happened while youngsters were on a home computer.[14]

Sex

- Forty-two percent of high school students admitted to having sex without a condom.[15]
- The abstinence education program *Choosing the Best* is 47 percent more effective at delaying a teen's first sexual encounter than condom-promoting sex education programs.[16]
- Adolescents who take virginity pledges are less likely to experience teen pregnancy, are less likely to be sexually active while in high school and as young adults, are less likely to give birth as teens or young adults, are less likely to give birth out of wedlock, are less likely to engage in unprotected sex, and will have fewer sexual partners.[17]

Understanding This Generation

The statistics are sobering. We don't need to convince you that the Internet, smartphones, and Wi-Fi are dramatically altering the parenting playing field. Children are growing up being bombarded with Internet messages and advertisements. We know a church youth minister who did an experiment. He randomly texted six teenagers from his youth group at 9:15 a.m. on Monday. That was thirty minutes into their first class period when all cell phones are to be turned off. He received answers from all six students in less than two minutes! Your children are living in a world filled with temptations, pressures, and bullying that you never dreamed of when you were their age.

The problem for our families, however, is not necessarily that society has become technologically saturated. The real issue is that society has grown from being secular to being increasingly anti-Christian. Today, public schools teach curriculum that often mocks Christian beliefs and values. Modern society does not obtain its views of the family, morality, or sexuality from the Bible. Rather, modern society upholds that people are free to do whatever they want—with exceptions, of course. If an artist wants to exhibit a grotesque picture that blasphemes Jesus Christ, it is praised as a work of art. But increasingly, putting out a manger scene at Christmas is being condemned as bigoted and hateful. Today, celebrities are enthusiastically cheered when they promote same-sex marriage, but if a business donates money to support healthy marriages between men and women, they run the risk of being boycotted. Our children are growing up in a society that is becoming increasingly *anti*-Christian. This will have profound consequences for our parenting.

In the midst of the rapid secularization of society, many parents sincerely want to raise their children to love and serve God. Many Christian parents yearn for their children to grow up experiencing God's blessing on their lives. Though the challenges are many, solutions *are* available. In fact, the blacker the pitch that society reaches, the more determined God is to use Christian families as lights on a hill (Matt. 5:14–16). God is just as interested in working through families today to extend His kingdom as He was with Abraham, Isaac, Jacob, Jesse, Mary, and Joseph.

In the following pages, we will give you tools to help your family be God-centered, God-directed, and God-blessed as you navigate through the many obstacles and challenges your family is facing. As you read the following pages, ask God to open your heart and mind to how He wants to guide and enable you to experience God's best for your family.

Questions for Reflection/Discussion

1. If you were to rate the current health of your family on a scale of 1 to 10, what number would you give it? Why?

2. Of all the issues identified in this chapter, which one concerns you most for your family?

3. What is one way you are using technology for the benefit of your family?

4. What is one way you find technology detrimental to your family life today?

5. In what ways are the Christian beliefs and values of your family currently being attacked? How might you better prepare your children for what they will be facing in a secular society?

Notes

1. See http://www.childstats.gov/americaschildren/famsoc.asp.

2. Susan Jones, "Fewer than Half of American Children Growing Up In Intact Families, Survey Says," CNS News (December 15, 2012), http://cnsnews.com/news/article/fewer-half-american-children-growing-intact-families-survey-finds.

3. See http://www.separation.ca/pdfs/divorcefacts.pdf.

4. See http://www.statcan.gc.ca/pub/11-008-x/2006001/9198-eng.htm.

5. Ibid.

6. Ibid.

7. See http://2011bullyingprogram.weebly.com/bullying-statistics.html.

8. See http://www.risk-within-reason.com/2012/03/06/bullying-facts-statistics.

9. See http://kidshealth.org/parent/general/body/overweight_obesity.html.

10. See http://www.helpguide.org/mental/internet_cybersex_addiction.htm.

11. Internet Pornography Statistics. Internet Filter Review, 2004.

12. Ibid.

13. "A World of Their Own," *Newsweek,* May 8, 2000.

14. "One in Five Kids Has Been Propositioned for Cybersex," *Legal Facts*, vol. 2, No. 3, 2000.

15. "Teens, Sex, & the Media," *Media Scope*, 2001.

16. Centers for Disease Control and Prevention, November 2004, www.cdc.gov.

17. Robert Rector, Kirk Johnson, and Jennifer Marshall, "Teens Who Make Virginity Pledges Have Substantially Improved Life Outcomes," The Heritage Foundation, September 21, 2004.

CHAPTER 2

Biblical Overview

The Greatest Challenge You May Ever Face

Think about the challenges you have faced personally in your life so far. Perhaps you had to overcome a serious illness. Maybe you grew up in a dysfunctional or abusive home. You may have been called upon to face a crisis or to start your own company. Perhaps you have cheered for a perennially losing sports team, and all of your friends make fun of you. . . . Life is filled with challenges. We contend that one of the greatest tasks you can ever undertake is the responsibility of raising up sin-prone, naturally self-centered children in a world filled with destructive allurements and pressures so that they turn out to be godly men and women. Simply put: raising children is one of the most challenging, yet rewarding undertakings on the planet.

Ronald Reagan is considered one of the better American presidents in the last century or so. He took on the Soviet Union in the midst of the Cold War. Through his leadership, the Iron Curtain collapsed. Developing a cordial relationship with Mikhail Gorbachev represented a herculean feat. Yet during that same time, Reagan was stymied by a strained relationship with his daughter, Patti. Reagan could take on his nation's most dangerous enemy successfully, but no amount of diplomatic skills could seemingly bring reconciliation with his own offspring. Sadly, this is true of many parents.

We conduct spiritual leadership conferences across America.[1] During a break at one meeting, a distinguished looking pastor who appeared deeply troubled approached us. We had been discussing how to be a spiritual leader in your home, church, and workplace. He had been a pastor for twenty-five years and was widely recognized as having successfully led some of the largest churches in his denomination. Still, he appeared deeply troubled.

He related to us that, while he had indeed enjoyed a stellar ministerial career, he was brokenhearted over his family. He had four children. He had led them to go to church every Sunday and to be heavily involved in its children's and youth programs. Yet now, as young adults, not one of them attended church. Two of them had renounced their belief in God altogether. He felt like a failure as a parent and as a leader. How could he continue to provide spiritual leadership to his congregation when he had failed so miserably to guide his own children?

Sadly, this man's experience is far from unique. Everywhere we go we meet grieving parents and grandparents who suffer daily from the knowledge that their offspring have rejected their most important values and beliefs. Some studies indicate that roughly 70 percent of children who grow up attending church with their family will walk away from church—and often God—when they become teenagers and young adults.[2] Churches today are filled with people who suffer regret, remorse, and resignation because of how their children turned out. As in every situation in life, it is always best to begin our understanding of parenting by looking at what Scripture says about the subject.

Parents in the Bible

The Bible is the most popular book ever written, and in terms of sales and readership, no book has sold more widely or been read by more people. There are numerous reasons for this. For one, God is the Author. Talk about a publishing coup, having the Creator of the universe put some of His thoughts down on paper! Second, the Bible is brimming with wisdom that has been tested and proven through the millennia. When you do what it says, you invariably live a blessed life! A third reason is that it is filled with compelling, exciting, and even romantic stories. It has something for everyone! But what makes the book so gripping is that it is brutally honest. It tells it like it is. It doesn't gloss over the mistakes and failures of its main characters. It shows us the heights to which God can raise people as well as the depths to which sin can plunge them. We know people such as Moses, David, and Peter as great heroes of the faith. But the Bible also concedes that Moses was a murderer, David an adulterer, and Peter a denier. Perhaps that's what makes the Bible such compelling reading. It tells the stories of ordinary people we can readily relate to. It reminds us that even the greatest saints in the Bible had feet of clay. And, just as God's grace was sufficient for the fallible humans who lived before us, it is equally capable of helping us overcome our own shortcomings and disappointments.

What is surprising about the Bible is this: despite the obvious importance that God places on the family, it is not as easy to find examples of good parents in the Bible as you might think. It is alarming how even some of the best-known men and women in the Bible fell short in the crucial area of being a good mom or dad. This becomes painfully obvious when we look at some of the parents in the Bible.

God

The first father figure we come across in the Bible is God Himself. Jesus told us to talk to Him by saying: "Our Father in heaven . . ." (Matt. 6:9). The first two people the heavenly Father parented were Adam and Eve. God provided them a delightful environment in which to live (Gen. 2:8–9). He supplied all of their physical needs (Gen. 2:18–22; 3:21). God spent regular quality time with them (Gen. 3:8-9). He offered them wise counsel on how to live an abundant life (Gen. 2:16–17). He also gave them responsibility (Gen. 1:26, 28). No father ever provided as much for his children or was more loving toward them than God was to Adam and Eve. Yet how did they respond? They chose to reject Him and His counsel. They became alienated from Him and even tried to hide from Him (Gen. 3:8). Ultimately their sin caused them to be separated from the beautiful home God had provided for them (Gen. 3:23). The first family in history experienced disaster!

Adam and Eve

Adam and Eve were the only two humans who ever experienced what it was like to be perfect. Unfortunately, by the time they became parents, they had allowed sin into their home. Once sin enters a family, it is insidious in its destructive power. The first parents had walked with God in the garden of Eden! They had perfect bodies that weren't filled with hereditary diseases and artificial preservatives. They had energy! Yet how did their children turn out? Well, their oldest, Cain, struggled in his relationship with God and with his younger brother Abel. This led Cain to eventually murder his sibling and live the remainder of his life in exile from his family (Gen. 4:1–15). The first children in history experienced disaster.

Noah

By God's own reckoning, Noah was the godliest man on the planet. Scripture declares: "Noah was a just man, perfect in his generations. Noah walked with God" (Gen. 6:9). When God determined to obliterate humanity from the face of the earth because of its grotesque sin, He went to great lengths to spare Noah and his family. Yet once the flood had subsided and Noah and his sons had become farmers, a family scandal occurred. Noah's son Ham humiliated his father in front of his brothers (Gen. 9:20–23). For the remainder of Ham's life, he lived under the curse of his father (Gen. 9:24–27). How could a man as righteous as Noah raise a son as disrespectful as Ham?

Abraham

By the time we come to Abraham, we feel we are in safer parental territory. After all, he is the founder of a line of patriarchs! From his descendants will ultimately emerge the nation of Israel and the Messiah. God made a covenant with Abraham that from his family all the families of the earth would be blessed (Gen. 12:1–3). Abraham raised Isaac, who would ultimately become a patriarch himself.

Yet even though he is upheld as a man of faith, not all of Abraham's parenting decisions should be used as a model of wisdom. God instructed him to leave his family in Haran and to go to a new land (Gen. 12:1). Yet Abraham inexplicably brought his nephew Lot with him (Gen. 12:4). This decision would lead to much grief and heartache in the ensuing years (Gen. 13:5–13; 14:12–17; 19). Then there was the time Abraham's faith wavered, and he took matters of becoming a father into his own hands. He had a son, Ishmael, through a woman who was not his wife. This son would become the father of the Arab peoples and engender much conflict with the Israelites for generations afterward (Gen. 17:18–25). Abraham would also lie about his wife, Sarah, claiming she was his sister (Gen. 12:10–20). As if that weren't enough, Abraham succumbed to dishonesty a second time, later in his life (Gen. 20:1–18). This character flaw of dishonesty would be passed down to his son and grandson. Certainly Abraham was a man of faith and a friend of God, but he was not a perfect father.

Isaac

Few babies have been more eagerly anticipated than was Isaac! His father waited twenty-five years for him! Isaac was a devout man of God who had two sons: Esau and Jacob. Isaac followed in his father's character flaws and claimed that his wife, Rebekah was his sister, just as his father had done twice before (Gen. 26:1–11). His younger son, Jacob, conspired with Isaac's wife, Rebekah, to deceive Isaac and to cheat Esau (Gen. 27:1–29). This understandably led to a bitter division between Isaac's two sons that forced Jacob to live abroad for many years afterward. The patriarch Isaac's home was torn asunder by deception and hatred.

Jacob

Jacob was a deceiver, but he came by it honestly. Following after his father and grandfather's propensity to deceive, Jacob would also resort to deceit when looking out for his own interests. It's not surprising that Jacob's ten older sons lied to him about the fate of his son Joseph when they sold Joseph into slavery (Gen. 37:31–36). Predictably, perhaps, when the tables were turned, Joseph later deceived his brothers as well (Gen. 42:6–24). Truly the sins of the fathers are passed down through the generations (Deut. 5:9).

What is significant is that though Abraham, Isaac, Jacob, and Joseph were God's chosen patriarchs for His people, each of their homes suffered conflict. The descendants of Abraham's sons Ishmael and Isaac would wage continual warfare against each other. Isaac's sons Esau and Jacob would experience enmity, as would their descendants. Jacob committed one of the worst parenting mistakes by showing blatant favoritism to his son Joseph. This, along with Joseph's exalted view of himself, infuriated his older brothers and drove them to discard their annoying little brother (Gen. 37:3–11). Even Joseph's sons would experience a dispute (Gen. 48:17–20). These were the founders of God's people; yet their homes were often anything but tranquil and godly!

Eli

By the time we leave the Pentateuch and arrive in the book of 1 Samuel, one might think we had entered a more enlightened era of parenthood. But things only grow worse! The old prophet Eli is the high priest as we enter the book of 1 Samuel. Hannah delivered her much-prayed-for son, Samuel, to him to be cared for (1 Sam. 1:24–28). Eli must have done a stellar job with Samuel, for the boy grew up to become a mighty man of God. But Eli didn't do so well with his *own* two boys. Scripture declares that his sons Hophni and Phinehas were corrupt and "they did not know the LORD" (1 Sam. 2:12). The beleaguered Eli heard of his children's immoral behavior as well as their greed and profanity. He attempted to stop them; yet they ignored the pleading of their elderly father (1 Sam. 2:22–25). As a result, God took their lives in judgment. It seems inconceivable that the top priest in the land could produce such wicked offspring.

Samuel

If any parent should have been alert to the danger of poor parenting, it ought to have been Samuel. After all, he had witnessed firsthand the pain that two wayward sons caused his mentor Eli to suffer. You would assume Samuel would have fervently sought to raise his offspring to walk closely with the Lord. Inexplicably, Samuel neglected his children, and as a consequence his sons Joel and Abijah made Eli's sons look like choirboys! They took bribes and so perverted justice that the Israelites demanded that Samuel appoint them a king, fearing his two corrupt sons would take over after he was gone (1 Sam. 8:1–8). Samuel proved blameless in his personal conduct as Israel's leader, but he failed miserably to raise his children to follow and honor his God.

David

David was a man's man. He single-handedly fought lions, bears, and giants. He led a band of battle-hardened warriors through perilous times until he ultimately ascended the throne of Israel. He defeated his nation's enemies. He organized his people's worship. He gathered the resources to build a dazzling temple for his God. But he repeatedly failed as a father.

His son Amnon raped his daughter Tamar, yet David did nothing about it (2 Sam. 13:1–22). In revenge, Tamar's brother Absalom murdered his half brother Amnon (2 Sam. 13:28–29), but again David did nothing (2 Sam. 13:37-39). When Absalom returned to live in Jerusalem, he spent two full years in the city without his father coming to see him (2 Sam. 14:28). Later Absalom initiated a revolt against his father, David, that threw the entire nation into civil war and ultimately led to Absalom's death (2 Sam. 16–18). At the close of David's life, his son Adonijah, Absalom's brother, promoted himself to be the next king even though that position had been promised to Solomon. Yet despite this flagrant self-promotion, David did nothing to rebuke his ambitious child (1 Kings 1:6). Only when a coup was imminent did David arise and thwart the schemes of his son. Even then, there is no record that he spoke to Adonijah or sought to guide him into making wise choices with his life. David enjoyed far more successes on the battlefield than he did on the domestic front.

Kings Jehoshaphat, Hezekiah, and Josiah

A puzzling feature of so many of the godly leaders of the Bible is how they could be so righteous and yet could raise such ungodly offspring. *Jehoshaphat,* for example, was one of the godliest kings to rule Judah. His father, Asa, had been a righteous king (1 Kings 15:11). Throughout his reign, King Jehoshaphat sought to honor God and to be at peace with the kingdom of Israel, ruled by the wicked King Ahab (1 Kings 22:44). However, in his desire to make peace with his northern brothers, Jehoshaphat allowed his son Jehoram to marry the daughter of Ahab and Jezebel. In his misguided effort at alliance building, Jehoshaphat sowed the seeds of his son's apostasy. For rather than following the godly example of his father, King Jehoram modeled his reign after his wicked father-in-law, Ahab (2 Kings 8:18).

King Hezekiah was one of the godliest kings to rule Judah. His father, Ahaz, had been unfaithful to God (2 Kings 16:2) and had introduced pagan worship into Judah. Yet, Hezekiah forsook his father's wicked example and served God wholeheartedly. Scripture says of him: "He trusted in the LORD God of Israel, so that after him was none like him among all the kings of Judah, nor who were before him" (2 Kings 18:5). Yet Hezekiah's son Manasseh became arguably the wickedest king ever to rule Judah (2 Kings 21:1-18). What a contrast! Judah's godliest king produced its wickedest.

Finally we see *King Josiah*. His father, Amon, was wicked, and his grandfather, Manasseh, was even worse. Yet as a boy, Josiah had a heart for God. He attempted to purge the land of the abominations his father and grandfather had introduced. Yet at his death, his two sons, Jehoahaz and Eliakim, both did evil in the sight of the Lord (2 Kings 23:32–37). Among the kings of Judah, it seems to be the exception that a godly king produced a godly successor.

Where Are the Godly Successors?

Scripture is filled with admonitions to teach our children to follow the Lord. As the Israelites were preparing to enter the Promised Land, God instructed the parents: "And these words which I command you today shall be in your heart. You shall teach them diligently to your children, and shall talk of them when you sit in your house, when you walk by the way, when you lie down, and when you rise up. You shall bind them as a sign on your hand, and they shall be as frontlets between your eyes. You shall write them on the doorposts of your house and on your gates" (Deut. 6:6–9).

God clearly intended for parents to talk about Him with their children *all the time!* Likewise, on the day the Israelite army crossed the Jordan River and commenced their invasion of Canaan, God made them stop and build a monument at the edge of the river so that in years to come, when their children and grandchildren asked what the structure was about, they could rehearse the miracle God performed on their behalf that day (Josh. 4:8–24). God was concerned that His activity in one generation not be lost on the next.

With God being so concerned about children growing up to embrace the faith of their parents, it is surprising how many did not. Or at least it seems unusual that children of spiritual giants did not follow in their parents' footsteps. It might be that the Bible is merely silent about people's children. For instance, Moses had a son Gershom (Exod. 2:22). When Moses returned to Egypt, he took his family with him (Exod. 4:20). Yet Moses trained Joshua to take his place, while Gershom disappears from the biblical record. Perhaps Gershom died of a childhood disease, or maybe he was not gifted to lead as Joshua was. The Bible doesn't tell us. What we do know is that when Moses needed to mentor an understudy to take his place, he didn't turn to his own children.

Likewise, Joshua famously declared: "Choose for yourselves this day whom you will serve, whether the gods which your fathers served that were on the other side of the River, or the gods of the Amorites, in whose land you dwell. But as for me and my house, we will serve the LORD" (Josh. 24:15). Truly noble intentions by one of the great heroes of the Old Testament! After such a bold declaration by that generation's most famous father, you couldn't help but be curious about how his children turned out, could you? Yet we never hear about them. All we are told about their generation is this: "When all that [meaning Joshua's] generation had been gathered to their fathers, another generation arose after them who did not know the LORD nor the work which He had done for Israel" (Judg. 2:10). Of course, this doesn't mean Joshua's children left the faith of their father. Maybe they were all prematurely killed off in a freak plague. Or perhaps they tried to dissuade the apostasy of their contemporaries but to no avail. What we do know is that when their generation turned from God, Joshua's offspring did not lead their generation to follow God as their father had done.

Gideon provides yet another example. He led his fellow Israelites to cast off the oppression of the Midianites and to drive them unceremoniously from their land (Judg. 6–7). For the remainder of his life, Gideon served as a judge over the people. However, Scripture testifies: "So it was, as soon as Gideon was dead, that the children of Israel again played the harlot with the Baals, and made Baal-Berith their god" (Judg. 8:33). Not only that, but Gideon's son Abimelech slaughtered sixty-nine of his half brothers in order to seize power for himself (Judg. 9:1–6). Tragically, after God did a great work through Gideon's generation, the next generation completely rejected the God of their fathers.

At times, parenting in the Bible can be utterly confusing. For example, King David loved God and enjoyed worshipping Him. Yet two of his children conspired against him. King Saul, on the other hand, was paranoid, disobedient to God's commands, and at times suffered spells of madness. Yet his sons, including the noble Jonathan, died fighting at his side against the Philistines on Mount Gilboa (1 Sam. 31:2). It is difficult to comprehend how an imbalanced, insecure father like Saul could raise Jonathan for a son, while David, considered one of Israel's greatest leaders, could rear Amnon, Absalom, and Adonijah. But such are the peculiarities of parenting!

Our curiosity causes us to wonder what the great prophet Elisha's children were like. Their father was one of the preeminent prophets of the Old Testament. But did he pass his mantle on to them as Elijah passed his on to Elisha? What were Daniel and Nehemiah's children like? Did they follow God as fervently as their fathers? Wouldn't it be great to know what the children of the twelve disciples did in their walk with God? (Yes, we are curious about the traitor Judas's children too!) Did they become leaders in the church? Perhaps they did. The Bible doesn't say.

The Bible on Parenting

So what can we learn from this rather dismal survey of biblical parents? *Raising godly children isn't easy!* Some of the greatest men and women in the Bible failed at it miserably. Does that mean it can't be done? Of course not. But it does teach us that parents need to carefully follow the instruction and guidelines of Scripture if they are to have any hope of succeeding. Read the verses below and see some of the wisdom the Bible provides for those who want to raise godly children:

- "I call heaven and earth as witnesses today against you, that I have set before you life and death, blessing and cursing; therefore choose life, that both you and your descendants may live"

(Deut. 30:19). Clearly God wants to bless both us and our descendants if only we will heed His commandments.

- "We will not hide them from our children, telling to the generation to come the praises of the LORD, and His strength and His wonderful works that He has done. . . . That they should make them known to their children; that the generation to come might know them, the children who would be born, that they may arise and declare them to their children, that they may set their hope in God, and not forget the works of God, but keep His commandments" (Ps. 78:4–7). God intends for parents to testify to their children what God has done in their lives.
- "The wise woman builds her house, but the foolish pulls it down with her hands" (Prov. 14:1). There are certain behaviors that can build up a family, and there are other actions that tear it down. Parents must decide which ones they will adopt.
- "Train up a child in the way he should go, and when he is old he will not depart from it" (Prov. 22:6). This has been a much-debated verse over the years! But it is declaring that what we do with our children when they are young has a lasting impact. We can build values into our children that remain with them the remainder of their lives.
- "Correct your son, and he will give you rest; yes, he will give delight to your soul" (Prov. 29:17).
- "Do not withhold correction from a child, for if you beat him with a rod, he will not die. You shall beat him with a rod, and deliver his soul from hell" (Prov. 23:13–14).

The Bible never worries about being politically incorrect! It urges parents to discipline their children so they are guided away from evil behavior and steered toward godliness. Better to suffer unpleasant moments while redirecting your children's improper behavior now than to suffer the heartache of having them reject your faith and values when they are adults.

Parenting Rewards

While parenting children can be hard work, the Bible does offer the following encouragement:

- "A wise son makes a glad father, but a foolish son is the grief of his mother" (Prov. 10:1).
- "The father of the righteous will greatly rejoice, and he who begets a wise child will delight in him" (Prov. 23:24).
- "Children's children are the crown of old men, and the glory of children is their father" (Prov. 17:6).

Nevertheless, parents should also take heed:

- "He who begets a scoffer does so to his sorrow, and the father of a fool has no joy" (Prov. 17:21).

The Perfect Father

The challenge for many parents these days is that they did not grow up in a home with healthy, godly parents, so they never had a good role model. Now as parents themselves, they often find themselves unsure of what to do. They might have a sense of what *not* to do, but they may never have witnessed good parenting up close. The encouraging truth, however, is that everyone has access to the model of a perfect parent, regardless of what kind of home they came from.

The Bible tells numerous stories about individuals, but it is primarily an account about God and His interaction with people throughout the generations. During the course of the narrative, readers catch glimpses of an amazing relationship between God the Father and God the Son. Let's take a moment to reflect on how the heavenly *Father* related to His Son.

As a twelve-year-old, Jesus already had a clear sense of what His Father stood for and what was dear to His heart. In a famous incident, Jesus' parents lost track of their young Son and were unaware that He had not accompanied them on their trip from Jerusalem to Nazareth. When they asked Jesus why He had remained at the temple, He explained: "Did you not know that I must be about My Father's business?" (Luke 2:49).

When Jesus commenced His public ministry and was baptized, Scripture tells us that a voice came from heaven declaring, "This is My beloved Son, in whom I am well pleased" (Matt. 3:17). The heavenly Father affirmed His Son publicly. We can only imagine the pleasure that must have given the Son!

It is also clear throughout the Gospels that the Father continually shared with His Son what was on His heart. When Jesus was questioned about why He had chosen to heal a lame man on the Sabbath, He responded: "For the Father loves the Son, and shows Him all things that He Himself does; and He will show Him greater works than these, that you may marvel" (John 5:20). The Father and Son regularly communed with each other. In fact, Jesus prayed that His disciples would "be one as We are" (John 17:11). After experiencing spectacular success, Jesus immediately took time to talk with His Father (Mark 1:35; 6:46). When facing difficult trials, Jesus spoke with His Father (Matt. 26:36–46). In fact, Jesus' entire life was spent seeking to bring glory to His Father (John 17:1). And, when Jesus' work on earth was done, the Father seated Him in a place of honor at His side (Acts 7:55).

Throughout this book we'll examine how God instructs us to parent our children, but His own example of relating to His own Son provides the supreme model of what godly parenting looks like. And not only does God *show* us what to do; He also *enables* us to do the same in our own homes.

Water, Wind, and Fire (A Story from Tom)

Our family lived on the west coast of Norway in the city of Stavanger for seven years. Being the same latitude as Anchorage, Alaska, summer days were long as the sun shone late into the evening. However, in winter the days consisted of only a few hours of daylight. There were times when the darkness became oppressive and depressing. One spring day, after an excessively long winter, we were at church. Suddenly a beam of sunlight burst through the stained-glass window, surprising and delighting the congregation. We resolved to hold a picnic at a lake to celebrate the return of the sun. After church, we rushed home to change into our picnic clothes, grabbed some hot dogs and snacks, threw in the quick grill (aluminum one-use grill), and headed to the lake to meet our friends.

Walking from the parking lot to the lake, I noticed a few trees with long wooden boxes attached to them. These contained what looked like extra-long metal brooms with long flat pieces of metal fanning out on the end. My Norwegian friend informed me that these were "fire whappers" (or whatever the Norwegian word for it was!). We had a great day at the lake, and just as we were waiting for our coals to burn out to discard the grills, we noticed the water rippling and bubbling in the middle of the lake. I was curious about what was causing this phenomenon. Even more disconcerting was that the dancing water was moving in our direction. I asked my Norwegian friend if we should be worried. He assured me everything was fine.

I hadn't noticed that high above the rippling water there were leaves swirling around in the sky. I grew nervous when I realized there was a wind funnel bearing down on us. Before I could warn my family, the wind funnel hit shore, picking up all the loose debris, twigs, leaves, and our barbecue grills. It savagely flung them into the air, spewing hot coals all around us. The coals landed in the tall grass, and the wind instantly whipped up a grass fire. I had a split second decision to make: stay near the water until the fire burned itself away or run to safety as quickly as possible. As I was about to gather my family and scamper up the pathway to safety, I spotted an elderly Norwegian woman. She had taken her beach blanket, dipped it in the lake water, and was beating the fire. Ashamed to be running away while leaving a lone octogenarian to fight the raging blaze, I soaked my beach blanket in the lake and, together with my oldest son, began beating and stomping the fire alongside her. My wife corralled the other two, or so she thought, to a safe distance away. In the commotion, the youngest child, Conor, got loose. Out of the corner of my eye, I spotted my stroller-sized child dragging a broken tree branch near the fire. He had seen other adults using tree branches as fire whappers, and he wanted to help. Once his mother caught sight of him, she dragged him kicking and screaming back to the water. I was proud to be working alongside my sons to save the forest and the cabins from being consumed. But with the wind still churning the fire, we were fighting a losing battle.

Then an amazing thing happened. To my left and right, Norwegians began popping up out of nowhere. They came running from neighboring campsites, many of them with fire whappers in hand. We surrounded the fire, and after forty minutes working furiously alongside each other, we beat the fire out, saving the forest and several nearby homes. As the last few embers were stamped to ash, the local fire truck slowly made its way up the road. Then, just as quickly as they had appeared, with barely a nod for a job well done, the soot-faced Norwegians departed. We were exhausted, and our adrenalin was in overdrive, but we were safe.

The story of the grass fire became lore in our family. It reminded us of how quickly a crisis can descend on an unsuspecting family. It also demonstrated how important it is for parents and children to work together when problems come. Finally, it demonstrated that when you need help, God is able to provide everything you need, even if from unusual places!

Conclusion

We're not sure what your family is currently facing. Perhaps you are experiencing a period of tranquillity and laughter in your home. Or maybe you are trying to put out a raging fire. Whatever you are going through, we believe God's Word can greatly help you. Throughout this book, we'll be looking at what Scripture says about guiding and building families. But from this quick overview, we can identify several truths.

- First, parenting isn't easy! Even if you love God with all of your heart, you will need to depend on God's wisdom, strength, and guidance if you are to succeed.
- Second, the Bible has much advice to offer to those who want to raise godly children. We are wise to heed its instruction!
- Finally, while we may not have grown up in a home where we saw godly parenting being modelled, we have a heavenly Father who is prepared to help us each step of the way in raising our children.

Questions for Reflection/Discussion

1. On a scale of 1 to 10, rate your current satisfaction with where your family is with God and with each other. If you are reading this book, it may indicate that you know your family could be doing better than it is. Take a moment to pray that as you read, God will open your understanding to the fresh work He wants to do in your home.

2. On a scale of 1 to 10, rate how you are presently doing as a parent. Now, what score do you think your children would give you? At what score do you think God might rate you? How does this make you feel?

3. What has been your greatest challenge as a parent? What are you doing to meet this challenge?

4. Which parent in the Bible do you admire most? Which one do you identify with most?

5. What might be two goals you have for your family as a result of reading this book? We pray that reading this book helps you to achieve them!

Notes

1. Blackaby Ministries International, www.blackaby.org.
2. Sam S. Rainer, "Going, Going, But Not Forever Gone?" in *HomeLife* (February 2009), 62.

CHAPTER 3

Our Home

The Trek North—Moving to Saskatoon

In April 1970, our family loaded up our Volkswagen van and headed north from Southern California to Saskatoon, Saskatchewan. Saskatoon is an agrarian city sitting in the middle of the vast prairies of western Canada. When we finally arrived on that historic spring day, we drove up to Faith Baptist Church and beheld for the first time the object of our quest—a neglected, white stucco, boxlike building. The entry door overhang drooped so much you couldn't open the front doors completely. There was a hideous, zigzagging crack running down the right side of the building. But what was more disturbing was the "For Sale" sign we discovered that had been sitting prominently on the front lawn. That sign summed up the hopeless despair into which the few remaining church members had slumped prior to our parents' acceptance of their invitation. Our young family was their last hope for survival, as they had voted to disband as a congregation had we declined to come. We had no idea what we were about to experience in that little church. What happened over the next twelve years would be the foundation for a book that would significantly alter the lives of millions of people around the world.

Many people have mentioned to us how intrigued they are by our family. Our father is now an internationally respected Christian leader and author. All five of his children entered full-time Christian ministry. He is currently praying that all fourteen of his grandchildren would serve God with all of their hearts. Our family is somewhat unusual (in more ways than one!). At times people who did not grow up in Christian or healthy homes may assume families like ours must have been a domestic utopia where perfect parents used a magical formula that always resulted in God's blessing. We want to debunk that delusion! We also feel it is important to be transparent with you regarding our personal backgrounds. The family in which we grew up was far from perfect. Yet, it exerted a profound impact on us that continues to this day.

Our earliest memories as children centered on church. Worship services, Sunday school, potlucks, and friends from church were central to our lives. That wasn't unusual, considering our father was the pastor. It had not seemed terribly unusual when, in a special-called family meeting, our parents informed us we were moving to Canada. However, our dad is notoriously optimistic! During that meeting, he excitedly told us about the enormous possibilities for ministry in Canada and about the snow we would have fun playing in. However, he somehow overlooked the facts that the church only consisted of ten people, and that the church building was the biggest eyesore in the city, and the kindest description of the church parsonage was "modest." (Luckily for the church there was no Google Earth street view back then!)

Those early days in Saskatoon taught our family much about perseverance. We learned to keep our eyes on God instead of on the problems that seemed to always be lurking around the corner. We can still remember attending Sunday school in those early days of the church. An elderly British accountant taught us kids in the church basement. Every spring, the winter runoff would cause water to seep into the building. We'd arrive early Sunday mornings with our father and mop up the water on the floor. Then as our Bible lesson commenced, we watched water steadily creeping back into the room. When the water finally reached the legs of the table where we were sitting, class was dismissed!

During those days, we also discovered what a church "family" is all about. We did not have any blood relatives within a thousand miles of us, so our church family became our "cousins," "grandparents," "uncles," and "aunts."

Even though our church was never in danger of being described as a megachurch, our father was highly respected and, in the case of some of our friends, held in awe. He wasn't overbearing, demanding, or super spiritual. In fact, he had a playful side that took diabolical delight in practical jokes. (He could *not* be trusted with firecrackers!) Our church was filled with new believers, and for many of them, our father was the first pastor they had ever met. He was still developing his understanding of the biblical principles that would one day be published in the book *Experiencing God*. But even in its embryonic form, our father's biblical teaching was as riveting as it was powerful.[1] The church of our youth was a beehive of exciting activity. The lights of the church seemed to be on around the clock, every day of the week.

In the 1980s there were swarms of teenagers, university students, Bible school students, and curious visitors trafficking through the building. There were dozens of mission churches in surrounding towns to which many of our church members drove on Sundays to teach, preach, sing, play musical instruments, and lead Bible studies. It was normal for people to come to know Christ throughout the week and be introduced to the congregation on Sundays. For our family, these days were especially exciting because we remembered how close the church had come to shutting its doors. It may have been at that early time in our lives that we first realized the dramatic impact one family could make on an otherwise hopeless situation.

Serious Times and Difficult Days

One of the most challenging moments for our family during the early years in Saskatoon was when our mother became seriously ill after our baby sister was born. At the time, we were not told how close she was to dying—at one point, the doctors had informed our father they did not think they could save her life—but the memories of taking cards and flowers to her in the hospital are etched in our minds to this day. We are not sure what was going through our father's mind at that time. He had five children between the ages of a few months and ten years old, no family to help him, a church to run, kids to feed and get to school, a baby to manage, and a wife in the hospital with a life-threatening condition. He certainly would have wondered why God brought him to Canada only to have his American wife become gravely ill. However, our father's mantra has always been, "Bring your troubles to God and your faith to the people."

Our home life was one of organized chaos more than disciplined calm. There were five kids with five schedules, five sets of homework, mountains of laundry, and a veritable army to feed at every meal, including numerous guests. Complicating those issues was a meager income with which to purchase food and a dad who seemed to be gone far more than he was at home. But we felt loved and safe. And, we knew God was working in and through our little church that miraculously kept growing.

Maybe it was the long, cold (we're talking Siberia cold) winters that toughened us up. Or perhaps it was due to the fact that we sat squarely on the lower end of the middle class (or the top end of poverty level) that strengthened our resolve to trust God in the good times as well as the difficult. One thing was certain: our parents were not quitters. Our father was a man of faith who regularly put his trust in God for all to see. Perhaps he got his steady nerve from his British father who survived the horrors of the First World War. When my dad was running a Bible college, he once asked a pastor to fly four hundred miles to Saskatoon once a month to teach classes. The pastor was uncertain whether the funds would be available to cover his airfare. Ultimately the man agreed to come, saying, "Henry, I don't have the faith that the money will be there, but based on your faith, I will agree to come."

Looking back, we're not sure how our mother held it all together in those days. She was (and is) a very strong woman. During our first month in Canada, she walked straight into a burglar at 2:00 a.m. as he was entering her bedroom. (The unwary thief's ears are probably *still* ringing from that scream!) She was not perfect (we have stories, but we are sworn to secrecy!), but she was our fiercest, most reliable, and loyal supporter. She was also the best cook we knew (her homemade cinnamon buns were legendary!) and a woman of prayer. She would later return to work part-time in order to obtain some of the items our little house needed, such as a paved driveway, a microwave oven, a dishwasher, finished bedrooms in the basement, and Christmas presents. You can read her perspective on our home in her book *Experiencing God Around the Kitchen Table*.

Almost African Missionaries

The missionary spirit was instilled into us as children in our earliest memories. Our father's first church was in a high-crime neighborhood in the Bay area of San Francisco. The local police regularly called on the young preacher to help them with difficult cases (including talking a man who had barricaded himself in his house with a gun while threatening to kill his wife, into turning over his gun). Our father's second church had been victimized by two church splits. In both cases, God used him to bring the congregation back to health and vibrancy.

Then our parents attended an international mission service and were challenged to go wherever God called them to serve. In obedience, they applied to their denomination's international mission board. They were preliminarily approved to serve at a Bible college in Africa. Then a problem occurred. Richard began to suffer unexplained fainting spells. Richard's brothers like to explain that a battery of tests were performed on his brain, but they could find nothing! Doctors suspected a brain tumor. The mission board suggested our parents not proceed until the medical issue was resolved. Had it not been for Richard's health, we would have all grown up in Africa! Instead, it was during the following year that Faith Baptist Church in Canada contacted our parents, and they were redirected north instead of east. Interestingly, once our family moved to Canada, doctors ran the same tests on Richard in order to continue his treatments, but they found nothing wrong.

Growing up in pioneer missions in Saskatchewan, we learned about making sacrifices for the cause of Christ. One sacrifice was living far from relatives. Our mother's sister's family served as missionaries to Eastern Europe when the Iron Curtain was still a menacing reality. Likewise, our maternal grandparents took early retirement and set off as associate missionaries to Zambia, Africa. We regularly received "aerogram" letters from our grandparents and marvelled at how a retired couple could make such a drastic change to follow God's will for their lives.

There were the inevitable squabbles between us kids as the four boys shared bedrooms in our cramped little bungalow. Our mother attempted on many occasions to have regular family devotions with us, but with such crazy schedules, dad's travelling, and his multitudinous responsibilities with the church and its missions, we were doomed to failure. Our father used to explain that it was more important to live out his faith for his family than to merely talk about faith from a book. He believed more lessons could be learned by implementing Deuteronomy 6:4–9:

> Listen, Israel: The LORD our God, the LORD is One. Love the LORD your God with all your heart, with all your soul, and with all your strength. These words that I am giving you today are to be in your heart. Repeat them to your children. Talk about them when you sit in your house and when you walk along the road, when you lie down and when you get up. Bind them as a sign on your hand and let them be a symbol on your forehead. Write them on the doorposts of your house and on your gates. (HCSB)

While having regular family devotions or making use of devotional books is a fantastic thing to do, our parents believed the most important thing they could do for their children was to daily live out their faith before us. While we doubted at times that our parent's methods of discipline were always fair (the older children received *far* more discipline than the younger ones, despite the fact they were *much* better behaved), and though our father could definitely have been home more, and though there were various parental practices that could have been improved upon, there was never any question that our parents truly loved God with all of their heart and would do whatever He told them. That left a lasting impression on us all.

Following in Big Shoes

Growing up, we never had the nicest house on the block (we weren't even in the top 100), nor did we sport designer fashions. All the same, we children sensed there was something special about our family. It wasn't that our father was a famous author, because that wouldn't come for many more years. It was that God was *real* in our home. We had front-row seats to observe God answer our family's prayers. We witnessed lives being changed because of what God was doing through us. We experienced broken people arriving on our doorstep and leaving changed.

You would have thought we were the wealthiest people in town by the confidence we had for the future. And though we have been deeply appreciative of the way our father's book *Experiencing God* has impacted people around the globe, we can't really say we were surprised. The book simply summarized the lessons God taught our parents while we were growing up in their home. We had watched those truths changing lives for years, and we knew that once those same truths spread beyond our family and church, countless other people would feel the impact as well.

Our father missed more than one of our ball games and band concerts over the years, but he had an uncanny way of showing up when God was about to doing something powerful in the life of one of his children. He was present when each of his five children gave their lives to Christ. He baptized each of them and performed their wedding ceremonies. He was present as we each surrendered to God's call into ministry and as we walked across the stage for each of our graduation ceremonies.

Our father, now in his late seventies, deals with a variety of physical challenges and does not have the energy or stamina he once had. His voice has lost its thunder, his body is no longer a slave to his will, and his memory is increasingly selective, but his love for God remains undiminished. His determination to faithfully serve his Lord remains strong. He enjoys spending daily time with God more now than ever before. His example has been the determinative influence in each of his children's lives. If you know our father, you will recognize his influence throughout the following pages. But before we delve into those truths, we need to tell you a little about our own homes.

QUESTIONS FOR REFLECTION/DISCUSSION

1. Could you discern God's activity in your home as you were growing up? If you could, what kinds of things did God do in your childhood home?

2. What did you learn about God by watching your parents?

3. What place did the church have in your childhood home?

4. Are you more focused on your career or on raising your children right now? Are there any adjustments God wants you to make?

5. How might God want to use your family for His purposes in the future?

6. How will your children look back on their time growing up in your home?

Notes

1. At Blackaby Ministries International we have literally hundreds of cassette tapes of Henry Blackaby sermons that were recorded at Faith Baptist Church beginning in the 1970s that are being formatted into MP3 files for downloading. You can access them from our Web site at www.blackaby.net.

CHAPTER 4

Richard's Family: A Study in Contrasts

I have always believed that the key to successful parenting hinged not so much on the *process* but on the *product*. That is, parenting is not about establishing the right rules and setting the most reasonable curfews. It centers on doing whatever is required to end up with children who honor God and you. If you are looking for a list of "Ten Sure-Fire Ways to Raise Great Kids," you may be disappointed after reading this book. That's because, though the Bible offers good advice on rearing children, much of parenting must be customized to the particular family. Families are unique. They consist of individuals and particular circumstances. Consequently, parents must seek God's wisdom to know what is best for their situation. At least, that's what Lisa and I discovered.

Our Marriage

Lisa and I have been married for thirty years. It hasn't been easy! If she had grown up on the North Pole and I in Antarctica, we could not have been more polar opposite. My family put the "B" in Baptist! We can trace Baptists back in our family tree all the way to John! OK, well, not really. But there are Baptist ministers and missionaries generously sprinkled throughout numerous generations preceding mine. My father was a Baptist minister. His father was a bank manager, but he planted Baptist churches. My great grandfather was a student at Spurgeon's

College in London under Charles Spurgeon. In fact, family legend has it that one wayward relative began to indulge liberally in alcohol and died suddenly at a premature age. Everyone speculated that having descended from generations of tee-totalling Baptists, this man's genetic constitution made him unable to handle the "imbibing" he was doing, and the alcohol killed him! (Of course, that's just a rumor.) Even my mother's parents were Baptist missionaries in Africa. It is quite clear that much of what I experienced in life was passed down from generations of God-fearing, church-leading ancestors.

Lisa's family, on the other hand, were devout Catholics. When Lisa's father died, five priests officiated at the funeral. Two of my wife's aunts were nuns. In fact, when Lisa was growing up, her family predicted she would become a nun herself (a prophesy I will forever be grateful proved false).

I spent my early childhood growing up in San Francisco and Los Angeles. I have lived in cities all my life. Lisa grew up in the agricultural town of Carrot River, Canada. Its population of a thousand people boasted more grain elevators per capita than any other town in the province. Lisa grew up in the western Canadian province of Saskatchewan. I grew up in a home with four boys and one baby sister who was tacked on at the end. Lisa was raised in a family of seven girls and one brother (who was understandably upset when he had to wear hand-me-downs!).

Another major difference between us was our parents. Lisa's mother came from French Canadian roots. My mother was an American from Oklahoma. Lisa's parents mostly limited their social life to occasional bridge games with quiet friends (with eight children, they were kind of busy!). My mother is an off-the-shelf extravert who regularly fed the multitudes passing through the minister's home. Lisa's father did manual labor most of his life. He could fix or build anything. He constructed the home Lisa grew up in and would periodically add on a room when more children arrived. He never traveled on business, and Lisa has no memories of her father being away from home overnight. My father is also a Canadian, but his bank manager father never taught him how to fix anything. As a result, my dad never taught *me* how to fix anything (I only passed Industrial Arts class in high school due to the mercy and long-suffering of my teacher, who did not want to see me return for another year). Dad often traveled to fulfill speaking engagements.

I recall one mealtime where my mother prayed for our father as he was speaking in a large meeting in Texas that day. It was the first we children knew our father was gone, and he had been away all week! These divergent views of our parents would provide some challenges for Lisa and me later in life.

Lisa and I did experience a few things in common. We both grew up in loving homes where family was considered important. Both of our homes abounded with laughter. My father afflicted his children with the world's worst puns. Lisa's father could put you into hysterics with his self-depreciating humor. Lisa and I were also born into families where religious faith was central. We also both grew up in homes within sight of the poverty line! The houses we grew up in were modest (and crowded), and money was scarce. Finally, and perhaps most importantly, both of our families opened their presents on Christmas *morning* and not on Christmas Eve, as some less civilized people do!

As a young adult, I concluded that four children would be a perfect family size, so I looked for who the lucky mother was going to be! Lisa, on the other hand, had watched a rather graphic film on childbirth during a health class in high school and henceforth concluded that zero children would make a perfect family. We would have some negotiating to do!

Our personalities are also diametrically opposed. I am rather task oriented, cognitive, focused, and a long-range planner. Lisa, on the other hand, loves a party and is always coming up with ways to make ordinary living a lot of fun. She is a feeler who for years assumed she had married someone who made Spock look like an emotional basket case! She is also, well, not exactly focused. In fact, she is extremely random. I'll give you one example. She uses a weekly pill organizer for her vitamins and medications. However, she cannot bear to be enslaved to always Tuesday's meds on Tuesdays, so she will randomly take pills from whichever bin she feels like on that particular day, which of course causes problems later when she can't remember if she took her meds or not! Thankfully, she's not as random as her sister Paulette who, after hosting a party at her house, found a full pot of coffee chilling in the refrigerator. And as for long-range planning? For Lisa, delayed gratification means the time you have to wait for UPS to deliver your online purchase. So you can imagine what it was like for us when we found ourselves as parents who needed to decide how we were going to jointly rear our three children.

Our Children

Let's face it: not all children are the same. Some have colic; others coo and gurgle continuously. Some blissfully sleep through the night; others are night owls. Some kids are hyper; others are calm. Some are loud; others are quiet. Some are girls; others are boys. Our first two children were boys. They did what boys do: played hard and loud. Our friends, whose children were angelic girls, thought our offspring were barbaric! You don't get to choose your children; you only get to choose your response to them!

Mike

We named our first child Mike (well, actually Michael, but he changed it to Mike as soon as he could). Mike's entry into the world did not go smoothly. He went into distress after Lisa underwent twelve hours of labor. After an emergency C-section, Mike entered the scene. Mike was good-natured from the beginning. He was a social animal with a vivid imagination. School provided some challenges since unless he was bound with duct tape to his desk, Mike could not remain seated for more than a few seconds at a time. This brought him to the attention of his teachers on a regular basis. Let's just say Mike never heard of the "Honor Roll" during his academic career! As Mike grew older, he tried his hand at various endeavors. He played some sports: soccer and in-line hockey. We tried to introduce him to music even though Lisa and I combined could not come up with one musical bone in our bodies. He took piano and clarinet but finally found his passion: drums (sorry next-door neighbors). Mike had his struggles, just like every child. As a teenager, he commenced a quest to become "cool." He changed how he dressed, dyed his hair several different colors (some at the same time), got a piercing or two, and formed a rock band. At age eighteen he was also diagnosed with Type 1 diabetes.

Today, as I write this, Mike is twenty-seven. He finished college, earned a master's degree from seminary, and is currently working on a PhD in Apologetics. He is the college/single adult minister at First Baptist Church in Jonesboro, Georgia, and has written a book with his younger brother, Daniel, entitled *When Worlds Collide: Stepping Up and Standing Out in an Anti-God Culture.* He is also engaged to a charming young lady named Sarah. He's working on his third book and has developed into an awesome public speaker.

Daniel

Our second child, Daniel, has always chosen his own unique path through life. He was born a month premature, but that is the *only* thing he ever did early! He is a laid-back child with a fertile imagination and a stubborn streak a mile wide! Daniel ran into some major challenges during middle school. He suffered from a severe sleep disorder that eventually made it impossible for him to continue attending school. We homeschooled him in order to help him sleep as much as possible. He later struggled to know what to do after he graduated from high school, which led to a year of international travel and mission work. Daniel is a brilliant child who struggles at times to put that creative mind to work when he lacks sufficient motivation. That led to his unfortunate propensity to skip classes and to put off doing his homework until the last minute (or Jesus' second coming, whichever came first). Daniel loves music and can play almost any instrument you find in a typical church worship band. He excelled in playing hockey and loves to follow sports. He is also an English nerd and takes great delight in reading Russian classic novels. (Like I said, he hasn't had it easy.)

Along with Daniel's sleep-disorder issues, he suffered various challenges while growing up. He was pulled from two different schools because of his health. Like his older brother, Daniel had to "find himself" as a teenager. During that season of life, he grew his hair long (giving Rapunzel a run for her money), he tried a few piercings, and played in his brother's rock band.

Despite facing health issues as well as moving to a different country halfway through college, Daniel completed university. He is completing a master's degree at Golden Gate Seminary in San Francisco, is married to his sweetheart Sarah, and is helping plant his second church. He is presently coauthoring a second book with Mike and is currently writing the second novel in a fantasy trilogy series entitled The Lost

City Chronicles. He is also looking at entering a PhD program that focuses on "Christianity and the Arts."

Carrie

Just when we felt like we were getting a handle on raising boys, God sent us our princess. Sweet little Carrie has endured the unrelenting torment of her two gross older brothers. After some astute parenting techniques in which we gently steered her away from wanting to be a ninja turtle or a Jedi knight like her brothers, she embraced the finer arts of ice skating and designer clothes.

Carrie is our family's health nut. She would rather endure a waterboarding interrogation than eat a doughnut or drink a soda. She exercises continuously and has run a half marathon. Carrie's kryptonite is worry. I don't know where she got it from, as she has been lovingly nurtured all of her life. She used to worry about being away from home overnight or attempting new things. She worried throughout college about flunking even as she piled up one four-point semester after the next. Carrie loves to shop, travel, write, and did I mention shop? She graduated from college and is currently enrolled in two master's programs, one for advanced writing and the other in apologetics from a seminary. She has a fine boyfriend (don't tell *him* I said that), and she just signed a contract with a publisher to write her first book.

So that is my family, at least for the moment. No grandkids yet, not that we haven't dropped plenty of hints. Each of our adult children loves their parents and God. All three are currently enrolled in seminary and feel called into some form of Christian ministry. The *process* wasn't always easy, but we love the *product* so far! I travel a lot, and so I was often away from home. Lisa is a softhearted, nurturing mother whose solution for most of our children's problems was to give them a gift so they felt better! I had to be the "heavy" in our home, and some of our kids, especially of the male variety, needed more "heavy" than others. Nevertheless, thus far, it has been exciting to see what God has done in and through our children.

Family Principles

We'll be giving you plenty of illustrations from our parenting experiences in the coming chapters, but for now let me summarize some of the principles by which we raised our children. These are not necessarily the identical rules you should follow in your home. I will simply relate what we did in our home and the kind of family, and children, that resulted.

1. Trust God throughout the process.

Lisa and I do not hold ourselves up as parenting experts. We have made far too many mistakes to see ourselves that way! Sure, we have worked extremely hard at parenting, but we also know that other parents have too and yet have suffered major disappointments. I am grateful that my parents regularly prayed for my children. I will be forever grateful that God, in His grace, chose to do in my children's lives what their parents were unable to do.

2. Keep the rules few but nonnegotiable.

We did a couple of pretty unorthodox things as parents. Perhaps one of the most controversial is that we had very few rules! Hey, you can't rebel if there is nothing to rebel against, right? Actually, we were aiming for character, not conformity. It has been said that it was when ancient Rome had the most laws that its society was most corrupt. We figured that if we kept pushing our kids to act with character, we wouldn't have to keep telling them how to behave.

3. Respect and support family members.

This *was* nonnegotiable. If your sister was competing in an ice-skating competition, you had better be there! If your sons' rock band was performing in a downtown café, you had to show up and, if necessary, jump up and down in the mosh pit (*man* was I ever sore the next day). As important as friends are to teenagers, they generally come and go, but family remains. When a friend came between two siblings, the friend had to go.

4. Church is not an option.

There were lots of options in our home. Bedtime, as our kids got older, was one. But going to church was not. At one point when Daniel was struggling as a young teen, he was reluctant to begin going to the weekly youth event at church on Wednesday evenings. We brought him to the church and he sat in the minivan in the parking lot the first week, but he was there! (We also encouraged half the youth group to go out and visit with him until he decided to try it out the following week.)

5. Don't be too proud to get all the help you can.

Lisa and I shamelessly asked other parents what they did with their children for discipline, vacations, and Saturdays. Every time we observed a family that seemed to be having a blast together, we'd probe the parents (and sometimes their kids) and find their secret. We applied this same principle when our kids struggled. At times, even though I tried to be a good father, my kids weren't all that receptive to what I had to say to them. So, rather than hunkering down and yelling louder, I'd find some "cool" person in the church my kids *would* listen to, and I'd have *them* say it! We didn't care what people thought when we told them our children were struggling. We figured the more allies we had, the better chance we had of ultimately experiencing victory.

6. We focused on what mattered.

Again, Lisa and I broke a lot of parenting norms on this one. And this is one of those principles you definitely have to customize to your own situation. For example, having your children keep their bedrooms clean and tidy is great. But how many teenagers do you know who do that? We encouraged them to, and I made more than one "comment" along the way, especially related to how Daniel's room could provide the perfect set for the movie *Revenge of the Swamp Creatures*. Yet unless we were prepared to engage him in daily battle about making his bed and putting the clothes on the floor into the laundry, it wasn't going happen. But do you know what? Daniel never did drugs, or smoked, or drank alcohol. He played on two different worship teams and became a leader in his youth group (once we convinced him to end his boycott in the parking lot!). So what *really* mattered? That he made his bed every day, or that he loved going to church and keeping his body "clean" of unhealthy stimulants? It just seemed easier to close his bedroom door sometimes and try to ignore the strange wildlife noises emanating from his room during the night . . . and to focus instead on what really mattered. Was it important for Daniel to be responsible and to clean up after himself? Yes. Was it more important that he had a close relationship with his parents and merrily marched off to church with us each week? You bet! By the way, now that he is an adult and living in his own place, he likes things neat and tidy! (If you'd like to read more on how we did this, check out *Putting a Face on Grace: Living a Life Worth Passing On.*)

7. We sought to create a home of joy.

Lisa and I, like a lot of parents, were concerned that our children might one day grow up and reject our faith or family values. How could we prevent that? We decided it would not be by surrounding them with rules and regulations. We determined that if our children were to wholeheartedly embrace our faith, it would be because our faith and lifestyle were a lot of fun! We wanted them to see that there is no better way to live than the Christian way. After all, it is easy to rebel against rules, but how do you rebel against the joy of the Lord? So we did everything we could to ensure that our home regularly resounded with laughter. (If you'd like to read about some specific things we did, check out my book *The Seasons of God.*)

Thanks for taking a moment to learn a little about my family. Tom and I felt it was important that you know something about our homes before we jump into a discussion of how to help your family experience God. We aren't experts, but by God's grace He has granted us some success in our families.

QUESTIONS FOR REFLECTION/DISCUSSION

1. How are you and your spouse different from each other? How has that been good for your children? What challenges has that caused?

2. List the top three rules in your home. Should those be the most important, or are you missing something?

3. How are your children currently responding to your home's rules? Does God want you to make some adjustments?

4. Is there joy in your home?

5. Are any of your children currently rebelling against something in your home? If they are, what are they reacting to?

CHAPTER 5

Tom's Family: Leading by Example

I took my time finding a good wife. I suppose I was picky and held out for the best one I could find. Kim and I married the month I turned thirty after I finished my college and seminary education. We both have degrees in education and share similar backgrounds, such as family values, the way we celebrate holidays, some favorite foods, a love of music, and an interest in travel. We both grew up in homes that liked to laugh and have fun. But we brought some differences into our marriage as well. All of my relatives were churchgoers, and many of them were pastors, missionaries, or church leaders. Kim's family had only a handful of churchgoers, and most were in business or farming. Kim brought to our marriage elegance, a love of reading, high academic standards, goal setting, a deep desire to always do her best, and a talent for creating a welcoming home. I brought the knowledge of how to fix and repair things (more or less—OK, mostly less), five musical instruments, and a love of her amazing cooking. She brought books; I brought tools. She contributed a sense of decorum; I instilled a sense of silliness. What was special for both Richard and me was that our father baptized our wives and was also their pastor for several years.

My Children

I'll be referring to my children from time to time in this book, so I'd like to formally introduce them to you here.

Conor the Courageous

My son Conor just turned thirteen and is heading down that slippery teenage slope. He enjoys music and sings in an audition children's choir, plays piano, and has been regularly asked to play the national anthem on the keyboard for his school assemblies (because no one else has the courage to do it). He used to talk about being a pilot when he grew up but now thinks managing a hotel would be a far more interesting career. He is a decent athlete, has a sharp sense of humor, and if we can overcome his passive-aggressive nature, I think he will turn out great. Conor will be the one to inherit all of my tools because he likes to fix things and figure out how they work, a trait he gets from his dad. Lastly, he has a quick wit and is extremely observant of what goes on around him, choosing to learn from other people's mistakes rather than making them himself.

Matthew the Conqueror

My son Matthew (Matt) has always had more than his share of testosterone. Some days we would tell him to go outside and run around the house twice, and then when he came back in panting, he would ask, "Now what?" Matt never had an awkward stage, and his superior height and athletic abilities led him to excel in basketball and soccer. He became the captain of both teams in high school. He has drawers bulging with "Player of the Game" T-shirts, shelves of trophies, ribbons, medals, plaques, and awards that bear testimony to his competitiveness. This past year he realized his dream when he accepted a partial scholarship to play as a guard at Trinity Western University. He managed to be the co-valedictorian in high school and score a number of academic and sports scholarships to help with college tuition. He has a wonderful ear for music (keyboard, drums) and a keen analytical mind. He keeps toying with the idea of one day becoming a pastor but currently is pursuing a degree in political science.

Erin the Pathfinder

Our daughter Erin was our firstborn and a perfect angel. Frilly dresses, dollhouses, pinks and purples, and lots of craft supplies filled her bedroom. Erin never complained or rebelled. She cheerfully obeyed and loved giving handmade gifts to her parents. It is dangerous to always assume everything is OK just because your child doesn't complain. We learned this lesson with Erin. She loves to shop, go to concerts, hang out with friends, and watch British dramas (*Dr. Who*, *Downton Abbey*). She hates it when someone is unhappy. She loves college. She also has a wonderful singing voice, plays piano, has a quick wit, and possesses a quirky sense of style that works well for her. When she finishes her degree in corporate communications, some company will be lucky to hire her.

Kim: The Glue That Keeps Us All Together

Kim, my wife, did not grow up going to church or with God at the center of her home life. She had to find her own way with God. As a teenager, she felt led to my father's church. She is a voracious reader and pursuer of God. You name the Bible study; she has probably done it, if not taught it. She has a sensitive heart for women at the church, so our family holiday dinners usually include a single mom or two and their children around our table. She is constantly going for coffee with people, praying with people, leading women's Bible studies, or preparing to lead a study. Her commentaries, study Bibles, books, and notes are usually evident when you visit our house. To me she embodies what a godly woman looks like. She lives what she believes. Both our home and ministry in churches have always been a partnership. Much of my success as a minister over the years is due to her prayers, service to others, and godly advice along the way.

High Expectations

We didn't want to be overbearing or unreasonable in our expectations for our children. Although we had high standards for their behavior, we encouraged them to express their individuality and to pursue their own interests. Honestly, who likes a bunch of rules forced on them?

We never posted rules on the refrigerator and didn't hand out rewards for good behavior. We are a family driven by love for one another. Clear expectations have helped us get there, but they have never been our primary focus. Much like God's family, the rules are there to help us enjoy life and to avoid trouble. In our family, as in God's, the priority has always been the love relationship, not the rules. The unwritten rules in our house are pretty simple.

1. Show respect toward one another.

We did not permit name-calling, lying, stealing, bullying, unreasonable teasing, or sarcasm. Our children were expected to: let others finish speaking before replying, not speak negatively about a sibling to a friend, and not gang up against each other. As parents, we knew we needed to demonstrate the kind of respect we expected our children to show us.

2. Family takes priority.

We encouraged our children to support each other's interests and activities as much as possible. We attended basketball games, piano concerts, choir performances, soccer games, and special events whenever we could. Sometime friends last a lifetime, but those are rare. I wanted my kids to understand that friends will come and go but family remains. I remind them not to treat their brother, sister, or parents in a way that they will have to apologize for later when they are adults.

3. God is the center of our home.

The debate in our home was never about whether we would go to church or not, but about what was appropriate to wear when we arrived. I asked Erin recently why she never resisted going to church when she was younger. She replied, "I never knew that was an option! Was I supposed to give you trouble?" In our home, God's name is used in prayers, discussions about theology, or in a respectful manner, but not in an empty or vain manner. I told my children that they could use whatever curse words they heard me say. So far I have not given them any ammunition! In our home, parents and kids are held to the same standards.

4. Home is a safe place.

People are always welcome in our home. Many of my children's friends come from broken homes or families in which the parents are at work when the children arrive home from school. We wanted our house to be a gathering place for our kids and their friends. Our house is not large, but it is comfortable and open for people to drop by. That being said, it is a shared space by all of us. We expect each family member, regardless of age, to clean up after themselves and to respect one another's property and personal space. We don't own a lot, but what we do possess we'd like to preserve for as long as possible.

5. Dinnertime is important.

We value eating together as a family, and only recently as our kids' work and basketball schedules interfered have dinnertimes been missed. We did not watch TV during supper except for the Olympics and other special occasions. Whenever one of our family members was absent from dinner, they were missed. We laugh, tease, joke, inform, and connect with one another during meals. Today, as our kids have crazy work and practise schedules, we have mandated Sunday lunches as family time and keep them sacrosanct.

6. Strive for good character.

We expected our kids to honor the curfew, be trustworthy and honest, and to stick to their convictions. My children understood that their character and trustworthiness determined whether or not I granted them certain privileges, like driving the car. I asked others about their driving habits. Continued positive reports allowed for repeated opportunities. My children were routinely reminded that every decision they made had a consequence—some would be positive, and sadly, others would be negative. I prayed that they would make wise decisions so they could enjoy the ensuing rewards. Periodically, other parents would comment on how well behaved my kids were. Of course, I was always proud to hear those comments, and I would always relay them to my children so they knew that others were noticing their character as well. I had a good chance to talk with one of my sons about the rewards of good character when he was invited to join another family for a week's skiing in the Austrian Alps! (Good character has its rewards!)

7. We're a family; everyone helps out.

Everyone had a role to play in our family. Family members were expected to do their chores without complaining and to pitch in when needed. Helping kids appreciate the effort required to keep a family functioning is important. It will certainly help them later when they move out on their own. Doing laundry, cleaning up, washing dishes, vacuuming, washing the car, pulling weeds, mowing the lawn—someone has to do all these things—and kids may as well learn how sooner than later so they are fully prepared to enter the world as responsible adults. We are a family, and families work together.

8. Clear communication is important.

This has become more important to me as my hearing gets worse, but clearly communicating with family members is highly valued in our home. Over the years my wife has used a *lot* of "sticky notes" left on the microwave to remind various family members of what they needed to know or do. Now we have text messages, e-mails, and Facebook in addition to answering machines and phones. I have helped my kids mean what they say and say what they mean.

9. Try to make a difference in other people's lives.

We have made it a priority to welcome hurting, lonely, and overlooked people into our home. Perhaps this is the "pastor" coming out in me, but it warms my heart when our kids include newcomers in their activities. I don't want to raise selfish, self-centered children, and when I see that sinister trait creeping in, I address it quickly. One day I took my son Matt with me to help a woman move out of her home and into an apartment. Matt asked why we were doing it. I explained that this woman's husband was an alcoholic who mistreated her. She had no family to help her, so we were going to be her family. Ten years later, this woman still remembers that day clearly and considers us her family.

These family rules must make sense to our kids, for they have not only embraced them, but they see where some of their friends' families could use similar expectations in their homes. For a school assignment last year, Conor wrote: "If I was in charge of my family for a day, I would hand over my privilege back to my parents because that would be too much for me to handle. There aren't many rules that I would make because all the rules that I would make are already in progress. My family is big and happy. I wouldn't change any rules."

By the grace of God, our parenting must be working. All three kids (so far) are doing well in school, sports, music, and church. They are generally responsible, helpful, respectful, dependable, and fun to be around. I suppose the fact that three families have asked us to be legal guardians for *their* children means our home is attractive. We are *not* a perfect family with perfect parents and perfect kids. But that is why the truths that follow are so compelling. They work with imperfect families! If they could help our family thrive, I know they can bless your family too.

Questions for Reflection/Discussion

1. What would you like your family to look like ten years from now? What specific actions are you taking to make that a reality?

2. Do you need to make any changes in how your children or their parents relate to one another to head off troubles in the coming years?

3. What is one thing you really like about your family relationships? What is one thing that needs to change in your home to increase your love and respect for one another?

CHAPTER 6

The Seven Realities of Experiencing God

When Henry Blackaby first wrote *Experiencing God,* the material startled thousands of Christians. Many people confessed that they had attended church all of their life; yet studying *Experiencing God* made them realize they had been practicing *religion* but not enjoying a *relationship* with God. These people attended church services weekly, but they were not encountering the living God. They completed their Bible readings but never heard God speak to them through His Word. They said prayers but never heard God's answer. They were in a relationship with Christ, but it was lifeless, stagnant, and boring. Then they learned that God is a Person who is actively at work in their world and who wants them to enjoy a loving, dynamic, life-changing relationship with Him. This truth radically changed their Christian life.

In this chapter, we want to outline the foundational truths of *Experiencing God,* known as the "Seven Realities." In the remaining chapters we'll apply these realities specifically to your family. Our father wrote *Experiencing God* as a result of extensive Bible study as well as reflecting on his own experience walking with God. As we have described already, he assumed the pastorate of a struggling church in Saskatoon, Canada. The congregation had only ten members remaining when he arrived. Yet God granted that church a vision for starting congregations across that vast province. Apart from God's guidance and provision, such an undertaking was ludicrous. The impoverished congregation trusted God to provide every resource required to call mission pastors for the new churches. Over the next twelve years, God led that church and its missions to initiate thirty-eight new mission churches and its missions to launch a Bible college to train pastors. God's active guidance and provision are the only explanation for what ensued. When our father put to paper what he learned about God, based on his experience, he developed the following seven realities.

Reality 1. God Is Always at Work around You

Eternal God has been working through the ages to accomplish His divine purposes. He chose to create the universe, and it was so. He decided to create people with whom He could enjoy fellowship, and it was done. When humanity sinned and rebelled against Him, God initiated a redemptive plan to restore people into a relationship with Him once more. Speaking of Himself, God declared: "I am God, and there is none like Me. Declaring the end from the beginning, and from ancient times things that are not yet done, saying, 'My counsel shall stand, and I will do all My pleasure.' . . . Indeed I have spoken it; I will also bring it to pass. I have purposed it; I will also do it" (Isa. 46:9–11). Whether you are aware of it or not, God is continually working around you to accomplish His will.

- He is constantly working to draw people to Himself through the activity of the Holy Spirit (Jer. 31:3; John 16:8–11).
- God uses circumstances to bring people to a place where they call upon Him for help and guidance (Jon. 1:4; Acts 9:3–5).
- God is always at work convicting people of their sin so they seek salvation and freedom (John 16:8).
- God is always working to conform believers into the image of His Son (Rom. 8:28–30).
- God works through people to share the gospel with those who have not heard it (Acts 1:8).
- God's Holy Spirit is helping believers know what they should pray for (Rom. 8:26–27).

The most important factor in our world is not what *we* are doing but what *God* is accomplishing. Our focus ought not to be pleading with God in prayer to bless our plans. It should be asking God to show us what He is doing so we can adjust our lives to His activity. Oswald Chambers observed, "Spiritual insight does not so much enable us to understand God as to understand that He is at work in the ordinary things of life, in the ordinary stuff human nature is made of."[1]

This reality has perhaps been the most revolutionary truth of the seven. It encourages people to never give up, regardless of how difficult the situation may be in their family, or church, or nation. For, regardless of whether we see it or not, God is working. And what God begins, He completes (Phil. 1:6).

Reality 2. God Invites You into a Love Relationship with Himself

God's nature is love. He cannot express Himself toward you in any other manner but perfect love. Because He wants to have fellowship with you, He will invite you into a deep, intimate, growing love relationship with Him. Scripture says:

> The one who does not love does not know God, because God is love. God's love was revealed among us in this way: God sent His One and Only Son into the world so that we might live through Him. Love consists in this: not that we loved God, but that He loved us and sent His Son to be the propitiation for our sins. . . . We love because He first loved us." (1 John 4:8–10, 19 HCSB)

All that we know about love comes from God (*not* from Hollywood!). He invented it! He *is* love! God demonstrated what true love looks like by reaching out to us even as we were rejecting Him. From God we learn that love includes forgiveness because God forgave our sins. We discover that love requires loyalty and fidelity because that is what God demonstrates to His people. We experience that love can include discipline for wrongdoing because God loved us enough to allow us to feel the consequences for our sins. We realize that love requires sacrifice as we consider, with wonder, the price God was willing to pay on our behalf.

The Bible provides the historic record of God reaching out to people with love in the hope that they would respond back to Him in like manner. Those who return His love are blessed and welcomed into His kingdom. Those who reject His love choose to live outside of a relationship with Him (John 1:12; 3:18). God's ultimate expression of love for us came when Christ made the supreme sacrifice for our sins.

- We should never question God's love for us because that was settled once and for all on the cross.
- We should never question whether or not God's plan for us is in our best interest since He only acts toward us in ways that reflect perfect love.

Even when God's own people repeatedly forsook and rejected Him, He never abandoned them. Rather, God drew them back to Himself by His love. He redirected them from harm through His discipline. He provided second, third, and fourth chances through His undeterred forgiveness. God is not satisfied until people love Him with all of their heart (Mark 12:30).

God could have created human beings with the same capacity for love as lizards, cows, or vultures. Instead, God built within each of us the innate desire to love and to be loved. He created within us a need that only He can meet. That's why, when we are sinning and out of fellowship with God, we cannot find contentment or experience true joy. Only when we love God and others are we living as God intended. How heartbreaking for God to offer so much and yet for us to ignore or reject His love (Jer. 7:13). You may be like many others who were taught to be religious but not to enjoy a love relationship with Christ. If that is the case, don't rest until you are experiencing the infinite joy that comes from loving God with all of your heart.

Reality 3. God Invites You to Become Involved with Him in His Work

The basis of any healthy relationship is the time that two people spend relating to one another. God is not content for you to believe in Him or to worship Him from afar. He wants to relate to you *personally*. God is not merely a doctrine to believe; He is a Person who wants you to become involved with Him in His eternal work.

God knows what is at stake for people who never hear about Him or who choose not to follow Him (John 3:16). Therefore, He works with a sense of urgency to redeem those who are living apart from Him. If you love God, you will share His heart. What concerns Him will concern you. And, as you relate personally to God, He will reveal His will to you. Jesus said to His disciples: "No longer do I call you servants, for a servant does not know what his master is doing; but I have called you friends, for all things that I heard from My Father I have made known to you" (John 15:15). The closer we draw to Christ, the more we learn about what is on His heart.

As God works in the world around you, He will invite you to join in His activity. He will invite you to become His hands and feet by which He reaches out to other people (Rom. 10:14–15). When God reveals to you what He is doing in someone's life, that is His invitation for you to join in His activity. This is the way God worked throughout the Bible:

- God invited Adam to participate in the naming and subjugation of the animal kingdom He had created (Gen. 2:19–20).
- God asked Noah to adjust his family to the cataclysmic judgment He was bringing upon the earth (Gen. 6:13–22).
- God invited Abraham to leave his country and to join God's activity in creating a holy people (Gen. 12:1–3).
- God invited Moses to leave his shepherding business and to join Him in freeing a nation from slavery (Exod. 3–4).
- God invited Joshua to join Him in claiming the Promised Land for His people (Josh. 1:1–9).
- God invited Mary and Joseph to participate in raising the Messiah (Matt. 1:20–25; Luke 1:26–38).

- God invited fishermen to join His redemptive work (Mark 1:16–20).
- God invited Paul to join Him in taking the gospel to the Gentiles (Acts 26:12–18).

God continues to invite people to join Him in His activity. If you keep your spiritual senses alert, you might be surprised at where God is working in your world and how He wants you to become involved!

Reality 4. God Speaks by the Holy Spirit through the Bible, Prayer, Circumstances, and the Church to Reveal Himself, His Purposes, and His Ways

This particular truth has proven difficult for many believers. That's because they have never been taught to recognize God's voice. Many new converts were informed that once they became Christians, they were to attend church each Sunday and to try and be good people. One day when they died, they would go to heaven and God would finally become "real" to them. As a result of such anaemic teaching, many sincere believers are unaware that God *wants* to communicate with them, to say nothing of being able to discern His voice. Consequently, many Christians have never heard God speak to them, even though they claim to have a personal relationship with Him.

Some Christian leaders argue that God has *already* spoken (as recorded in the Bible), and there is nothing more He needs to say. Some people equate God speaking to His people today as equal to God dispensing new revelation, so they are wary of any active role the Holy Spirit might play today in *applying* Scripture to people's lives. These same people typically struggle with the concept of a *personal relationship* with God because any meaningful relationship between two people requires two-way communication. God is not a mute observer, sitting passively in the backseat of our life while we take the wheel. He is almighty God who will relate to us in the same manner in which Jesus related to His disciples (John 14:16). Jesus said, "My sheep hear My voice, I know them, and they follow Me" (John 10:27). This verse certainly applies to our salvation, but it also encompasses our entire relationship with the Good Shepherd.

The moment you become a Christian, the Holy Spirit enters your life and assumes the same role Jesus exercised with His disciples (John 16:7). Just as Jesus guided His disciples to know what to do and believe, so the Holy Spirit will lead you to experience the fullness of the Christian life. Depending on your particular need, the Holy Spirit will be your Guide, Comforter, Advocate, Defender, and Friend. The Spirit will direct you in the path you should take (Ps. 25:4–5; John 14:17, 26; 15:26; 16:13) and what you should say (Luke 12:2). The issue is not whether or not God is speaking to you; the question is whether or not you are hearing what He is saying. There are four primary ways the Holy Spirit communicates with people. These are the Bible, prayer, circumstances, and other believers. Let's look at those.

God's Spirit will speak to you through the pages of the Bible.

God's Word is living and active (Heb. 4:12). The Holy Spirit uses it to provide guidance, convict of sin, reveal truth, and address the needs of your heart. If you do not spend time reading and meditating on God's Word, you remove the primary instrument through which God guides His people. It is essential for Christians to regularly submit their lives to God's Word so He can address any area of their life that is not in alignment with Him (Eph. 5:26). This involves more than merely pausing for a moment to collect a comforting devotional thought for the day. This includes allowing God's Word to wash over your heart and mind so it transforms your thinking and behavior. Every time you open your Bible, be prepared for God to speak directly into your life.

God will speak to you as you pray.

Prayer is a conversation between God and people. We relate to God in prayer as children relate to their father (Matt. 6:9). Through prayer we share our concerns, joys, love, fears, and questions with Him. Sometimes we simply bask in His presence (Ps. 63:1). However, while many Christians have been taught to present their petitions to God, they are not always aware that prayer is a *conversation*. If we chatted with our friends like we talk with God, we wouldn't have friends for long! No one likes to have friends who do all of the talking!

This is God's invitation: "Call to Me, and I will answer" (Jer. 33:3). The Bible says, "The LORD spoke with Moses face to face, just as a man speaks with his friend" (Exod. 33:11 HCSB). The most important thing that is said in prayer is not what *you* state but what *God* declares! He already knows what you are going to tell Him. On the other hand, you have no idea what He might say to you. Prayer is not primarily a time for you to convince God to do something about your concerns. Rather, it is a sacred moment when God impresses upon your heart that which is on His heart. It is when God opens your understanding to what He knows is important and when He guides your life into the direction He intends for you to go. Prayer is not a boring religious exercise, nor is it a self-indulgent litany of our concerns. It is an opportunity to draw near to God and to hear His thoughts. What an amazing invitation!

God speaks through the circumstances of life.

God is capable of speaking to you through any circumstance in your life. At times we can neglect to read our Bible or to pray, but it is more difficult to avoid our life's circumstances! God does not necessarily *cause* every situation in our life, but He certainly will *use* them.

For example, a job offer and a chance encounter with a friend are circumstances. So is being downsized at work or being diagnosed with a tumor. Apart from hearing from God, these situations can appear to be wonderful or devastating. However, only as we hear from God can we truly understand our life's circumstances. For example, losing our job typically appears to be negative: how will I make my house payment? Where will I find another job? But God may intend to use that experience to build humility and faith into your life to a degree you never knew before. Perhaps God wants to demonstrate the extremely practical ways He can provide for your needs. Losing your job could be one of the greatest things to ever happen in your Christian life. That is why it is crucial for you to hear God's voice in the midst of your life's circumstances.

Sometimes it may appear as if doors of opportunity are closing before you. Yet, you cannot know that for sure unless you hear from God. Likewise, just because a door appears "open," it does not mean you should walk through it. You must seek a word from God.

There are many circumstances you may face for which there is no Scripture verse that speaks directly to the issue. That is when you must rely on the Holy Spirit to take Scripture and apply it specifically to your situation. When you learn to live with your spiritual eyes wide open, you will see the mighty hand of God at work all around you.

God speaks through the church body.

We are individuals, but we were not designed to live a solitary life. God did not create us to be independent but interdependent. God intends for every Christian to join a body of believers called the Church (1 Cor. 12:12–31). If you were designed to be an eye, then you need to share what you are seeing with the other members of the body. If you were made to be an ear, you must heed what the eye tells you it is seeing. You cannot know fully God's will for your life if you are not relating closely to other believers.

Jesus said we must be careful how we treat other Christians because He resides within each one (John 13:20). Because Christ resides within every believer, it is possible to hear from Christ every time you talk to another Christian. At times you can become so enmeshed in the circumstances of your life that you no longer have a clear perspective. God may send another believer to share a clear word with you that helps you know God's view of your situation (2 Sam. 12:7). Be certain you maintain close relationships with other believers through whom God can send you a clear, timely message.

Reality 5. God's Invitation for You to Work with Him Always Leads You to a Crisis of Belief That Requires Faith and Action

When almighty God shares His heart with a creature of dust, it is going to cause a crisis! However, a "crisis of belief" is not identical to a *crisis*. We typically view *crises* as something negative. No one but a masochist wants one of those! Everyone will face difficult moments in their life whether they are Christians or not. A *crisis of belief*, however, is a moment when you are confronted with a decision of whether or not you will trust God and obey what He says. God initiates God-sized endeavors! When God invites us to join Him in what He is doing, it is naturally going to stretch us in our human frailty and weakness. This is why it is called a crisis of *belief*. Scripture indicates that apart from faith, it is impossible to please God (Heb. 11:6). Therefore, God will ask you to do things that require faith. When you face a *crisis of belief,* you must believe God is who He says He is. The way you prove your belief is by stepping out in obedience. Notice what this looked like in the lives of people in the Bible:

- Childless Abraham may have believed God was powerful, but he faced a crisis of belief when God told him at age seventy-five that he was going to become the father of a multitude (Gen. 15:1–6).
- Moses might have believed God could use anyone for His purposes; however, he faced a crisis of belief when God told him—someone who wasn't a good public speaker or leader—to be His spokesman (Exod. 4:10).
- Joshua might have believed God was all-powerful. But he faced a crisis of belief when he stood outside the formidable walls of Jericho without any siege equipment (Josh. 6).
- Peter, Andrew, James, and John might have been God-fearing fishermen, but they faced a crisis of belief when Jesus told them to leave their business and to follow Him (Mark 1:16–20).

Our faith will be constantly tested by the situations and people we encounter each day. As Christians, our faith is based on what we know to be true about God. Each step of faith we take builds on the foundation of the previous steps we have taken. Joshua could trust God to defeat Jericho because he had seen God do amazing things previously in the desert. Moses could trust God to deal with the Red Sea because He had already seen God produce ten plagues in Egypt. Elijah could trust God to send fire down upon Mount Carmel because he had experienced God's faithfulness throughout his years as a prophet (1 Kings 18:20–39). As we experience more of God, we will be able to trust Him with increasingly difficult circumstances. However, we will never become immune to crises of belief because God is always prepared to accomplish still greater things in our life than we have previously known!

Reality 6. You Must Make Major Adjustments in Your Life to Join God in What He Is Doing

We cannot stay where we are and go with God at the same time. When God asks us to follow Him, we must get up from where we are and move to where He is going. We must adjust whatever it is in our life that prevents us from obeying God's instructions. It could mean:

- changing our schedule,
- adjusting our routines,
- moving to a new city,
- giving up a job,
- becoming involved in a new ministry,
- adjusting our finances to support a mission cause,
- adopting a child or taking in foster children, or
- a thousand other things.

Most people dislike change. They would rather keep what they know than step out into the unknown. But if you are going to move from where you are to where God wants you to be, you must make adjustments. Your problem will be that your way of doing things is not God's way (Isa. 55:8–9). Every time you join God in His activity, you must set aside your ways and adopt God's ways. Too many Christians are trying to accomplish God's work using *their* methods! That doesn't work! (Just ask Abraham or Moses! [Gen. 16; Exod. 2:11–15]). That's why you must make adjustments. God will align your thinking, methods, and finances so you can do His work His way, for His glory.

Reality 7. You Come to Know God by Experience as You Obey Him and He Accomplishes His Work through You

This is our ultimate aim: to experience God in new and profound ways. This involves infinitely more than attending church on Sundays! Knowing God experientially was the apostle Paul's driving ambition (Phil. 3:7–10). His wish for every Christian was "that you may know what is the hope of His calling, what are the riches of the glory of His inheritance in the saints, and what is the exceeding greatness of His power toward us who believe, according to the working of His mighty power" (Eph. 1:18–19). Anything less than knowing Christ in this manner is to shortchange your Christian life.

The key to experiencing God this way is obedience. Some people claim to believe God, but they don't obey Him. This is impossible. Jesus asked: "But why do you call Me 'Lord, Lord,' and not do the things which I say?" (Luke 6:46). Obedience is the doorway to experiencing God. Every time you do what God tells you, you will move into a deeper walk with Him. Each time you disobey, your Christian walk will stagnate. If you are faithful in the little God asks of you, He will give you more (Matt. 25:14–30). You can experience as much of God as you want. You just have to obey Him.

A Mother's Plea

One mother had a particularly challenging teenager who was rebelling against the faith and morals he had been taught at church. The woman felt deeply burdened for her wayward son, yet everything she tried ended in failure. Even as she carried a heavy load herself, the woman became aware that there were other mothers in her church who were having a similar experience. Their teenagers refused to attend church and were getting into trouble at school and with the law. These women grieved over their children and had begun to lose hope. God led this mother to contact the others and invite them to join together to pray each week for their children. The mothers bonded together as they pled with God to perform miracles in the lives of their children. Over the next year they began to witness the seemingly impossible occurring. One by one, these rebellious teens began to experience a heart change. They started to apply themselves in school. Each of them graduated, some going on to higher education. They all turned from the destructive path they had been racing down and began attending church once more. God's invitation to a solitary mother had not been earth-shattering. No seas parted. No passports were required. She simply believed that with God all things are possible. Then she started making whatever adjustments God asked of her. When she did, families all over her church were gloriously restored. Only heaven will know the eternal impact of one woman's obedience.

Where Are You?

The Seven Realities are not a magic formula. They are simply the pattern God has used throughout Scripture as He has worked in people's lives. At times we can linger on one reality. Perhaps we reject God's invitation into a deeper love relationship. Maybe we face a crisis of belief in which we cannot bring ourselves to trust God for an issue in our life. Or we may know what God wants us to do but be unwilling to make the necessary adjustment to obey Him. The degree to which we experience God will largely be determined by how fervently and fully we embrace God's work in our life.

Throughout this book, we'll examine how you can experience God working in your family's life. In addition, we'll look at how you can help your children experience God in their lives. Next let's look at the high calling and amazing privilege God grants to us in parenting our children.

QUESTIONS FOR REFLECTION/DISCUSSION

1. If you were to guess where your Christian life is at present, which of the realities would you say you are in right now? Why is that?

2. Have you experienced God speaking to you in the past? If so, what did He tell you?

3. Were you taught that Christianity was primarily a relationship or a religion? How might you cultivate a deeper relationship with Christ than you already have?

4. Are you presently experiencing a crisis of belief? If so, what are you struggling to believe God for?

5. Are there adjustments you need to make if you are to move forward in your walk with God? If so, what are they? What is stopping you from making those adjustments?

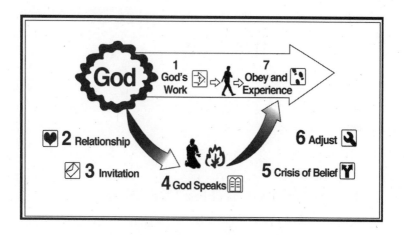

Notes

1. Oswald Chambers, *Disciples Indeed* (London: Oswald Chambers Publications Assoc. and Marshall, Morgan and Scott, LTD, 1955, 1967), 15.

CHAPTER 7

Roles Parents Play

Hands Off My Daughter! (A Story from Tom)

I dreaded the day my daughter Erin started dating. We talked it over with her and tried to delay it as long as was possible. (I couldn't convince her to do high school and college at a convent, though I tried.) One day I nearly had a heart attack. I learned Erin was getting "friendly" with a boy I didn't know and, worse, didn't like!

One afternoon my wife dropped me off at the high school to help coach basketball for my son's eighth-grade team. I happened to walk past the bus stop and saw Erin there with a boy's arm around her waist. WHAT?! I was instantly hostile. Who *was* this boy? Why was *he* touching *my* daughter? Where's my bullwhip? When Erin saw me, she quickly stepped apart from the boy, his hand dropped to his side, and I smiled the faintest smile I could manage as I walked past, giving the boy the ol' *disapproving father* glare. A few minutes later I texted her, "That hand thing—not good! We'll talk at home."

Erin was seventeen, and I could no longer control her world as I did when she was three. We had recently moved home from overseas, and I did not yet know her new school friends or how she was spending her free time. We had built a lot of trust between us over the years and I expected her to be responsible. But I believed she was going down the wrong road. I knew she needed wise counsel. I also understood I could no longer make decisions for her.

I am big on "consequences" for our choices, so that's how I approached our talk that night. Using my best Gandalf impersonation, I began, "Every choice has consequences. . . ." I asked if she felt this boy was the type to help her achieve her life's goals. She thought for a minute and said, "No." I asked her if he was helping her grow deeper in her relationship with God. She admitted it was the opposite. I asked if his life was heading in the same direction as her life. She said, "no." He was working an hourly job at a grocery store and appeared to have little ambition, and she planned to go to college to work on a corporate communications degree. I asked about his home life and learned that his mother had left when he was twelve and died of cancer two years later. His father's girlfriend lived with him, his brother was experimenting with homosexuality, and his home life was not based on Christian values. Our home, on the other hand, was stable, Christian, education oriented, and God-centered. My daughter began to recognize that many of her values were opposite to his. I could see how the young man would be attracted to qualities he saw in my daughter. I felt sorry for what he had endured in life so far, but my daughter being his girlfriend was *not* the solution to his problems.

As I sat on her bed talking calmly and quietly, the answers to my questions helped bring clarity to her relationship. My last question was, "So what do you think is the best choice you can make in this relationship?" She said, "I probably need to break up with him." Inside I danced and jumped four backflips, but outside I was quietly supportive. I wish I could say it happened the next day, but it didn't. It took time. It was hard to realize she was no longer a playful little six-year-old organizing her dollhouse. She had grown into a beautiful, intelligent, young woman who was on the verge of adulthood and no longer depended on me like she once did. She definitely still needed a dad, but the role I would play from this point forward would be drastically different from the past.

All the World's a Stage

In a typical day, parents wear many hats and play a variety of roles in their home. Your day may begin as a **Chef:** set out breakfast for incoming children while spreading out three sets of sandwiches for lunches. One child only likes butter on the bread; the other, mayonnaise. One likes salami; another tuna; the third prefers peanut butter. One likes Jarlsberg cheese; the other, cheddar; and the other, Velveeta! One likes a particular granola bar; another prefers chocolate rather than vanilla pudding. One enjoys apples (green, not red) over oranges, and so on.

Next you serve as the **Fashion Expert:** "Does this shirt go with these pants?" "Where's my jacket?" "Are there any clean socks?" "I can't find my shoes!!!" Next the **Hair Stylist:** "Will you help me with my hair?" "I can't get this cow lick to lay down!"

On to the **Day-Planner:** "Can Ryan come over after school?" "I have to go to a birthday party Saturday; can you pick up a gift for me?" And then the **Chauffer:** Drive to school, practices, rehearsals, friend's homes, shopping, etc. Once you return home, you morph into the **Launderer, Grocer, Bill-Payer,** and **Lawn Maintenance person.**

If you are like us, you enter each day wondering which "hat" you must wear to meet your family's needs. Here are some other roles parents can play in their children's lives. You can probably think of more:

Advocate	Teacher	Caregiver	Protector
Advisor	Cheerleader	Financier	Personal Assistant
Coach	Drill Sergeant	Consultant	Medic
Maid	Spiritual Leader	Mechanic	Fashion Expert
Purchaser	Entertainer	Party Planner	Social Coordinator
Hair Stylist	Repairman	Negotiator	Therapist

Different Roles at Different Times

We must play a variety of roles in the lives of our children. Our tasks change depending on our children's needs and ages. Not all of us feel prepared to do everything our children need us to, but we try our best. Here are some definitions and duties of some of the most basic roles parents play.

Advocate: One who upholds or defends a cause or who intercedes on behalf of another.

An advocate is someone who actively pleads the case of another. Lawyers do this for people in court as they defend their client's rights.

Parents advocate for their children when they need someone wiser, more experienced, and knowledgeable. Satan is the father of lies (John 8:44). The unbelieving world will continually hurl untruths at our children. It is up to parents to uphold the truth for their children.

Our father once met with a high school math teacher on behalf of one of his children. All but two students in the class were failing. The teacher refused to consider his "teaching" was the problem. Our father simply said, "As a teacher myself, I know I have not *taught* until my students have *learned*. I do not teach materials; I teach students. What is it going to take to help my son learn what you claim you are teaching?" Children need advocates!

Teacher: One who instructs others.

Diligent parents are continually teaching their children what they need to know to thrive in life. Whether it is social manners or explaining why the leaves fall off trees in autumn, we are constantly answering the inexhaustible "why" questions to satisfy the curiosity of our children. We teach so many things, such as:

- how to read and write
- how to repair things that are broken
- how to navigate technology (TV remotes, computer, stereo, etc.)
- how to clean and pick up after yourself
- how to behave and show proper manners and respect for others
- how to dress yourself and how to dress for special occasions
- how to wear makeup or how to shave and do your hair
- how to do homework, study for tests, and write papers for school
- how to pray and read the Bible

The list can seem endless. But it is our responsibility to pass on important information and skills to our kids (Deut. 4:9; 11:19; Ps. 78:1–7). If *we* don't teach our children the important issues of life, someone else will!

Caregiver: One who attends to the personal needs of another person.

If you carry a lot of Kleenex tissues and hand sanitizer wherever you go, you know the role of a caregiver (Jer. 30:17; 1 Pet. 5:7)—potty training, wiping faces (and other parts), bathing, dressing, feeding, and all those tasks our little ones can't manage on their own. We also care for our sons or daughters while their broken bones heal or as they recover from illness. As they grow, we must cry with them when they break up with a boyfriend or girlfriend, help through disappointments when they don't make the team or lose an important game, or encourage them when they don't get the job they applied for. This role never ends, as parents exert great influence on the emotional well-being of their children throughout their lives. (We're grown men, yet we still feel the need to let our mom know when we are having a bad day!)

Protector: One who protects; a guardian. (A Story from Richard)

When my (Richard's) son Mike was in kindergarten, he was timid about going to school. He was our oldest and had never left the safe confines of his home like that before. So, I took him for the first couple of days. The kindergarten students were required to line up on the playground before they were marched in to class. Mike found himself standing next to a rather ill-mannered little boy. This ruffian decided it would be great fun to thrust himself into my son Mike so that, like dominoes, the children in line behind him would ripple backward as each child banged into the next.

I had been discreetly standing off to the side so as not to embarrass my firstborn. I was wearing mirrored sunglasses and a black trench coat. I should mention I also stand six feet two inches tall and weigh comfortably more than two hundred pounds. When I saw the bully bang into my son the first time, I was alarmed but maintained my composure. Perhaps this hooligan would be satisfied with his antics just one time. But seeing he had knocked half a dozen of his classmates to the ground the first time, he gave an extra hard heave the second time that caused eight students to stumble. My son was timidly bracing himself for the next collision. That was too much. I descended upon that child and lowered myself menacingly into the little thug's face. "I wouldn't do that again if I were you," I muttered through clenched teeth. I slowly walked a few paces away and then turned and glared at the boy. He instantly turned angelic. Problem solved. Of course parents can't rush to the aid of their child every time someone is unkind to them. But in that early period of my child's schooling, my son learned that his father would be quick to protect him if the situation was called for.

Our children need protection today more than ever. Whether it is from a bully on the playground or a stalker on the Internet, dangers abound. At times our children's friends can be manipulative, or schoolteachers can label our children improperly. As our children grow older, they may need us to look out for them on a team road trip or at a school party. They may even need us to protect them from themselves. The world is a dangerous place. Children need someone who is alert to the dangers they are facing.

Advisor/Consultant: One who helps others make the best decision when considering many options.

You will be asked a thousand times by your children (particularly daughters), "How does this look?" (Dads, be careful how you answer that one!) Your children will ask you to edit their papers, help them with science projects, and choose essay topics. Further, you will need to advise them concerning awkward issues with friends, choices of classes, scheduling glitches, body hygiene (awkward!), appropriate music, and choice of friends to hang out with. Interestingly, one of the roles of the Holy Spirit in *our* lives is as an advisor to guide us in the paths we should take for our own benefit (John 14:26).

Cheerleader: One who seeks to inspire others to greatness.

Sometimes our children question their abilities or lack confidence. They can become weary with practice and need encouragement to "push through" to the end. They may require active support if they are to go beyond what they think they can do. Children face the constant temptation to settle for less than God's best. Performance anxiety, fear of public speaking, cowering before a stronger team can paralyze our kids. But having a personal cheerleading section can give children the confidence they need to face their fears and achieve their best.

We have both spent countless hours cheering on our children at sporting events. Their team members all knew who their parents were because we were the loud, zany adults in the stands at every game. I (Richard) once went to cheer for my son Daniel while he played an outdoor hockey game in twenty-three-degrees-below-zero weather. I had to stand beside the boards of the rink to cheer. I grew so frozen that I thought my internal organs were frosting over! Every time Daniel left the ice, I scurried to the car I had left running and tried to defrost. As soon as Daniel was back on the ice, I frantically climbed out of my vehicle and cheered loudly for my son. I am amazed that cheerleading stint didn't end in pneumonia. But my son saw to what lengths his parent would go to support his efforts. Those times are priceless. Everyone needs someone to cheer for them.

Financier: One who guides others in managing money.

Whether or not you are a financial guru or not, there are some basics of money management you will need to teach your children. You should teach them to tithe their earnings to God as well as to manage a budget. You should encourage your children to save and to avoid using credit. Perhaps more importantly, we need to help them to develop a healthy view of money and possessions (Heb. 13:5; 1 Tim. 6:10). We should also teach them how to apply for jobs, ace an interview, and be outstanding employees. Stewardship of resources will apply to many areas of life.

Personal Assistant: One who organizes and manages personal details for others.

When our kids are young, we make most of their decisions for them. We keep their schedules and establish their routines. We make their appointments, check to see if their assignments are completed on time, and double-check to ensure they have their equipment and uniform ready for the next game. Some children seem to require a *team* of administrative assistants to keep their lives organized!

Coach: One who instructs and inspires others to achieve their goals.

You will have to help your kids know how to catch a ball, be a team member, play an instrument, dance, sing, ski, skate, ride a bike, dive into a pool, and drive a car. You must provide advice on how to get along

with others, study for exams, and how to be gracious winners and los-
ers. You will need to regularly encourage them to always give their best
effort, regardless of what others are doing. You may also be called upon
to be a "player-coach," where you get out on the field and show your
kids by example.

Drill Sergeant: One who instills discipline, respect, and the appreciation for conformity and routine in others.

There are inevitably occasions when children simply don't feel like
doing what they should. Getting up for school on a cold winter's day,
doing homework when a popular sitcom is playing, and taking a shower
each day can sometimes provide herculean challenges. You will occasionally need to "remind" them that they need to clean their room, make their
bed, get to school on time, do their homework, finish their chores, and
"get a move on" when they are running late. This particular parental role
is not the most enjoyable, but it can pay huge dividends if you produce
self-disciplined children who know how to do a job well and on time.

Medic: One who attends to the medical needs of others.

As a parent, you will be observing and assessing symptoms, suggest-
ing medications, and prescribing rest. You'll inevitably have to console a
child who has been hurt, take kids to the emergency room, and discuss
their medical issues with the family doctor. Occasionally this role can
consume enormous amounts of time. There are few times your children
will appreciate you more than when they are sick.

Maid/Cook

You know the routine! Doing laundry, making beds, vacuuming
bedrooms and playrooms, ironing clothes, cooking meals, making
lunches, providing snacks, doing dishes, baking cakes, making cookies,
hosting parties (and cleaning up after them). Parenting is not for the lazy
or selfish! Sometimes it is just a lot of hard (never-ending) work.

Spiritual Leader: Moving people on to God's agenda.

Sometimes parents want the Sunday school teacher or youth pastor
to play this role on their behalf, but nothing can replace parents helping

their children to know and love God. We need to point our children to God's answers to life's issues that are found in the Bible. We must teach our children to pray and turn to God in times of trouble. Parents shape their children's attitudes about church and ministry. Parents will also affect their children's view of God, especially God as a "Father." That is one role we cannot abdicate or be careless about.

Parents Must Grow Along with Their Children

As children advance into each stage of life, they need their parents to mature in their roles along with them.

Toddlers

Young children need hands-on, involved parents. We are *controllers* at this stage of their life. Parents of preschoolers must: organize playtime, dress their children, choose TV/video shows, mandate nap time (yay!), and maintain the schedule throughout the day. Discipline is relatively straightforward at this age. Young children should have a healthy respect for authority and an aversion to the consequences of bad behavior. And of course, toddlers need lots of love as they develop their identity and character.

Children

As our children mature out of the toddler stage, they assume greater responsibility for themselves. Rather than being underfoot all day, they go off to school, lessons, and sporting events. Now they come home from school asking to play at a friend's house or handing us a birthday party invitation to reply to. Rather than telling our kids what their schedule is, they are telling us what they want to do and where they need to go. We still provide plenty of guidance, but increasingly they are couched as suggestions rather than mandates. We were the primary adults in our toddler's world. Our older children are influenced by a wider circle of people, such as friends, schoolteachers, coaches, music instructors, youth leaders, and pastors. Our role must change from *controllers* to *managers*.

Teens

Teenagers require different things from us than do our toddlers or middle-school children. Let the roller coaster begin! We may feel as if we need a master's degree in child psychology, mental health, behavioural sciences, conflict negotiations, stress management, and sports nutrition! During these occasionally turbulent years, our teenagers no longer need us (or want us) to tell them what to wear, what music to listen to, or what they should eat. New roles are required as we help our teenagers navigate life, love, jobs, career choices, responsibilities, disappointments, and relationships. Though they are becoming young adults, teenagers still need tremendous amounts of affirmation and support as they face increasing pressures and dangers. Raising teens can be especially challenging for parents who struggled themselves as teenagers and who may still carry scars from that era themselves. At this point, parenting moves from *management* to *consultant*. We can't *make* our adolescent offspring do very much. This stage of parenting can only be successfully navigated with large doses of divine wisdom, patience, and long-term strategies.

Young Adults

As our children mature from teenagers into their twenties, our relationship with them changes once more. Make no mistake; twenty-year-old children *still* need parents! That's because several of the most crucial decisions your children will ever make often occur during this period of life. They may decide: whether to earn an advanced degree, whom to marry, and what career to choose. This is certainly not a time for parents to wash their hands and exclaim, "My job is done now; they are adults!" Think of your investment! You spent twenty years guiding and nurturing your children into adulthood. You can't throw away their future simply because they turned eighteen! A poor choice in marriage partners or unwise career or education decisions can cripple your children and their possibilities for the remainder of their lives.

In parenting young adults, our role can shift from *consultant* to *friend*. They are adults now, and if you did your job well, they will share many of your values, passions, and perspectives. They may also hold your religious, political, and economic views. They may approach parenting their own children (your grandchildren) with the same priorities you used on them. They will be fun to spend time with because odds are good they will also share a similar sense of humor (unless you are like us and your children adamantly reject your love of puns!), and they will of course share many family memories with you (either for good or for bad).

The key is for parents to grow with their children. We know great parents of preschoolers who, unfortunately, kept talking to their teenagers like they were preschoolers. Baby talk to a baby can be cute. Baby talk to a sixteen-year-old can be annoying! One of the reasons parenting teenagers can be challenging is not merely because adolescents face greater issues but also because their parents don't keep up. By the time their children need them to navigate unprecedented challenges and difficulties, their parents are hopelessly out of date and out of touch.

God's Character Matches the Needs of His People

It is fascinating to observe the progression of God's revelation to His people, newly freed from slavery in Egypt, as they gradually learned how to be a holy people. God was always involved with His people, first as a Deliverer, then as a Protector, then as a Provider, then as a holy God. By some counts there are more than 650 names of God (Father, Son, Spirit) in the Bible. Each one represents a role God plays with His people. Look at the following names as they relate to the role of parent:

Avenger	1 Thess. 4:6
Advocate	1 John 2:1
Author of Peace	1 Cor. 14:33
Chief Shepherd	1 Pet. 5:4
Comforter	John 14:26
Commander	Isa. 55:4
Consuming Fire	Deut. 4:24; Heb. 12:29
Counselor	Isa. 9:6
Deliverer	Rom. 11:26
Everlasting Father	Isa. 9:6
Fortress	Jer. 16:19
Friend	Matt. 11:19
God Who Sees	Gen. 16:13

Healer	Exod. 15:26
Judge	Isa. 33:22; Acts 10:42
Prince of Peace	Isa. 9:6
Provider	Gen. 22:13–14
Shepherd	Ps. 23:1
Strong Tower	Prov. 18:10
Teacher	John 13:13
Who Is Present	Ezek. 48:35

God played widely divergent roles according to what His people needed. There were times when they needed Him to be a caregiver who provided food and water. On other occasions He protected His people from their enemies, guided them around danger, judged their sin, punished their rebellion, forgave their sin, encouraged them to obey, and much more. There are many similarities between how our Father in heaven treats His children and how we should relate to ours. Pity the children who only have one-dimensional parents!

Your Role

From all the different roles you play as a parent, which do you think is most important? While you might have numerous titles racing through your mind, we'd suggest your greatest role is not even on the above list. That's because it's your identity as a *child* of God. It has been said that "good leaders are good followers." It could also be said that "good parents are good children." Regardless of your age, your identity is ultimately defined by your relationship to your heavenly Father. Throughout your life you will be dependant on Him, seeking His guidance and provision as well as fellowshipping with Him and loving Him. When your children observe what kind of child you are to God (and to your own parents), they will see how they should act as well. Every role you play is one your children may eventually need to perform as well. Hopefully you are setting an outstanding example before them.

QUESTIONS FOR REFLECTION/DISCUSSION

1. What is the most challenging role you currently have as a parent?

2. Can you honestly say that you would be comfortable having your children copy your relationship with God? Why or why not?

3. What kind of child are you to your parents (if they are still living) and to your heavenly Father? What kind of example are you providing your children?

4. What has been the most challenging adjustment you have made in your parental role as your children have grown up? What adjustments do you still need to make?

5. Which role do you most depend on God to play in your life today?

6. What is one parenting role that you need to overhaul and update? Make specific plans to begin doing that this week.

CHAPTER 8

God Is Always at Work around Us

Kids, Games, and the Work of God

When we were children, the two of us could play for hours. At one point we could be exploring a prehistoric jungle while trying to avoid child-eating dinosaurs. The next minute we and our merry band of GI Joes would be fighting bad guys. Then we'd be desperados frantically trying to make it to the Mexico border before our mother cornered us and exiled us to our afternoon nap. But invariably, our favorite game to play was Church.

We went to church every Sunday and watched our revered father preaching from the pulpit and ministering to the people. Inspired by his example, we would conduct our own services in our tiny bedroom. We would transform our bunk bed into a platform and pulpit. Tom would be the worship leader, and Richard would be the preacher. Our mother would be the hardened sinner. Since we only had enough floor space for one chair, our congregation was quite meager. But, seeing as our mother was generally the only person available, and in light of the fact we knew she desperately needed a fresh encounter with God, we always enlisted her as our congregant.

Tom would lead the congregation in singing. Our mother would faithfully bellow out the lyrics, and we would enjoy a moving song service. Once that was done, Tom would announce, "And now our pastor is going to come and preach God's Word to us today." Richard would mount the pulpit and pull out his Children's Picture Bible. Because Richard was illiterate at the time, his sermons were not exactly complex. He would invariably preach the same sermon in every service regardless of how many times our tiny congregation met. However, he always preached with passion and a sense of urgency. The title of his message was "The Sin of Spanking Your Children." As Richard warmed to his theme, he would solemnly declare, "There may be some of you here today who have committed this horrible sin, and now God is convicting you to repent of your evil deeds and return to God!" We'd always feel compelled to extend an altar call so any sinners present could immediately find peace with God. When no one "walked the aisle" during the first two verses, Richard would pause the singing and declare: "Now folks, we're not in any hurry today. We're going to continue to sing until *everyone* has been made right with God!" Finally, to bring closure to the ordeal, our mother would dutifully make a public decision, committing herself afresh to be a better mother in the future. We'd then close the service, rejoicing in God's goodness that day.

While this was all a lot of fun while we were kids, an interesting thing happened. Over twenty years later, Richard became the pastor of Friendship Baptist Church in Winnipeg, Canada. Guess who he called a year later to be the worship and education pastor? Tom. The first time our mother attended church where her two oldest children were serving, Richard was sorely tempted to preach on how parents ought to treat their children! But he refrained. Since then, we have both moved on to work at Blackaby Ministries International, where we speak and write together today.

Could our mother have had any idea as she watched her two oldest children playing church that she was being given a glimpse into the future? Even as she might well have wondered what her children would grow up to become, she was unknowingly being given a sneak preview. God was already stirring in our hearts in ways none of us understood. Does this mean that every childhood game is a foretaste of the future? Well, depending on what your kids are currently playing, we certainly hope not! What is true is that God is always at work in and around our children's lives. But there is a crucial issue: Is it possible for God to be working in our children's lives and yet for us to miss it? Unfortunately, it is.

Jesus and Children

Of the Seven Realities popularized by *Experiencing God,* undoubtedly the most revolutionary truth is this: *God is always at work around you.* The reason some people struggle with this reality is because there are times in our lives when we do not see anything happening around us bearing any resemblance to the divine. Since we don't notice God doing anything around us, we assume He must be working at a different address than ours. But the truth is that God *is* at work. We need the Holy Spirit to open our spiritual eyes so we can see what He is doing (Mark 8:17–18).

During a busy time in Jesus' ministry, a group of children kept swarming around Jesus, wanting to be near Him. How annoying! Everyone was excitedly watching to see if Jesus would perform a miracle, or say something profound, or pass out baskets of food once again. Instead, Jesus seemed preoccupied with the pesky children who wouldn't leave Him alone. Jesus' disciples felt responsible for crowd control during these public events. They assumed He needed to focus on the influential people of that city or to prepare His next message. In the Middle Eastern culture of that day, children were to be kept at a respectful distance from the men. So the disciples attempted to shoo the irritating gadflies away from their Rabbi. Jesus, however, instead of rebuking the uninhibited children, chastised His disciples. Scripture says Jesus was "greatly displeased" at the Twelve for preventing the youngsters from coming to Him (Mark 10:13–16; Matt. 19:13–15; Luke 18:15–17). Apparently Jesus perceived something His associates did not. The disciples saw annoying children bothering the adults. Jesus recognized God's hand at work in the youngest generation, drawing them to the Savior.

God *is* at work in your home. It is imperative that you not miss what He is doing. There are at least four ways God works in your children's lives. Let's look at each one.

1. God Works in Your Child

Every human being has a divine purpose. No life is an accident, nor is any person redundant. The Bible teaches that God knew us long before we were born (Ps. 139:15–16). While we were still in our mother's womb, God understood our full potential (Jer. 1:5). Which raises an extremely important point: How much potential is there in one person God chooses to put on the planet? You might see a normal-looking baby, sleeping in her mother's arms. But what does God see? What could God do through the life of one person? What victories could God achieve over the enemies of humanity through that individual? What medical cures could God lead someone to discover? What invention could that person create that would alleviate suffering for millions of lives around the world? God knows.

Some children, such as Moses, Samuel, John the Baptist, and Jesus, were answers to people's prayers. Parents rejoiced at their coming because they offered hope for the future. Other children arrived into the world to parents who had no clue what their child could or would become.

Abraham Lincoln's father apparently looked upon his big, strapping son as cheap labor. He worked his son almost to death on his farm and then rented him out like a mule to other farmers in an effort to pay off his debts. Abraham so resented his father for the way he treated him that he didn't invite him to his wedding, nor did he attend his father's funeral. Abraham's father never saw the brilliance or statesmanship qualities in his son that would one day make him one of his nation's greatest presidents.

George Washington's mother believed her son was forever indebted to her. She continually harassed him about visiting her and taking care of her. Consequently, George did everything within his power to avoid her, even when she lived on his property. His mother clearly did not see in her son the general of the revolutionary forces, her nation's first president, and an outstanding leader.

The Duke of Wellington was pulled from school when his parents' finances grew lean. They kept his two brothers in school but withdrew Wellington because he showed so little promise. His parents could never have imagined their unpromising child winning his nation's greatest battle and becoming its prime minister.

Winston Churchill's parents regularly ignored him. They saw little promise for his future and rarely spent time with him.

King George VI's father continually ridiculed him because he stuttered, was bowlegged, and left-handed. His father would have been astonished at how his son led Great Britain through the most gruelling war in its history.

In contrast, Tim Tebow's mother was encouraged to abort him. While pregnant, she suffered severe health issues that caused the fetus to experience a severe placental abruption. Doctors believed the child would be stillborn and urged the mother to have an abortion to preserve her own life. But, believing God had a purpose for her unborn child, she refused, even though it placed her own life in grave danger. She could not have known that twenty years later, as a professional football player, he would impact millions of people through his Christian witness. But God knew.

As children grow up, God is active in their lives, working out His divine purposes. For young children it might be as simple as the Holy Spirit's developing in your child a tender heart toward God and His Word. Perhaps as a parent, you notice how carefully your child listens during the pastor's sermons. Or perhaps your child begins talking about spiritual matters with you and you detect God gently working in his or her life.

God at Work in Richard's Daughter (A Story from Richard)

Three years ago our ministry held a conference on revival in Atlanta. We had three generations of Blackabys speaking. We also had two generations from Billy Graham's family: Anne Graham Lotz and Will Graham. It was a great meeting, and we received plenty of positive feedback. My daughter Carrie, who was a second-year university student, attended. She doesn't often get to be with me in such meetings, so it was a special treat. However, because our ministry was hosting the event, I carried a lot of responsibility and was greatly distracted.

Upon our return home after the conference, I went to my office at home to catch up on e-mails. Carrie stuck her head in the door, wanting to visit. She asked how I thought the meetings had gone. Thinking she might be curious to get the "inside scoop," I began explaining my observations on the plenary sessions, relating some of the comments we received on evaluation forms. Suddenly, I sensed I was totally "missing it." The look on Carrie's face suggested that she did not care much about what the enrollment or book sales amounted to. So, I stopped my analysis and asked her what *she* thought of the meetings.

After offering the obligatory comments about how good it was, she said, "Dad, this weekend I realized that God is calling *me* into some form of ministry too." I was caught by surprise. Carrie's two older brothers had already felt God calling them into some form of ministry, but Carrie had always shown a greater proclivity for *shopping* than for church work! (After all, shopping appeared to be her area of spiritual giftedness!) But at that moment I realized that in the commotion of a hectic conference schedule, while I worried about logistics and my own presentations, God was quietly dealing with my daughter. A lot of great things resulted from those meetings, but what I treasure most is what God did in my daughter's heart.

Of course we can't peer into our children's minds to see what God is doing there, so parents must watch for clues that a divine work is occurring. We do this by observing their behavior, carefully listening to what they say, praying with and for them, and being sensitive to what the Holy Spirit alerts us about them.

2. God Is at Work around Your Children

Not only will God work in the heart of your child, but He will also seek to involve them in His activity. There are numerous stories in the Bible describing how God invited children and youth to join His activity. Perhaps Moses' parents wondered what God was doing when the daughter of Pharaoh plucked their child out of the bulrushes and adopted him as her own (Exod. 2:1–10). One wonders what Jesse mused when his youngest son killed a lion and a bear while defending the flock (1 Sam. 17:34–35), or when he learned that his young son had killed the fearsome giant Goliath (1 Sam. 17:49). We can't help but speculate what the boy's mother told him upon learning he had taken the lunch of fishes and loaves she had packed for him and surrendered it to the Rabbi Jesus who wanted to feed the multitude (John 6:8–9). In hindsight, it's clear that God had a special purpose for these children. Unfortunately there are times when God is working through the lives of young people, but the adults are oblivious to what is happening.

Missing the Work of God

Our father was once speaking at a church during its Sunday morning and evening services. At the close of the morning service, he extended an altar call. An elementary-aged girl came to the front of the auditorium, kneeled at the stage, and began praying. Our father felt impressed to go up and pray with the young girl. She was asking God to help her best friend become a Christian. At the close of the evening service, that same girl walked down the aisle with another young girl in tow. It was her friend she had prayed for that morning. The friend was coming to ask Christ to be her Lord and Savior. At the close of the service, the pastor dutifully introduced the young convert to the people and began to go through the normal protocol of having the church vote to receive her as a new member. Our father called out to the pastor, "You're hiding the activity of God!" He then explained to the congregation what had happened that morning. God had been working in that young girl's life, giving her a burden for the salvation of her friend. God answered her prayer, and that evening that friend prayed to become a Christian. The adults in the service were merely going through the formality of inducting a new church member onto the church roll, but none of them had recognized the wonderful work God had done that day. The pastor and the congregation, ultimately repented of their spiritual carelessness and pledged to be more alert to what God was doing in their midst. Unfortunately, this happens all the time. God is often at work in the lives of young people, but we do not recognize what is happening.

Two Dangers

There are two primary dangers parents face when it comes to God working through their children's lives. The first is, as we've seen, when parents miss what God is doing. The second is when parents impose their own will on their children rather than being sensitive to what God intends to do.

Do you remember Mrs. Zebedee, the mother of James and John? She had some definite ideas about what she wanted her two boys to do! (We can only imagine how she behaved at Little League games!) She asked Jesus to let her two sons serve as His right- and left-hand men (Matt. 20:20–22). Jesus' response was, "You do not know what you ask" (Matt. 20:22). If Jesus had granted this ambitious mother's request, her two sons would have been impaled on crosses at the left and right of Jesus. At times, the worst thing God can do for us is to give us what we keep asking for!

The problem is that parents often mistakenly assume that they know what is best for their children. *Of course* they need to go to the same university their parents attended, or join the family business, or enter a profession that will earn them a lot of money, or live in the same county when they are adults so the grandchildren are close. Well-meaning parents can assume that what they want for their children must also be what God wants. It is wise to remember the words of Isaiah: "'For My thoughts are not your thoughts, nor are your ways My ways,'" says the LORD. 'For as the heavens are higher than the earth, so are My ways higher than your ways, and My thoughts than your thoughts'" (Isa. 55:8–9). If we have not clearly heard what is on God's heart for our children, it is likely that we are settling for less than His best for them.

Opposing God's Work (An Example from Richard)

I was once leading a conference with my father for a wonderful group of missionaries serving in Europe. One afternoon we had a sharing time. Many couples came to the microphone and recounted heartbreaking stories of how their own children's faith had suffered while they were serving in foreign countries and sharing the gospel with others. Some of the missionary children had become involved in drugs. Others had rejected the Christian faith. There was not a dry eye in the room as parents related the suffering they had endured. The missionaries grieved that their children, after watching their parents travel the globe to tell others about Christ, had chosen to reject Christ themselves.

There was one couple standing at the end of the line to speak who appeared deeply troubled. After all the agonizing stories that had already been told, I could not imagine what suffering these parents had endured. Then they told their story. Their oldest son had grown up with his family on the mission field. He was in his final year of high school and was trying to determine what God wanted him to do with his life. One day he told his parents that he wanted to spend his first year out of high school volunteering somewhere in the world where there was poverty so he could help people and share the gospel with them. His mother quickly demurred, arguing that he needed to go to college and that it would be wasteful to expend a year of his life that way. The youth approached his parents later and said he would like to enter medical school. By gaining this expertise, he could one day enter a country that might be closed to Christian missionaries. Once again, his mother opposed his plan, claiming they were poorly paid missionaries and medical school was extremely expensive. Was there not a cheaper degree he might pursue? Finally, one evening the young man told his mother he had just received a desperate call from a teenage girl. The young woman sounded suicidal and had desperately reached out to him for help. He was on his way to meet with her. "You can't go and see her!" the mother protested. "I don't trust that girl, and you can't meet with her at night." She forbid him to leave the house.

That afternoon during the conference, the mother finally realized what she had been doing. Unlike many of the other missionary couples whose children were drifting away from God, her son was earnestly seeking to do God's will. However, it was the boy's own mother who consistently opposed everything God was initiating in his life. The mother wept as she realized the greatest deterrent to her son's walk with God was not Satan, or atheists, or ungodly friends, but his own mother. She, a loving mother and Christian, had often prayed that her son would grow up to serve the Lord, but was bewildered at the realization she had consistently been her son's greatest roadblock.

If parents are not careful, they can unwittingly oppose or hinder the very work in their children's lives that they have been praying for.

3. God Is at Work around Your Home

God is not only working *in* your children and *through* them, but He is also at work *around* them. Wise parents continually keep their spiritual senses attune to what is happening in and around their house and family.

Jesus once rebuked His disciples for being oblivious to God's work around them. God the Father had performed a miracle to feed five thousand men and their families with a handful of loaves and fishes. Then

Jesus performed a similar miracle feeding four thousand. Yet despite all they witnessed, the disciples were still disoriented to God's activity. Jesus asked, "Is your heart still hardened? Having eyes, do you not see? And having ears, do you not hear?" (Mark 8:17–18).

It's possible for God to be working all around our family and yet for us to miss what He is doing. We were fortunate to have a mother who stayed home during our childhood years. Part of the reason was because with five children to coordinate, feed, and shuttle, our Grand Central Station required a stay-at-home mom! But our mother also believed her ministry was to respond to what God was doing around her family.

As teenagers, we had our "lair" in the basement where we hung out with our friends. We'd often come upstairs to raid the kitchen for snacks only to discover one of our friends sitting at the kitchen table talking with our mother. He had come over to hang out with us, but upon being greeted at the door by our mother, she had commenced a lengthy discussion about his life and how he was spending it! Some of our friends never made it downstairs! We had two friends who lived across the street from our house when we were growing up. Their parents were divorced, and they lived with their father. When they needed somewhere to eat lunch on school days, our mother agreed to take them in and commenced ministering to them every lunch hour. Our house always teemed with neighborhood children when we were growing up (especially just after our mother pulled homemade cinnamon buns out of the oven!). Her attitude was: If these children's parents don't want their kids to hear about God, they can keep them away from my house!" Our friends heard a lot about God!

The same truth applies in our children's schools. God is at work there too, and wise parents try to be alert so they can join in His activity. Both of our wives were favorite volunteers at our children's schools. One year Lisa received a call from Daniel's teacher one week before school was to commence. The teacher explained that renovations to her classroom were running late, so her class could not meet in it during the first week of school. She had scheduled field trips for every day that first week. The teacher had heard Lisa was a great volunteer, so she was calling to enlist her services! Richard, on the other hand, took a shift as a parent volunteer at his daughter Carrie's kindergarten class one afternoon and had to go home immediately afterward and crawl straight into bed from exhaustion!

God is at work in our children's schools. Some of our children's friends come from hurting, broken homes. Other children have never been to church and have only heard God's name uttered in their home when it was being blasphemed. Still other children are lonely or hurting and desperately looking for someone who cares about them. Schools, whether they are public or private, are enormous mission fields for families that want to be on mission with God.

School and Casseroles (An example from Richard)

Do your children struggle with mornings as much as ours did? We're not sure if it was because their breakfast cereal was laced with sedatives, or what it was; but compared to our children, molasses looked like the Roadrunner when fleeing Wiley Coyote. One morning was particularly gruelling. Lisa kept encouraging the kids to pick up the pace and get ready for school. They stared blankly at her. "Hurry!" she urged. By the time Lisa pulled up to the school in our car, the school bell had rung and children were making their way to their classrooms. As Lisa helped her kids cross the street, she noticed Daniel's schoolteacher, Mrs. Smith, pulling into the staff parking lot. Anyone arriving *after* the Blackabys was *really* late!

Lisa's first thought was to look the other way and not embarrass the teacher by making it obvious she was aware of her tardiness. But Lisa felt impressed that she should find out why the teacher was unusually tardy. As Lisa walked quickly alongside the teacher, the frazzled woman explained what had happened. She was a single mom with two school-aged children. In the middle of the night, she awakened to a strange sound only to discover her oldest son in the midst of a seizure. Terrified, the woman raced him to a hospital emergency room and stayed up all night waiting for test results. The woman did not attend church and was unsure where to turn for help.

That day, Lisa sensed God had an assignment for her. She went home and began baking! I like to joke that Lisa has the "spiritual gift" of casseroles! After school that day, Lisa showed up at the teacher's doorstep with a homemade meal and words of encouragement. God wanted to comfort a distraught woman that day, and He chose to use an ordinary mom to do it.

The question is not, "Is God at work around my family?" The question is, "Have you recognized where God is working?" (Because He *is* at work!)

4. God Is at Work in Parents

When it comes to the role of parents in their children's lives, we could summarize it in two ways. *First,* parents support and participate in God's activity in their children's lives. *Second,* parents oppose and counteract the secular world's negative influence on their children. The harsh reality is: just as God is constantly at work in your home, so is the world's ungodly influence. More than likely your home is permeated with worldly values and perspectives that flow through social media, television, Internet, movies, music, billboards, and your children's friends. The world's values are diametrically opposed to God's. That is why the apostle Paul urged believers to "not be conformed to this world, but be transformed" (Rom. 12:2).

The challenge is that even as you train up your children to walk in righteousness, your children's friends and classmates may be trying to indoctrinate them with opposing values and viewpoints. You must be walking closely enough with your children to know what they are encountering. You must be able to recognize signs of the world, or God's activity, in your child's life.

What makes parenting so challenging is that each child is unique! One-size-fits-all parenting doesn't work! You may have worked hard to be a good parent to your firstborn. Then, just when you think you are starting to "get the hang of it," you have a second child who is diametrically opposite to the first one! Back to the drawing board! Some children will readily accept parental guidance while others stubbornly insist on doing everything their own way. Parents must fashion a unique and workable relationship with each child.

What makes things even more interesting is that the same qualities and characteristics in your children that exert a positive influence can likewise be their Achilles' heel. Being a sociable child can also lead your daughter to be easily influenced by her friends. Being an obedient child can lead your son to be easily led astray by deceitful classmates. It is imperative that parents know their children well so they are attentive to issues that inevitably arise.

A Challenge to Grow

As your children mature, their problems and temptations become more complex. It is one thing to help your preschooler learn how to share a toy with her friend in the nursery. It is quite another issue to teach your teenage daughter about moral purity or your son about avoiding Internet pornography.

That is why we commend you for reading this book. Wise parents are constantly learning and growing so they are prepared for the next stage their children enter. Just because you were successful with your children's previous stage of life is no guarantee you will obtain the same results in the future, especially if you fail to keep growing.

A word of caution is in order here. We know parents who insist that their children adapt to them rather than the parents adjusting to their children. After all, they are the parents, the adults in the household. They are in charge. It is the children who should adapt to the leadership style of their parents and show due respect in the process! As you might expect, this approach doesn't work very well.

We recommend the opposite. *You* are the mature person in the relationship, so it stands to reason that *you* should do the adapting. Your faith in God is presumably stronger than that of your child, so you should be the first one to go the extra mile. I (Richard) recently talked with a frustrated set of parents. They had developed the unhealthy habit of arguing with their daughter. She seemed so irrational and irresponsible to them that they were continually criticizing her choices and descending into yelling matches with her. They confided to me that they were worried that their daughter, having made so many poor decisions, might walk away from the Christian faith. I gently asked them what their daughter witnessed of the Christian faith when she interacted with her parents. They were critical, argumentative, and sarcastic toward her. I suggested that since they had been long-time Christians, they ought to be modelling Christian maturity to their daughter. The problem was that as their daughter progressed to teenage issues, her parents had lagged behind in their growth as parents. Now they were bewildered at how to relate to their teenage daughter who had been so sweet and compliant as a young child.

We talk with many discouraged parents who worry that they have grown too old or out-of-date to successfully relate to their teenage or adult children. Yet the truth is that, just as God seeks to grow up children, so He is fully prepared to bring parents to maturity as well. Before you give birth to your first child, God will be working in your life to prepare you for parenthood. It may be that one of the reasons God took twenty-five years to give Abraham his promised child was because it took that long to prepare Abraham to be the kind of parent required to raise a future patriarch.

As you welcome the first baby into your home, God may well be working on eradicating selfishness in you that could hinder you from being the caliber of parent he wants you to be. People are born with a natural tendency to be selfish. That has to be purged if we are going to raise our children well. Some people enter adulthood filled with anger, or with a sarcastic tongue, or a lazy streak. All of that has to go if we are going to be in a position to help our children experience God.

If God grants you more than one child, the Holy Spirit will seek to make whatever character adjustments are necessary in you to help you be successful. If you have both boys and girls, you will require additional fine-tuning! We grew up in a family with four boys and then one baby sister at the end of the line. Understandably, we were quite comfortable roughhousing and "trash talking" with our sons! But our daughters were another story! As men (and "manly men," we might add), we both had to learn how to relate to our sweet little daughters. That involved additional growth on our part! Thankfully God, and our wives, helped us make the adjustments in our parenting so we could effectively raise our sweet daughters.

Conclusion

God *is* at work around you! And He is actively at work in your family. You must learn to recognize God's activity whether it is in, through, or around your home. It is also critical that you quickly respond every time God chooses to do a fresh work in you as a parent. In the coming chapters we'll look closely at what this looks like.

QUESTIONS FOR REFLECTION/DISCUSSION

1. Where do you see God working in your family right now?

2. If you don't recognize where God is working presently, why do you think that is?

3. What might you do to identify where God is at work in your family? Consider:

- Going away for a weekend with your spouse and praying and talking about where God is at work.
- Taking each of your children out for a meal and asking them probing questions that might reveal God's activity in their lives.
- Taking time to pray in an extended way over each of your family members and asking the Holy Spirit to enlighten your understanding to His activity around them.

4. Could it be that something in your life is hindering God's work in your family? If it is, take immediate action to remove the impediment.

CHAPTER 9

God Calls Us into a Love Relationship

Wind in My Face (An Example from Tom the Sea Captain)

My family tries to coordinate our schedules during the summer so we can take a week's vacation together. This past summer we rented a small vacation house in Penticton, British Columbia, situated between two lakes. We enjoyed the beaches, floated down the canal between the lakes, visited the summer music festival, ate great food, and checked out an amazing farmer's market spread across three city blocks. But the highlight was renting a small ski boat for tubing, something we had never done before. Each of the family members had their chance to ride in the water tube. Thumbs-up signal was for "go faster and crazier"; thumbs down signal was for "slow down, you are scaring me to death." I enjoyed bouncing my teenage son around and seeing him laugh and scream as I pulled him back and forth across the wake behind the boat. I loved stopping in the middle of the lake just to jump in the warm water with my kids and watch them do flips off the side of the boat. But the enduring memory of that time was looking over at my youngest son, Conor, as we drove into the sunset, wind whipping his blond hair and a huge smile on his face as he sat looking out from the front of the boat. He turned around and said, "Dad, this is the best day of my whole life!" At that moment I felt like I had finally achieved a long-standing goal as a dad, which was to help my kids enjoy life and to appreciate being together as a family. We have to work hard to schedule those times now with busy college schedules, part-time jobs, sport camps, fund-raisers, and church activities, but it's so worth it. Building a love relationship takes intentional and consistent effort. No one is better at that than God. His goal for us is to enjoy Him and to delight in being a part of His amazing family.

Mommy Help!

"Mom, I need help with my hair!"

"Dad, I need more contact lens solution."

"Mom I need a sack lunch tomorrow."

"Dad, I need a ride to school early for practise in the morning."

"Mom, I need $20 for school photos."

"Daddy, I need help to spread my jam on my peanut butter."

"Mommy I need help to wipe my . . ."

It seems that every time we turn around, our children need something from us. To a certain extent it is nice to be needed. Good parents want to provide for their needs and to help them thrive. Every child has different kinds of needs:

1. *Physical needs,* such as a safe home environment, eating a balanced diet, proper clothing, adequate sleep, and safety from harm

2. *Emotional needs,* such as feeling wanted, a supportive family, freedom from manipulation and emotional abuse, and a stable/predictable home life

3. *Spiritual needs,* such as connecting with our Creator, fellowship with other Christians, support and encouragement in our faith, and good models of Christlikeness

4. *Psychological needs,* such as affirmation, laughter, acceptance, being told the truth, and a healthy home environment

The Ultimate Need

There is one particular need, however, that when met, addresses all the others: love. Perhaps that is why love is foundational to the two greatest commandments (Matt. 22:38–39). Out of His infinite love, God created us with a need for love. Significantly, of all the creatures God created, only humans have the capacity to return love to their Creator (unless, of course, we count puppies). This is part of what it means to be created in God's image (Gen. 1:26).

God calls each member of your family into a love relationship with Himself. This is not something that can be forced on your kids, nor can we respond to His love *for* them. We can only create an environment for our kids to want to follow our God. Have you noticed that whether it is cars, jewelry, sports, books, classic movies, guns, crafts, flowers, vacation spots, or fast-food restaurants, children often like the same things their parents like? Richard has faithfully cheered for the Buffalo Sabres hockey team for more than forty years. They have never won the Stanley Cup (though he will be quick to tell you they *should* have, several times). But guess what? Richard's son Daniel is an avid fan too. They both get the NHL cable station simply so they can watch their beloved Sabres play on TV. Daniel has Sabres paraphernalia and devotes many hours to learning about their young players developing in their farm system and about the renovations to the players' locker room. Why, you might ask? Is it a rare genetic brain disorder passed down from father to son? Well, maybe. But if the truth is told, Daniel loves the Buffalo Sabres because his *dad* does. More often than not, our children will grow to love what their parents *genuinely* care about. How sad when our offspring can enthusiastically chant all of our college football cheers and recite lyrics from our favorite songs and movies, but they show little interest in our God. When we enjoy God, love to be with His people, appreciate His blessings, and find great pleasure spending time with Him, our children notice. They know what we *really* care about.

Remember when Jesus met some of His disciples at the Sea of Galilee after He had been resurrected? He intended to use them to spread the gospel message across the world. But there was one thing He wanted to settle with Peter first. Three times Jesus asked Peter, "Do you love Me?" (John 21:15–17). Jesus knew that if Peter didn't get his love relationship with Jesus settled first, nothing else in his life would matter. Every one of us has to honestly answer that same question.

Campfire Chat (An Example from Tom)

I was once asked to bring the devotional thoughts in the morning and the fireside chat in the evenings at a summer youth camp. I brought my son Conor with me so he could ride horses, run the ropes course, and practise some archery. During one of the fireside chats, I mentioned the importance of putting God first in our life. I said even though my wife and children meant everything to me, if I had to choose between my relationship with them and my relationship with God, I would choose God. On the way back to our car that night, Conor looked up at me with a quizzical look on his face and asked, "You would give up your *family?*" I thought for a moment and replied, "It's not that I don't dearly love my wife and children, but the Bible tells us to love God more than anything else in the world." He said, "Oh, I know. And that's the way it should be."

Abraham had an opportunity to teach his son Isaac a similar lesson (Gen. 22:9–12). Isaac was the son of promise, the one through whom a nation was going to be built. He was also probably spoiled, the only son of older parents, and had everything he wanted. (After his parents waited twenty-five years for him, can you imagine the toys stockpiled in his nursery when he was born?) Once Isaac became a teenager, his father took him to the top of Mount Moriah and proved to God, and to his son, that nothing was more important to him than God. Isaac saw firsthand that his father's relationship with God superseded everything else. Seeing his dad's dedication propelled Isaac to make a similar commitment himself. On that historic day, Isaac learned far more from his father's actions than from his words. What would your children say is the most important thing in your life? (They can tell, by the way.)

One of God's harshest rebukes of His people was for abandoning Him for false gods. It grieves God when His children turn away from Him. One of the Ten Commandments specifically warns, "You shall have no other gods before Me" (Exod. 20:3). God understood what it was like to have rebellious children! Listen to what God had to put up with from His people:

- "Therefore, fear the LORD and worship Him in sincerity and truth. Get rid of the gods your fathers worshiped beyond the Euphrates River and in Egypt, and worship Yahweh." (Josh. 24:14 HCSB)
- "The Israelites did what was evil in the LORD's sight. They worshiped the Baals and abandoned the LORD, the God of their fathers, who had brought them out of Egypt. They went after other gods from the surrounding peoples and bowed down to them. They infuriated the LORD." (Judg. 2:11–12 HCSB)
- "When Solomon was old, his wives seduced him to follow other gods. He was not devoted to Yahweh his God, as his father David had been." (1 Kings 11:4 HCSB)
- "And in every single city of Judah he made high places to burn incense to other gods, and provoked to anger the LORD God of his fathers." (2 Chron. 28:25)
- "I will pronounce My judgments against them for all the evil they did when they abandoned Me to burn incense to other gods and to worship the works of their own hands." (Jer. 1:16 HCSB)
- "They have returned to the sins of their ancestors who refused to obey My words and have followed other gods to worship them. The house of Israel and the house of Judah broke My covenant I made with their ancestors." (Jer. 11:10 HCSB)
- "But you have done more evil than all who were before you, for you have gone and made yourself other gods, and molded images to provoke Me to anger, and have cast Me behind your back." (1 Kings 14:9)

The Israelites would have loudly protested that they still loved God. After all, they continued to observe the Sabbath. They celebrated religious holidays and donated offerings at the temple. Their schedules were filled with religious activity. But God saw their heart. He knew how they really felt about Him. He recognized that they had other priorities and loyalties than Him. God described Himself as "a jealous God" (Deut. 5:9). He will tolerate no rivals for our affection. He is dissatisfied with lip service or the occasional donation in the offering plate. He will settle for nothing short of us loving Him with *all* of our heart, soul, mind, and strength (Mark 12:30). We may attend church every Sunday. We may loudly proclaim our belief in Christian doctrines and uphold moral standards, but God knows where He stands in our priorities.

Disconcerting Questions (An Example from Tom)

Two of my three children have admitted to me at different times that they were unsure if God existed, or that it didn't seem like prayer actually worked, or they didn't get anything out of the Bible when they read it. This was disconcerting, since both of them had prayed for Christ to save them from their sins, had been baptized, and were members of the church. I realized they were at an age where they were ready to own their relationship with God. They were separating their belief from their parents' faith. I admit I was a little nervous. But I also remembered doing the same thing when I was a teenager. I had to come to a place where God was real to me, not just to my mom or dad. I could no longer believe God existed because they said He did. I wanted to know for myself that He loved me and had a plan for my life.

I assured both of my children that God had placed them in a Christian home so they would be introduced to Him at an early age and would have a good foundation upon which to know Him. I recounted various times throughout their life when we had prayed for them and God had answered in unique ways. I reviewed our family history and showed them how God had clearly cared for us, led us, guided us, and blessed us as we loved and followed Him. But just as Joshua required his people to choose which god they would serve (Josh. 24:15), they would have to make their own decision to surrender their lives into God's loving hands. Though they have experienced different spiritual journeys, both came to a place where it seemed best to honor God and follow Him. Now their faith is their own. Presently I am preparing to have that same discussion with my youngest son one day soon and am praying a lot in the meantime.

Owning Our Faith

Mike and Daniel Blackaby, in their compelling book *When Worlds Collide: Stepping Up and Standing Out in an Anti-God Culture,* assert that seven out of ten teenagers in the church today will walk away from church.[1] This statistic worries many Christian parents. Inevitably there are times when our children will express reluctance to attend church or to participate in youth programs or Bible studies. In these moments, parents may fear that their child is turning their back on their faith and on God.

Most children will experience times where "church" isn't appealing to them. However, some of those children may never have possessed a genuine faith in God in the first place. There are numerous well-meaning parents who sincerely desire for each of their children to come to a saving faith in Christ. These parents bring their children to every church meeting and Bible study they can. They make their kids do their nightly Bible readings and say their prayers. All of this is fine, but at times parents, and their churches, inadvertently water down what it means to become a Christian in their attempt to ensure all of their children make decisions for Christ.

The most oft-used invitation to salvation these days goes something like this: "Today, if you will ask Jesus to come into your heart, He will save you from your sins, and you will go to heaven when you die." Often the preacher will instruct everyone to bow their heads and close their eyes. Then he'll say, "While no one is looking, just raise your hand briefly if you want to ask Jesus to come into your heart right now." Several hands furtively shoot up and then back down. The speaker assures those who raised their hand that they are now destined for heaven when they die. When the children's parents hear of their decision, they are delighted and relieved that their child is now a believer. The child is soon baptized and added to the church membership roll. Being promised that "once saved, always saved," the youngster attempts to be a good Christian by going to church and trying to be "good."

This practice, though it brings great relief to parents, is dangerously misleading. For one, this type of conversion "prayer" is totally inadequate. It does not include repentance. Jesus will not enter your heart if you refuse to repent of your sin (Acts 2:38; 3:19). Second, there is no mention of placing your faith in Christ. Without faith, you cannot be saved (Rom. 10:9–10). Third, it mentions nothing of Christ's lordship (Luke 6:46). Without repentance, faith, and surrender to Christ's will, people will not experience conversion.

The Bible says it is evident who has been born again and who has not. Just look at the fruit of peoples' lives. Jesus said: "For every tree is known by its own fruit. For men do not gather figs from thorns, nor do they gather grapes from a bramble bush" (Luke 6:44). When people become Christians, they do not merely have their name added to the Book of Life. To become a Christian, you must be *born again*. Your entire orientation and nature changes. The Holy Spirit enters your life at conversion and begins to transform you from a sinner into a saint. To use Jesus' analogy, if you are transformed from an unregenerate apple tree into a converted orange tree, it will be obvious! How? Your life will begin to produce oranges! But if you claim to have been transformed into an orange tree, but all your life produces is apples, you are merely a deluded apple tree. Unfortunately, there are many children who continue to produce apples in their lives, but their parents hold fast to the hope that their children are in fact now orange trees. The evidence simply isn't there.

I (Richard) once met a sincere couple who were grieving over their son's spiritual condition. He had prayed the "sinners prayer" when he was seven and had been baptized into their church soon afterward. But at age fifteen, the boy rebelled and turned his back on God. He was now thirty-two and had never looked back. These sincere parents pled with him to return to his faith. They gave him Christian books and Bibles, but he refused to read them or to discuss spiritual issues with them. They told me: "We keep telling him he is a Christian and he needs to *live* like one, but he won't listen to us. What else can we tell him?" I understood that these parents desperately wanted to believe that even if their child never darkened the door of a church building again, he would one day go to heaven due to his childhood decision. But the parents were not doing their son any favor by assuring him that though he was living as an unregenerate person, he was actually a saint. It is absolutely critical that we help our children experience a true, authentic, born-again experience in which they repent of their sins, place their faith in Christ, and wholly yield their lives to obey Christ. When people are truly born again, they *stay* born again!

There comes a time in each person's life when they must own their faith. They can no longer relate to God through their parents' convictions or trust in God because their relatives do. They must establish their own personal relationship with God, for they are the only ones who can surrender their lives into His hands. It is our prayer that every Christian parent will live in such a way that their children will feel compelled to love and serve the God of their parents. It is heartbreaking to hear parents lament the fact that they brought their kids to church, but they never brought them to Christ.

Your Faith Is Paramount

Living out an authentic and genuine love relationship with God before your children is the most important thing you can do as a parent. You may be wondering right now if *you* have ever truly given your life to Christ. Some can pinpoint the day and hour when they were "born again"; others see it as a process over time. The *how* is not as important as *that* you are a Christian. If you are unsure about your own spiritual condition, you must begin here and settle that all-important question once and for all. Only then can you help your family have Christ at its center.

How *Can* We Know We Are Saved?

Here are three simple tests you can use to see if a person's heart has been transformed by the indwelling presence of God:

1. When we are saved, God promises to place His Holy Spirit in us, affirming that we have been born again. If you are not aware of the presence of God in your life; if you are not feeling conviction for your sin; if you have no desire to worship God, study His Word, talk to Him in prayer, or be with His people, then God is not in the center of your heart and life (2 Thess. 2:13; Eph. 1:13; Rom. 8:11).

2. One of the roles of the Holy Spirit is to conform you into the image of Christ (Rom. 8:29). That means your attitude will become like Christ's (Rom. 12:2; 1 Cor. 2:16), your behavior will reflect Christ's (Col. 2:6; 1 John 1:7; 2:6), and your character will bear testimony to the Spirit's presence in you (Gal. 5:22–23). You should be growing in love, joy, peace, patience, goodness, kindness, gentleness, faithfulness, and self-control (the fruit of the Spirit). The Bible claims a good tree cannot bear bad fruit (Matt. 7:16–18). If the fruit of someone's life is contrary

to Christ's character, you know something is amiss. Paul says, "Now the works of the flesh are obvious: sexual immorality, moral impurity, promiscuity, idolatry, sorcery, hatreds, strife, jealously, outbursts of anger, selfish ambitions, dissensions, factions, envy, drunkenness, carousing, and anything similar. I tell you these things in advance—as I told you before—that those who practice such things will not inherit the kingdom of God" (Gal. 5:19–21 HCSB).

3. The Bible says that how we treat others reveals what our heart is like toward God. We cannot hate others and love God at the same time (John 13:20; 1 John 2:9; 4:20). Our thoughts and actions toward other people will reflect our love for God. We should always be trying to draw others to God's love through us, not disrespecting them, judging them, criticizing them, and pushing them away. Jesus said, "You have heard that it was said, Love your neighbor and hate your enemy. But I tell you, love your enemies and pray for those who persecute you, so that you may be sons of your Father in heaven" (Matt. 5:43–45 HCSB). Our relationships with others reflect our relationship with Christ.

If your children have no desire to attend church and no interest in honoring God with their lives, then you need to continue praying for their heart transformation. Don't keep trying to force religious activity upon them when what they need is a relationship with Christ!

There are times, however, when children, especially teenagers, may choose to reject their earlier faith and commitments in order to live according to the world's values and ways. In this case the issue may not be their *salvation* but their *obedience*. The prophet Jonah had a problem with obeying God. In fact, he ran in the opposite direction from where God told him to go (he ended up with a whale of a story!). It wasn't that he didn't know God; it was that He did not want to do what God said. Some children may follow in the steps of the prodigal son. That particular child needed to come to his senses before he finally returned to his father (Luke 15:13). The prodigal was still a son, just a wayward son. If Christ does indeed dwell within our wayward children, then He will be continually wooing them back to Himself.

Jesus told a parable about a farmer sowing his seeds by hand (Matt. 13:1–23). It was an ordinary event in the life of a farmer, but the spiritual application is relevant to our children as well. The seeds scattered by the farmer fell on four different types of soil.

1. *Pathway*—The soil was hard, so birds came and ate the seeds before they could take root (God's Word had no impact on the person's heart at all).
2. *Rocky soil*—The soil was shallow and rocky. The seeds sprang up quickly, but because they only had shallow roots, they died in the hot sun before they could mature (God's Word created some interest but withered in the heat of the day).
3. *Weedy soil*—The soil was good, but it was so full of weeds that when the plants began to grow, they were choked to death by the competition (the Word began to exert an impact on the person's life, but the life was so conflicted with cares, concerns, and temptations that God's Word eventually was snuffed out).
4. *Good soil*—The soil was fertile and deep, and the seeds grew strong roots and produced between thirty to a hundred times what was sown (God's Word was welcomed, so it produced much fruit in the person's life).

Each of the four types of soil received the same seeds, but only in one of the four soils did the seed grow to maturity and bear fruit. Helping our children get past a shallow relationship with God into a deeper walk with Him is our goal. We must do everything possible to cultivate the soil of our children's hearts so their childhood conversions grow, mature, and produce lasting fruit over the ensuing years. That's why we need to watch our children's hearts carefully. We must remain alert to any hardening or "weeds" creeping in. If we allow our children to remain bitter toward a friend who disappointed them, their heart can grow hard. We'll need to help them process hurtful experiences so they maintain a warm, vibrant walk with God. When we begin to hear our children talking excitedly about things of the world, such as Hollywood romances or cute boys at high school, but they show no interest in God, we recognize we have some "weeding" to do! Wise parents tend to the soil of their children's hearts so they are receptive to the next seeds God sows in them.

Consider What Your Children Witness

Unfortunately, not all churches are stellar examples of what God intended His people to be like. Many children are being taken to churches that are dry, ritualistic, divided, boring, and lifeless. For these young people, church is something you endure, a religious duty to perform each week, but it has no meaning or relevance for them. They may not see how the church makes any meaningful contribution in their parents' lives either. For such children, "going to church" merely involves being a nice person, giving some money in the collection plate, singing a few songs, and enduring a boring speaker each week.

Until God becomes personal to them, they will always see church as a ritual, a routine, and a religious activity, but not a place to encounter the living and loving God. It is critical that you take your family to a healthy, growing church because your children will tend to view God through the lens of their local church. If church is boring, then God is boring. If church is exciting and innovative, so is God. However, you may not have many viable options for healthy churches where you live. That is when your personal walk with God in your home will have even greater significance!

Finding a Church Family (An Example from Tom)

When we moved back to North America after living in Norway, Kim and I had to find a church to attend for the first time in our marriage (I had always been on staff before). It was somewhat disappointing how difficult it was to find a church that preached God's Word accurately; encouraged its people to develop a personal, growing walk with Christ; modeled love among its members; and actively strengthened Christian families. We took our search for a new church home extremely seriously because we knew how impactful it would be on our family. Kim and I knew there were things we wanted in a church, but it was more important to us that our children feel connected to it. We were willing to forego some of our own preferences so our children had a positive experience.

During those days we concluded that the church was not responsible for discipling our children. That was our responsibility as parents. It took almost two years to finally settle on a church family. During that

time we had a lot of family devotionals and family prayer times to help
our kids stay connected with God. We even had our own family worship services while sitting around the piano! Our children heard what
God was saying to their parents as we took turns sharing with them.
As parents, we learned how to communicate our faith to our kids more
effectively both in word and in deed.

Ask Yourself Some Questions

Our homes must have a faith in Christ that is alive, meaningful,
personal, growing, authentic, and attractive. Ask yourself:

- Do I have the peace Christ promised in my life? (John 14:27;
  Phil. 4:7)
- Do I demonstrate the joy of Christ's presence in my life? (John
  15:11; 16:24)
- What does my behavior reflect about my love for God? (Mark
  12:30)
- How often do my children hear me pray? (Eph. 6:18)
- How well do I represent God's love to my children? (John
  13:34)
- Do I put God's kingdom first in my life and in my home?
  (Matt. 6:33)

Hopefully you are doing well enough in these areas that your children could not use your example as an excuse to turn away from God.
Authentic, genuine, growing, personal faith is central to demonstrating
a love relationship with God to our children. When our children watch
the joy we have in relating to Christ, they ought to feel compelled to
embrace Christ for themselves.

Prodigals Want a Party

The Bible does not provide many details regarding the home
in which the prodigal son and his older brother were raised (Luke
15:11–32). They must have been relatively well-to-do as the family had
servants, nice robes, and a family ring. There was also enough money to

give the younger son his inheritance early without destroying the family business. We know the boys were expected to work, since the older son had returned from working in the fields when he discovered his younger brother had returned. What is interesting is that both boys were looking for essentially the same thing—a party. The younger son decided to find it in a faraway land where he squandered his money on loose living, eventually becoming destitute. The older brother longed for a party, too, and resented his father for never throwing one for him. Both failed to appreciate what they had in their father. The younger son assumed he could only find happiness by embracing what the world offered. The older son was around his father all the time, but he didn't *know* him and, therefore, failed to *enjoy* him. While this parable is generally used to portray God's amazing grace for sinners who find their way home, there is an underlying issue. Both children were looking for a party. They wanted to experience joy in their lives. Of course, our children want that too. Some of our kids will assume that to find it, they must leave the church, and the faith, and greedily gulp up all that the world has to offer. Others may continue to sullenly go to church, but they find no joy in their relationship with their heavenly Father either. Parents must help their children understand that there is incredible joy available in their relationship with their heavenly Father if only they will get to know Him.

Would you say your home is characterized by love and joy? Do you have times when you sit and laugh together or celebrate one another's accomplishments? Does your family know how to throw great parties? (For a discussion of joy in the home, check out Richard's book *The Seasons of God*.) We both strived to develop homes that reverberated with the joy of the Lord. We wanted our kids to understand that the essence of the Christian life was not the rules you had to follow but the relationship you got to enjoy. Both of our wives excel at organizing parties and helping our kids enjoy life and family. For several years in a row, Tom's family had to announce the dates of his son's birthday party months ahead so his friend's families could plan their spring break vacation accordingly! Over the years, our houses have been transformed into pirate islands, enchanted forests, truck stops, hippie communes, towns from the wild west, and Cleopatra's palace! Who says Christians can't have fun? The key, of course, is not the amount of money you spend or the decorations you put up, but the irrepressible joy that bubbles up within each family member who has come to know and experience their amazing heavenly Father.

Answering Machine Man (A Story from Tom)

Having lived in an international community in Europe exposed our children to many different cultures, nationalities, and accents. Few people have the ability to nail an accent like my son Matthew. He listened carefully to his friends in school and has dead-on imitations. From Asian Indian, to Chinese, Scottish, Irish, proper British, Italian, German, and particularly Norwegian, he can get us rolling on the floor with laughter in only a few minutes. We have let Matt record our answering machine messages for many years now, changing from Norwegian to Irish to whatever comes into his mind at the time. It is fun to hear the messages on the machine when the person calling has a hard time speaking because they are laughing so hard at the recording. Our family likes to share our joy with those who cross our path!

There needs to be love and joy in our homes. The daily pressures are, well, *daily*. Nevertheless, there are a multitude of reasons for families to have fun, to celebrate God's blessings, to enjoy their children, to sing, and to party. You will find that few children want to avoid a home that is filled with love and joy. It is natural to rebel against rules, criticism, unreasonable expectations, perfectionism, and micromanaging parents. But why would you rebel against a joy-filled home? "I'm outta here; everyone is just too happy in this house!" Not likely. Our kids ought to grow up experiencing the joy of a vibrant walk with God. Let's plan some spiritual parties and celebrate God, our friends, and the wonderful blessings God has given us!

Conclusion

Christianity is not primarily a religion. It is a relationship. The relationship is not based on dread or manipulation or uncertainty but on love (Jer. 31:3). A love relationship between you and God always leads to joy (John 15:11). This is what God is constantly pursuing with you and with your children. Living out of the "overflow" involves entering each day profoundly aware that almighty God loves *you*. God's presence in your life ought to be like a spring of living water that continually bubbles up within you (John 4:14; 7:38). Growing up in a home in which the parents are continually basking in the joy of God's presence is an incredible experience. May you never be satisfied until that is the experience of each of your children.

QUESTIONS FOR REFLECTION/DISCUSSION

1. Which words would best describe your current relationship with Christ?

> Loving
> Growing
> Vibrant
> Joyful
> Distant
> Strained
> Unreliable
> Dull
> Lifeless
> Exciting

2. Is your walk with God attractive to your children? Why or why not?

3. Could you say with all honesty that you love God with all of your heart, mind, soul, and strength?

4. What is the compelling evidence that you have been born again?

5. Write down the names of each of your children. Beside each name, list the clear evidence that they are or are not born again. If some of your children are not currently believers, put their names in your Bible and pray fervently and daily for their salvation.

6. What would you say most characterizes your home?

> Quiet
> Joyful
> Disciplined
> Frantic
> Fun
> Godly
> Busy

Noisy
Loving
Studious
Struggling

7. What fond family memories do you have from your own childhood that you are trying to recreate in your own home?

8. Do your family members enjoy being with one another? What do you think has contributed to the current atmosphere in your home? What needs to happen for your family to reclaim its affection for each other?

9. Do your children enjoy going to church? How might you help your family to get more out of church?

Notes

1. Mike Blackaby and Daniel Blackaby, *When Worlds Collide* (Nashville: B&H Publishing Group, 2011), xix.

CHAPTER 10

God Invites Us to Become Involved with Him in His Work

Missed Opportunities
(An Example from Richard)

When my children were in elementary school, I held a demanding job as the president of a seminary. I had to put in long hours at the office (or at least I *thought* I did). However, I didn't want to always be coming home late at night or missing dinner with my family. So, I developed a schedule in which I arrived at the office early each morning so I could return home at a reasonable time. I reasoned that my family would be snuggled in their beds during those early morning hours anyway, so it wouldn't cost them anything if I were already at the office. For years I arrived to work before 6:30 a.m. By 4:30 p.m. I was on my way home.

There was one problem. I was often exhausted by the end of the day. During those years, my teenage son Daniel became infatuated with basketball. I put up a net in our driveway, and he was forever shooting baskets. As soon as I would drag my weary bones into the house after another day at the office, Daniel would be enthusiastically asking me to come out and shoot some hoops with him. All I could think about was reposing in my La-Z-Boy recliner until dinner was served. Typically I'd make a "deal" with my son. "Just give me ten minutes to rest, and then I'll come out and play," I would plead. I would fall heavily into my chair and then desperately hope that Daniel would forget how to tell time! Sure enough, he'd be back, right on cue. "Dad. It's time!" "Son, just five more minutes. I had a *really* hard day today . . ." This routine occurred daily.

One day I entered the house and flopped into my chair, waiting for the negotiations to begin. Nothing. *Good,* I thought. *Perhaps Daniel hasn't noticed I'm home yet.* But then as I lay with my eyes closed, I began to hear a faint noise. At first I couldn't discern what it was. Then, it dawned on me. The sound I was hearing was the dull thumping of a basketball being bounced on the driveway outside . . . My son hadn't bothered to ask me to join him. In that moment, I sensed God speaking to me. I had been going to work early so I could be "available" to my family. But snoozing in a living room chair was not going to win me any "Most Accessible Parent" awards! God was working in my teenage son's life, and I was missing a marvelous opportunity to get in on the action. I hurriedly climbed out of my chair, threw on my tennis shoes, and made my way out to the driveway to join my son.

Sadly, that scenario is what many well-meaning parents experience. They *want* to be involved in God's activity in their children's lives, but they keep missing divine appointments that come their way. I personally vowed that if God was doing something in my children's lives, I didn't want to be sawing logs in the den when He did!

God Invites Us to Join Him in His Work

We should never lose our wonder at the amazing truth that almighty God chooses to involve *us,* mere creatures of dust, in His eternal work. God has an unlimited number of angelic beings prepared to instantly carry out His commands. Magnificent warrior archangels such as Michael stand perpetually at the ready to undertake any task their King commands. Faithful messengers such as Gabriel are continually alert to deliver divine messages promptly and accurately. God need only think, and it is done. *God has absolutely no need for people.* Yet, out of His infinite love and gracious condescension, God chooses to involve us—His frail, fallible creatures—to join Him in conducting His work.

Perhaps we should first consider exactly what the "work" is in which God allows us to participate. Not everyone views that word favorably!

For some, it connotes drudgery, toil, and tedium. Yet that certainly does not describe God's activity! God's purposes bring glory to Him through His creation. When God first created the universe, everything in it magnified Him (Rom. 1:20). As each star, planet, and creature fulfilled its divine purpose, it pointed directly back in reverential awe to its Creator. But then sin entered into humanity. People, the apex of creation, foolishly rebelled against God and chose to live in defiance of His ways and commands. The consequences were as immediate as they were horrific (Rom. 6:23). People suffered alienation from God and from one another. Violence and murder tore asunder the beautiful creation God had so lovingly assembled. The creation that had once eagerly embraced its divine purpose and brought glory to God now lived in terminal, desperate, rebellion against the only One who could give it life.

Since the epic fall of humanity, God has been steadily working to restore His creation. He does this by defeating sin, restoring fellowship with His creatures, and enabling people to experience abundant life (John 10:10). It is to this end that God is continually working. When God invites you to join Him, it is to bring Him glory by accomplishing His redemptive purposes in people's lives. As God sets people free, His kingdom expands. As people once again experience their divine purpose, they bring glory to God.

God wants *your* children to experience the fullness of life He designed them for. Sin, however, will rob them of God's best, just as it has cheated every person in history. God is therefore working to set your children free from their sin so they are free to enjoy fellowship with Him. Just as God called judges, prophets, apostles, teachers, evangelists, and preachers to become involved in His divine activity, so He will invite parents to join in His work to see that their children avoid the perils of sin and embrace abundant life.

What Joining God's Activity Is Not

Sometimes it is as important to understand what a thing is *not* as to know what it *is*. Well-meaning parents often misunderstand what God is asking them to do, and as a result, they invest their efforts in the wrong activities. The following are examples of the kind of work God is not asking us to do.

1. Resident Critic

Children generally have an innate sense of enthusiasm and hope. There is an invigorating freshness to youth who believe they can do anything! But to those of us who are older (and theoretically wiser), what seems like optimism to a teenager can sound a lot like naiveté to us. Hearing our children go on and on about how they will one day become a fireman or ballerina or action hero or rock star can grow wearisome for parents who realize how much work, effort, and luck is required to succeed in certain fields. So, some parents feel the need to give their kids a regular dose of "reality." Whenever their children begin speaking of their dreams, their parents hastily remind them that they are clumsy, or have big feet, or can't carry a tune, or don't have a scholarship or wealthy parents . . . Such parents genuinely believe they are helping their offspring by steering them away from idle dreams and on to more realistic ambitions. However, it is tragic when parents serve as their children's dream killers.

2. Substitute Holy Spirit

Some parents don't trust the Holy Spirit to do His job in their children's lives, so they give the third member of the Trinity a helping hand. Such thoughtful parents regularly lecture their children on how they should be living. Helpful articles warning against everything from obesity to pornography are shared for their offspring's edification. Lest the Holy Spirit be unable to bring adequate conviction over sin, these zealous parents leave no stone unturned in their efforts to ensure their children feel suitably guilty for any perceived or potential wrongdoing. Rather than allowing the Holy Spirit to work the sermon preached by the pastor on Sunday into their child's soul, these parents re-preach the message to their captive audience over Sunday lunch, with extra emphasis that was missed during its first delivery. While these parents might claim to trust God, their actions disclose the truth that they believe they, rather than the Holy Spirit, are responsible for their child's Christlikeness.

3. Judge, Jury, Warden

At times, parents can feel that their full-time job is meting out suitable punishments for their children's infractions of the family rules. While certainly there are times when parents must discipline their children as they guide them into godly behavior, that ought not to be the dominant feature in a Christian home. We have witnessed families where the prevailing conversation at the dinner table was on the various "sentences" each of the children were currently serving because of missed curfews or carelessly done chores. Some households are filled with shouting and recrimination for the children's continual shortcomings. One misguided mother was concerned that her teenage daughter was getting involved with the "wrong" crowd. When the miscreant returned home past curfew one night, her "punishment" was to be told she could not attend the Wednesday night worship time for teenagers at her church! The mother "reasoned" that because her daughter loved going to church on Wednesday evenings, it would be a perfect way to punish her for her misdeeds.

Sadly, many children who grow up in Christian homes come away with the skewed perception that Christianity is fundamentally about following rules and being forbidden from having fun. The majority of the conversations with their parents concerning Christianity always center on how they are not measuring up. Sadly, some parents act more like prison wardens than dispensers of blessing.

4. Religious Purist

There are parents who spend tremendous energy diligently ensuring that their children are protected from less-than-perfect churches. If the pastor does not use the "correct" Bible translation, or if the youth worship team leads the young people to sing songs that are not theologically sound, or if there is too much fun, and not enough Bible study or too much Bible study and not enough fun then the parents noisily yank their children from the program and zealously begin looking for another congregation. Such families may attend a multiplicity of churches over the years in their vain quest to discover a congregation that functions in an acceptable manner. Children growing up in such homes are regularly inundated with observations and criticisms of their minister's shortcomings and their church's deficiencies. When children are indignantly withdrawn from their church every few years, their parents may assume they are teaching their children to prize sound doctrine and God-honoring worship, but they may in fact be teaching their children to quit church every time they experience something they don't like. While sincerely wanting their children to have an edifying and doctrinally correct church experience, these misguided parents fail to recognize that with every criticism they launch at their church, they are planting nefarious seeds in their children's hearts that could one day spring forth into full-grown apostasy. Parents ought to beware when they find themselves continually speaking negatively about the church or its people. While the adults may think they are upholding a high standard for the church, their children may decide, based on what they heard, to chuck the faith and its people altogether.

5. Freedom Giver

These parents believe each child needs to find their own way to God. They don't want to force them to go to church, or demand they go to youth group, or require them to participate in church activities. Often these parents were forced to attend church when they were young, so they refuse to do the same to their children. Sometimes they feel each religion has its merits, and their children need to find which one is right for them. They believe it is OK to force them to clean their room, brush their teeth, take a shower, treat their possessions with care, and do their chores; but when it comes to "religious" things, they don't want to give any direction or pressure their kids in any way for fear they may rebel. The truth is that children *need* direction when it comes to matters of faith. Neglecting to help your children in the most important issue of life is gross negligence, and it tells them you don't consider faith in God to be as important as brushing their teeth.

Summary

The sad truth is that there are many well-meaning parents who fear that without constant diligence and a firm hand, their children could one day enter the burgeoning ranks of young adults who are leaving the church annually, despite their devout upbringing. Paradoxically, by raising their children on their own agenda, rather than joining God in

His activity, these parents facilitate the exodus they dread. God does not ask us to do everything we know to do in order to be good parents. He asks us to do everything He tells us. This means allowing God to take the lead in raising our children. We can trust Him with our family. He loves our children more than we do! And He knows what He's doing. He's had experience! The key is to recognize where God is working and then, when He invites us, to join Him in His activity.

God Is at Work

There are many places where God is at work in our world. He is certainly active in local churches. He is engaged in many Christian ministries that serve around the world. God is working in the market-place as well as in many places that might surprise you. But for many families, the most exciting reality is that God is not just accomplishing His purposes in evangelistic crusades held in massive stadiums or among pioneering missionaries reaching remote villages for the gospel; He is also working in their own home. There are at least three major areas where God is active in families.

1. God Works to Produce Godly Character

One of our favourite stories is that of Agostino di Duccio. In 1464, he was enlisted to produce a sculpture that would be placed along the roofline of the Florence cathedral. It was to join statues of Joshua and Hercules that had already been sculpted. The artist was given a large block of marble, and he commenced his work. However, in 1466 Agostino abruptly abandoned his project, and the partially sculpted marble sat forsaken in a courtyard for ten years. The stone was described as "badly blocked out and supine." In 1476, Antonio Rossellino was commissioned to salvage the marble and complete the project, yet he soon abandoned the effort as well. The marble block, rejected by its master sculptors, sat outside in the cathedral courtyard for twenty-five more years, scarred, rained upon, and seemingly beyond repair or hope. In 1500, officials consulted with experts, including Leonardo da Vinci, to see if there was any hope in salvaging "The Giant" as the marble slab was nicknamed. Finally, in 1501, twenty-six-year-old Michaelangelo was contracted to attempt to save the project. Early in the morning of September 16, the young artist commenced his work. He would not finish until 1504. When he set down his chisel, the statue of David remained, representing one of the greatest masterpieces by human hands. What had seemed beyond hope or repair, in the hands of the master became a breathtaking achievement.

Likewise, God seeks to take the sinful, selfish, scarred characters of our children and systematically fashion them to look like Christ. The apostle Paul claimed that God takes every experience in our life, both painful and pleasant, and uses them to sculpt our characters into His masterpiece (Rom. 8:28–30). Because humanity is permeated with sin, we don't have to teach our children to be selfish (Rom. 3:23). They exit their mother's womb hollering for people to meet their needs. Likewise, have you noticed that no one had to teach your children to lie or to steal cookies from the jar when mom wasn't looking? Perhaps you observed that you didn't have to enroll your children in boxing lessons for them to learn to fight with their siblings. It's innate. What *does* require instruction and training is for your kids to learn to always tell the truth and to be thoughtful of others.

God knows that children who fail to learn to be honest and thoughtful will experience a difficult life, may inflict pain on others, and might not be able to enjoy a satisfying marriage. In addition, their children may be destined to continue the miserable legacy into the next generation. What's worse, if your children never learn to address their sin problem, they may never recognize their need for the Savior, which could be catastrophic. Therefore, God will invite you to join Him in His work to produce Christlike character in your offspring.

We can tend to focus on behavior. God concentrates on character. The reason is simple. Character drives our actions. If we are selfish, we'll act selfishly. If we have a dishonest character, we'll behave deceitfully. God doesn't focus on symptoms. He always zeroes in on the heart of the matter.

As parents, we can easily become distracted by outward manifestations and inadvertently miss the real issues. For example: a mother is having coffee with her friend at her house. Every few minutes her child interrupts the conversation and insists on showing his mother what he is playing. Embarrassed at her son's rudeness, the woman repeatedly reminds him: "Billy, what do we say?" "Excuse me," the boy exclaims before launching into another animated discourse on his current activities. The mom mistakenly assumes that the key issue is for her son to demonstrate proper manners by saying "Excuse me" before he interrupts. The truth is that her son's primary problem is not that he forgets to say "Excuse me" but that he is self-centered and thoughtless of his mother and her guest. By focusing on his manners, the mother is teaching her self-centered child how to use "magic words" to get what he wants.

Likewise, two siblings are continually bickering. Each time, the father loudly exclaims: "Hey, you two! Stop fighting! Why can't you get along?" The father assumes he is being an "involved" parent because he intervenes each time his children quarrel. The reality is that the siblings have never been challenged to examine their heart toward the other. If each one genuinely loved the other, they wouldn't argue in the first place. But as long as their father merely acts as a referee, the fighting continues (to say nothing of the fact that their house is continually filled with shouting!).

God instructs us to "keep your heart with all diligence, for out of it spring the issues of life" (Prov. 4:23). That is why God is never satisfied with merely adjusting outward behavior. People can say the correct things even though their heart is far from God (Matt. 15:8; Luke 6:46). That's why God always addresses character issues. If, for instance, your ten-year-old son says something unkind to his eight-year-old sister, you might be tempted to say: "Jonathan! I told you never to talk to your sister that way! If you do that again, you are going to your room!" However, God might instead prompt you to say something like: "Jonathan, I am really surprised at you. You are normally so loving and kind to your sister. That doesn't sound like you. Your sister loves you so much, and you are normally such a good older brother." In this case you are appealing not to his actions but to his character. God may use your words to reinforce in your son a kind disposition. As his character develops, his insults to his sister will dissipate.

Once people become Christians, Christ begins living out His life in them, seeking to transform them so they have His character (Gal. 2:20; 5:22–23). Christian parents ought to work in partnership with the Spirit. As the Holy Spirit works in our children's lives, we become instruments in God's hands to fashion our children's character. Whether your children are ten or fifty, you can participate in God's work to make your children like Jesus.

Richard's son Daniel got married three years ago. Before the wedding, Richard took his adult son out for lunch to offer some fatherly advice. Richard could have dished out various tidbits of wisdom on how to "fight fair" or effective communication skills. Instead, Richard spoke to his son about character. He pointed out that as the man of his house, Daniel would always need to demonstrate kindness, gentleness, and patience to his wife, Sarah. He would need to be a leader who always took the initiative in doing what was right. He would also need humility to save him from becoming too proud to say he was sorry. Richard's son was twenty-two; yet God was working through his father to further develop his godly character. A man with godly character is an awesome husband! When you focus on developing character, you don't have to provide an extensive list of rules and regulations. People of character will find a way to do the right thing whether they have been told what to do or not.

2. Being on Mission

Not only does God seek to develop godly character, He also invites your family to be on mission with Him. There are numerous examples in the Bible of God initiating His call on people's lives when they were children. For example, Moses must have had a sense of divine calling early in his life. His mother and older sister Miriam would have told him about his miraculous escape from death as an infant and the fortuitous way he was adopted by Pharaoh's daughter and trained in Egypt's finest schools. Young Samuel would have known his life was in answer to his devout mother's prayers and that he had been dedicated at birth to the Lord's service. When an angel told Manoah and his wife they were going to have a special son who would defend his people, they prayed, "O my Lord, please let the Man of God whom You sent come to us again and teach us what we shall do for the child who will be born" (Judg. 13:8). Their son Samson did not always live up to his divine calling, but he clearly had one on his life nonetheless. John the Baptist's parents knew before he was born that God had a special purpose for his life (Luke 1:5–25). God told the young Jeremiah, "Before I formed you in the womb I knew you; before you were born I sanctified you; I ordained you a prophet to the nations" (Jer. 1:5). Scripture indicates that God intends for His people to live their lives on mission with Him (Exod. 19:6; 1 Pet. 2:9–10).

After God rescued the Israelites from slavery in Egypt, He declared: "For you are a holy people to the LORD your God; the LORD your God has chosen you to be a people for Himself, a special treasure above all the peoples on the face of the earth" (Deut. 7:6). Almighty God had a unique purpose for His people. Sadly, the first generation of liberated Israelite slaves never fully grasped the magnitude of their divine calling. They were continually distracted by various temptations and by false gods. As a result, even though the Israelites had been marvelously rescued from bondage, they were eventually discarded in the wilderness because of their rebellion and unbelief. Instead, God turned to the next generation and commanded them to follow Him so He would use them to accomplish His purposes in Canaan. God instructed the Israelite parents to rehearse with their children the special purpose God had for them (Deut. 6:1–9). As long as the Israelites obeyed God and yielded to His purposes, God blessed them and worked powerfully through them. However, when God's people forsook their divine calling, God punished them and eventually obliterated them as a nation, first under the Babylonians, then later under the iron fist of the Roman legions. The success of God's people hinged on their response to God's call on them.

God has a purpose for your children. He intends for them to be on mission with Him. For your children to experience the fullness of God, they must learn God's purposes for their lives. They need to understand a lesson the Israelites perpetually failed to grasp: God does not merely bless us for our own sake but so we can be a blessing to others.

Wise parents will raise their children with a sense of divine purpose. They may not be called into full-time Christian ministry, but they are all called to be salt and light in their world (Matt. 5:13–16). We know families who spend their Christmas vacation, and money for presents, going on a mission trip each year. Grandparents take each grandchild on an international mission trip so they can experience the thrill of spreading the gospel in a foreign culture. Other families regularly volunteer at a homeless shelter or soup kitchen.

As we were raising our children, we continually reminded them that God had a purpose for each one of them. It was not necessarily that they were supposed to become pastors or international missionaries, but we assured them that God wanted to use their lives to make a positive contribution to their world. We believe God calls people to serve Him as businesspeople or schoolteachers just as He calls others to be ministers and evangelists. The key is to understand that God appoints people to be businesspeople not merely so they can acquire a lot of money but so they can provide a Christian witness in the marketplace. He calls people into education so they can do more than put in their thirty years until retirement. He intends for them to exert a lasting impact on their students.

A Greater Vision than Video Games (An Example from Richard)

Most parents assume that each of their children could do something special with their lives if only they would walk closely with the Lord, work hard, and perhaps get a few lucky breaks (like winning *American Idol* or "a national talent show"). But life has a way of cruelly knocking the childhood dreams out of our children. My son Daniel faced several significant challenges in his life during high school. He suffered a sleep disorder that left him exhausted most of the time. He also faced several discouraging experiences at school. By the time he graduated from high school, he was not exactly preparing to conquer the world. He did not have the confidence, or sense of direction, to enter university. Daniel was a bright, multitalented young man; but with no sense of purpose for his life, it seemed he was in danger of wiling away his days eating snacks and playing video games.

Lisa and I sensed we needed to help our son elevate his view of his life potential a little higher than maintaining his winning streak playing Mario Kart. We could have marched him to the nearest McDonald's and insisted he become gainfully employed. We might have forced him to enroll in university (I am not sure we could have made him *attend*, but we probably could have made him enroll!). We could have argued with him constantly, trying to help him see how he was wasting his life. But we sensed that Daniel needed to gain a higher view of his life than merely toiling in school or striving to earn money. Teenagers who spend hours a day watching TV and playing computer games don't necessarily suffer from laziness but from an absence of a sense of divine calling.

People who understand that God wants to use their life for His purposes are far less likely to waste their time.

Ultimately, we chose for Daniel to spend his first year out of high school doing international mission work. To that point, Daniel had spent the bulk of his life in a quaint, middle-class, predominantly Caucasian town where he had never suffered from any greater want than occasionally running out of cheese for his homemade nachos. I knew some amazing people around the world who were living their lives at peak levels and changing their world. They graciously agreed to host my sloppy, directionless eighteen-year-old for up to three months at a time.

Daniel spent time in Botswana and helped a missionary who was seeking to reach college students for Christ. He toured South Africa and witnessed the oppressive life of those living in townships where AIDS was epidemic. He spent three months in Athens, Greece, volunteering in refugee camps. He served on a medical mission boat that went down the Amazon River ministering to the poor in tiny villages. He also helped work with the youth in his Uncle Tom's church in Stavanger, Norway. He concluded his sojourn with his church-planting uncle and aunt in Germany. Over the course of that year, Daniel sat in humble cottages on the Amazon River while grieving parents showed him the remains of the swimming trunks their two-year-old was wearing when he fell into the river and was eaten by piranhas. He worked with refugees whose lives were endangered in their home country but who were unwelcome in any other. He walked streets on which he was in the minority for not being HIV positive. He worked with teenagers whose wealthy parents were unaware of the emotional turmoil and angst that their children were undergoing. To say it was eye opening is putting it mildly!

Throughout Daniel's odyssey, Richard regularly e-mailed him and asked what God was showing him. The world was far more diverse and extensive than Daniel had experienced in his childhood. He had also been moved by how many people desperately needed a message of hope. Daniel felt invigorated by leaving his comfort zone and making a difference in people's lives. He could not imagine merely returning to his former life of boredom. He had experienced the exhilaration of being used by God to make a difference in people's lives, and now he was addicted to it.

Since that epic trip, Daniel has been on additional forays to the Philippines, South Korea, Greece, Israel, England, and France. He finished college, earning an English degree, and went on to seminary where he is preparing for Christian ministry. Now he's looking at a PhD in apologetics. In addition, he wrote a book with his older brother Mike entitled *When Worlds Collide: Stepping Up and Standing Out in an Anti-God Culture* that encourages teenagers and young adults to live their lives in a manner that impacts the world for Christ. Daniel traveled with me and my father to the Philippines where he met the national president and spoke to rallies of thousands of people. Daniel also had a vision of writing a fantasy trilogy that would not only be entertaining but would introduce issues of faith to readers who might never darken the doorway of a church. Volume 1, *Legend of the Bookkeeper,* has already been published, and the next two are scheduled for release soon. What happened to Daniel? I wish I could say, "Good fathering!" But in reality, he simply had the opportunity to learn that God was inviting him to be on mission with Him. Daniel hasn't looked back since!

Of course, you may think, *Well if I had enough air miles to send* my *children around the world doing mission trips,* they *might also feel called into Christian ministry!* Well, that might be true. But we have found that the key is how parents help their children focus on God's call. Richard recently sent his college-age daughter on a mission trip to inner-city Orlando. She worked with the homeless, and she was deeply impacted by that. The key is getting your kids to see the world around them and to discover how God wants to use their lives to change the world.

3. God Works to Bless Others through Your Children

A third area where God invites families to join Him in His work is in blessing others.

When God called Abraham to join Him in His work, He promised, "And in you all the families of the earth shall be blessed" (Gen. 12:3). God intends for our lives to bless others! Your school, workplace, and neighborhood ought to be a better place because you are in it. In an interesting study of Millennials (those born between 1980 and 2000), it was discovered that nearly 90 percent of them believe it is their responsibility to make a positive difference in their world; three out of four feel it is their role to serve others; and six out of ten think they will make a significant contribution in their lifetime.[1] Many in that generation have been imbued with a sense that their life should impact their world for good.

The problem is that, to put it mildly, people are born selfish. We tend to be far more interested in *being* blessed than in *imparting* a blessing. Richard's wife, Lisa, used to teach a four-year-old Sunday school class. One Sunday, Rebecca wanted the toy Madi was playing with. "Madi! *Jesus* says to share!" Rolling her eyes, Madi replied, "Oh, that was *last* week's lesson!" (Lisa had a lot of teaching still to do!) The reality is that being a blessing does not come naturally to most of us! God has to teach us how.

An Example from Richard

As every parent does, we had to teach our children how to share and be thoughtful of others. Children come out of the womb assuming that everything in life is about them. They expect people to meet their needs. Some children grow up continuing to expect that they are the star attraction at every family gathering. At some point, wise parents help their children learn how to give rather than always to receive.

One way we tried to teach this to our children was during their birthday parties. Some children are taught that their birthday is the one day each year when they are the center of attention, the recipient of all gifts, and the most popular person on the premises. I know one eight-year-old boy who assumed that because he was the birthday boy, he should win all of the games played at his party. When he began losing to some girls, he became furious and loudly began accusing his birthday guests of cheating. His embarrassed mother finally had enough and banished him to his room for a time-out. The party became far more enjoyable once the birthday boy was in exile.

To avoid such circumstances, we began teaching our children, while they were very young, that their birthday parties were a time to bring much happiness to their family and friends. Our children were trained that they were the *host,* not the prima donna, and that their job was to ensure every guest had a great time. If one of their friends from church did not know their friends from school, our child was expected to help everyone feel welcome. After opening every gift, our child was expected to genuinely thank the giver (even if they had two of the same toys stashed in their closet already). Our family worked hard to ensure the parties were *a lot* of fun and that every child went home with a "goody bag" brimming with candies and prizes. Once all the guests had returned home, we would review the extravaganza. We wanted to know if our child had fun. Our second question was always, "Did your friends enjoy themselves?" Of course we wanted our children to have a good time on their birthdays, but we also wanted to teach them how to "spread the joy" to others whenever it was in their power to do so.

The problem with children who never learn to be oriented toward blessing others is that they become self-focused, insensitive adults. You see this at times at weddings. "Bridezillas" are young women who assume that their wedding day is "their" day and everyone is present to pay them homage. I have known brides who were radiant on stage, but none of their bridesmaids were speaking to them by the end of the ceremony! These brides basked in the attention on their special day but gave scant thought to the comfort and needs of those who had traveled great distances to attend. The bride may have had a dozen bridal showers thrown for her to which bridesmaids were expected to attend and required expensive bridesmaids dresses from her attendants but then failed to adequately express her appreciation for all her best (soon-to-be former) friends did for her. Such disastrous, yet all too common, an occurrence reveals two things: first, if we do not teach our children to be thoughtful of others while they are young, they will be thoughtless of others when they are older; and second, even when our children are old enough to be married, they still can benefit from parents who continue to coach them to have success in the most important moments of their life.

Taking One for the Team (An Example from Richard)

It's not always easy to teach our children to be thoughtful of others. I'll never forget one particular adventure. I received a distressed call from a pastor in a city five hundred miles away. He had no money for a vacation, and his family was under severe stress. They needed a break! Lisa and I decided to invite the pastor and his wife, along with their three children, to our house where we could provide them a respite. We briefed our children in advance that we wanted to be a blessing to our guests. I cautioned our kids that I did not want them to be selfish with their toys. I urged them to let the other children play with whatever toy they wanted, and if anything was broken, I'd replace it when our guests departed. One day my son Daniel came running up to me exclaiming, "Eddie just broke my wooden sword!" I frantically tried to silence Daniel before our friends overheard his loud complaints. "Daniel!" I hissed under my breath, "I told you I would replace whatever was broken!" "I know," he responded, "but he broke it over my head!" (That was a long week!)

Parents Must Join in God's Activity

It's critical that parents join God in His activity in their family. God *is* at work. We need only to recognize what He is doing. It is possible for God to be at work in our children's lives and yet for us to miss it. Jesus' twelve disciples were companions of the Son of God; yet they did not fully comprehend the divine activity occurring around them (Mark 8:17–21). Likewise, God can be at work in our own children, and yet we miss it because we are not paying attention.

One of the dangers for parents is that they focus on the wrong things. For example, we know a dear mom who regularly prayed for her daughter to grow up to be a godly young lady. Of course, we know that often the way to develop Christlikeness is through suffering and hardship. If you pray for God to make your daughter godly, are you prepared for God to do what it takes to make her that way? This mother's daughter competed in an ice-skating competition. The daughter had worked hard and practiced much. But she lost. The young girl handled it well, but the mother was devastated. She asked: "Why would God let this happen? I prayed every day that God would help her to win." This sincere mother was praying for her child's godliness but looking for her daughter's happiness. Sometimes you can't have both. Had the mother looked carefully, she would have noticed that her daughter, though disappointed, was graciously accepting defeat and was determined to try harder the next time. The mother's prayers were being answered!

The key for parents is to both watch for God's activity and also to develop a close relationship with their child so they don't miss what God does. When parents talk regularly and meaningfully with their child, they get a front row seat to observe God at work! When Richard's son Mike was a young boy, he was enamoured with GI Joes. He would play with them for hours. After he began school, Richard was interested in what his son was learning and what new friends Mike was making. Mike, on the other hand, was often more excited about what he would play after school! When Mike would arrive home, Richard would begin plying him with questions about his day at school. What had he learned? Could he read and write yet? Were there bullies? Was his teacher nice? Had he decided what college he would attend in thirteen more years? Mike would immediately begin recounting the amazing adventures his GI Joes had experienced and how they had successfully commandeered Barbie's Playhouse and turned it into a command post. Richard would interrupt him and try to return the conversation to matters that he felt were of greater consequence.

One day Richard had just interrupted Mike's discourse on his action figures when his wife, Lisa, called him into the kitchen. (Richard knew this usually meant he was about to either receive some helpful parenting advice or be peeling potatoes.) Lisa whispered to Richard, "You know, if you let your son talk to you about whatever is on his heart at age six, he'll still be coming to tell you what is on his heart at age sixteen." Sound advice. The truth was that most of Richard's conversations with his children were based on what *Richard* was interested in. Richard cared about progress in school and achievement. Mike cared about having fun! Rather than always controlling the conversations with his children, Richard began trying to listen more and to detect God's activity while his children shared what was on their heart.

Of course, your children will not always share what they are think-ing when it is convenient for you! When Richard's son Mike became a teenager, Richard tried his best to be a good listener. He would greet Mike when he returned home from school and begin peppering him with questions: "So how was your day today?" "Good." "Well, why was it good?" "Because." Anything interesting happen today?" "No." "Anything you'd like to talk about, son?" "No, I just want to go to my room. Bye, Dad." These kinds of conversations could be exasperating! Often when Richard had time to talk, his children weren't interested. But do you know what would inevitably happen? Mike would become a chatterbox around 11:15 that night! Richard would be in bed, weary from a long day's work. In would bounce Mike, bored and wide awake.

He'd flop onto the bed and exclaim, "Dad, let's visit!" "Mike!" Richard would protest, "it's after eleven o'clock! Where were you at 4:30 when I had time to talk with you?!" The reality was that after a long day at school, Mike had wanted some time to himself. He wasn't ready to open his heart up to his parents. But now, at 11:15 p.m., like many teenagers, his biological clock had kicked in, and he was finally prepared to discuss issues. Richard had to make a crucial decision at this point. Was he only going to be involved in his children's lives on *his* timetable? Or would he be prepared to join God's activity in his children's lives at whatever time worked for them? Some parents only want to join in God's activity when it is convenient! Needless to say, Richard went to work in the morning tired on more than one occasion!

One of the reasons parents miss God's activity in their children's lives is because the parents talk *at* their children instead of talking *to* them. Listening always provides greater insights into God's activity than does talking (or lecturing). It is critical that we discern where God is working in our children so we can quickly adjust our lives to His activity. We have no idea what might be at stake in our children's lives. They may be wrestling with God's call into ministry, or they may be facing a temptation that could ruin their life, or their friend may be pressuring them to participate in a harmful activity. More is generally happening in our children's lives than we realize! That is why we must make it a priority to be in dialogue with our children and with God so we discern what is going on.

Summary

God *is* at work all around you and your family, and He will invite you to become involved in His activity. The key is for you to keep your spiritual eyes open to what He may be doing. It could surprise you!

QUESTIONS FOR REFLECTION/DISCUSSION

1. Make a list of each of your children. Under each name list "Character," "Mission," and "Blessing." Then jot down ways God is presently developing their character, their sense of personal mission, and their ability to bless others.

2. Consider the last couple of conversations you had with one of your children. How would you rate them on a scale of 1 to 10? What percentage of the conversation were you speaking and what percentage were you listening? How might you improve those percentages?

3. Do you need God to open your spiritual eyes and ears so you better recognize His activity in your home? Perhaps you need to take time to pray and ask God to do that today. Take time to read through the Gospels and notice how Jesus related to people. Then watch to see how Jesus is relating to your children in the same way.

4. Have you been watching for the wrong things in your children? While you have been watching for one thing, has God been doing something else?

5. Have your children been giving you clues as to what is happening in their lives? They often won't come out and say it, but they will offer hints if you are listening carefully! Review the recent comments your children have made.

6. Over the next week, schedule a special time with each of your children in which you can engage in an uninterrupted, quality conversation with each child.

Notes

1. Thom S. Rainer and Jess W. Rainer, *The Millennials: Connecting to America's Largest Generation* (Nashville: B&H Publishing Group, 2011), 36–37.

CHAPTER 11

God Speaks by the Holy Spirit through the Bible, Prayer, Circumstances, and the Church to Reveal Himself, His Purposes, and His Ways

A Mother Listens

During a mother's quiet time one day, she sensed God impressing upon her the need to spend time with her daughter. She was extremely busy at that time, but the prompting was so compelling that she decided to make time to spend with her child that day. She picked her daughter up after school, and they drove to a mall to hang out. On the way, she asked her daughter about her day and what was going on in her life. Their family was dealing with a lot of transition at the moment, and it had been difficult for the daughter. She replied briefly but then confided that a friend of hers was "cutting" herself (self-injury is a cry for help, a way of dealing with pain or disappointment rather than being suicidal). The mother asked who it was, but the daughter replied she had given her word not to say anything. The mother felt God telling her to press a little deeper, so she gently asked her daughter for more details. Soon the daughter confided that she also was trying self-injury, more out of curiosity. The mother was able to guide her daughter into a more healthy way of dealing with her pain. She found some helpful Christian websites. Together, they spoke to the school counselor who was well aware of the self-injury trend at the school and provided some excellent resources for them. Had the mother ignored God's warning, she would have missed a critical moment in her daughter's life, and the problem might have grown worse. It is critical that we hear what God has to say to us. There is too much at stake for us to miss a word from God.

God Speaks

Few biblical truths are more important or more misunderstood than this: God speaks to His people. For many Christians, the concept of God speaking seems illusive. Occasionally we hear people say, "I've never heard God speak to me." In truth, the problem is generally not that God isn't *speaking*; the issue is often the person's *hearing*. There are some Christians who believe God no longer speaks to people, or that He has fully communicated His will to us in the verses of the Bible. While God does speak through the Bible, He has innumerable ways of communicating His will to us. In these difficult and confusing days in which we live, we can't afford to miss anything God has to say.

When you become a Christian, the Holy Spirit takes up residence within you (1 Cor. 6:19). Your body becomes the temple of God. By His Spirit, God will convict, teach, direct, impress, and speak to you in order to guide you into His will (John 14:23; 1 Cor. 3:16; Eph. 2:22; 2 Tim. 1:14).

Sometimes we expect God to speak to us in one particular way. Perhaps He once spoke to us through a Bible conference we attended or a devotional book we read, and now we always go back to that same source whenever we want to hear another word from God. In the Bible, God rarely did the same thing twice. However, if we are not careful, we may inadvertently close ourselves off to many of the ways God wants to communicate with us.

For example, Janet has a difficult decision to make and decides to copy Gideon's method for hearing from God. She puts out a "fleece" to confirm she is going in the right direction (see Judg. 6:36–40). But God's answer could have been found in the devotional thought Janet was scheduled to read that morning during her quiet time. Janet, however, was in a hurry and skipped her Bible reading that day. Then while she was listening to a Christian radio program in the car on the way home from work, the speaker gave a clear word from God that would have provided direction to Janet's situation, but she was distracted by a slow driver in front of her. Later, in the home group Bible study that week, God inspired the group leader to share truths that pertained exactly to Janet's questions. But Janet chose to stay home that night to get caught up on some work around the house.

Because Janet assumed God would speak to her the way He had before, she missed three other ways He was providing guidance. In the end, Janet chose to simply weigh the pros and cons of the decision and then proceed with her own best judgment. The role of the Holy Spirit is to "guide [us] into all truth" (John 16:13). We must be prepared for Him to guide us any way He chooses.

It is extremely important for parents to model "seeking God" for their children. Parents should do this not only in times of crisis but also in everyday situations.

- When we read family devotions with our children, we ask, "What do you think God is saying to us through this verse?"
- We pray not only for intervention in our life situations, but we thank Him for how He has answered our previous prayers. The way God answers our prayer is His means of telling us once again how much He loves us.
- When we arrive home from church, we take time to debrief with our children what God said to them in their Bible study time and through the sermon that morning.
- At the dinner table we share ways God guided us during the day. We also invite our kids to relate how God led them.

Jesus Take the Wheel (An Example from Tom)

One summer, my family had a chance to drive down to Italy for a few weeks' vacation. It was a hot day, and we were returning from visiting an aquarium. The air-conditioning was going full blast when all of the sudden every warning light on the dashboard came on, the A/C went warm, the steering became laborious, and I knew we were in trouble. I said to my family, "Someone pray for a gas station to show up real soon." My wife prayed, and wouldn't you know it, within less than a block, we pulled into a gas station. I knew if I turned the engine off it would not turn back on again, so I backed the car into a parking spot that was easily accessible to a tow truck and turned the engine off. Sure enough, the primary engine belt was gone. Being a Sunday, the gas station was closed, and I had no clue who I should call for help in Rimini, Italy. How do you even pronounce *mechanic* in Italian? *MiKANniko?*

I explained to my family that we needed to pray for God's help. Just as we said, "Amen," a car pulled up to the gas station. A young man and woman got out, unlocked the office, and went inside. I chased after them, hoping they could understand English. They were a little startled by my abrupt entrance, but fortunately the woman understood my meager attempt at sign language, pitifully pointing to my broken car. She called a tow truck that towed our vehicle to the only mechanic open that day. The mechanic found that a small wheel that drove the belt in my British Vauxhall minivan was broken. He grimly announced, "We have no such part in *all* of Italy!" I called my wife and told her to pray with me. Then I called my mechanic back home, who informed me that my van was made by Citroen, a vehicle commonly found in Italy. Looking up, I saw a Citroen dealer across the street! In less than a day, the car was repaired—and quite inexpensively too. My three kids were able to see their dad turn to the Lord in a time of crisis and watch as God answered every one of our prayers, almost immediately. The half-day we spent waiting for repairs was worth it for my kids see how God cares for His children in their time of need. So what was God saying to us through that event?

1. He knows what is going on in our life each moment of the day.
2. He can take care of us even when we have absolutely no clue what to do next!

3. God can set in motion anything and anyone He chooses to help us at any time and any place (and often in the most creative ways!).

4. He has put people in our lives for a reason, and we should not hesitate to call on them when we need to.

Now God did not speak to me through a burning bush. But His Spirit *led* me to call my church member back in Norway to get the information I needed. He *answered* every one of our prayers within minutes. And He *reminded* us of His great love for us by the way He cared for us.

When we talk about God "speaking" to us, we mean God *communicating* to us in a way we understand. It would be incorrect to assume God only speaks in an audible voice, as He did to some people in the Bible. The testimony of Scripture is that God used numerous means to communicate His will to people (Heb. 1:1). Other words or phrases that could be used instead of *speaking* to us would be:

- *Leading us*—as in "God led me to pray for an old friend today, and just as I finished praying for him, the phone rang, and it was that same person on the other line!"

- *Impressing upon us*—as in "the missionary spoke about what God was doing in her place of ministry, I felt impressed to give to her the unexpected bonus check I received from work that day."

- *Compelling us*—as in "I don't normally do this, but I feel compelled to take the day off work to drive you to your medical appointment tomorrow."

- *Revealing to us in His Word, in a dream, in a vision*—as in "I read the Scripture passage in my morning devotional, I suddenly came to understand something about God that had been bothering me for weeks," or "As I was praying for God to work in my wayward daughter's life, God showed me how my own attitude was a major part of the problem," or "I had the most vivid dream last night. It was as if God was sitting right next to me through the tough meeting I was scheduled to have today. I feel at peace about it now."

Think about how God spoke to various people in the Bible:

- Moses: face-to-face, as one man speaks to another (Exod. 33:11)
- Joshua: through an angel of the Lord (Josh. 5:14)
- Gideon: an angel and fleece (Judg. 6:12, 37)
- Joseph: three different dreams (Matt. 1:20; 2:13, 19)
- Elijah: still, small voice (1 Kings 19:12)
- Balaam: donkey (Num. 22:28)
- Israelites: spoke from the fire (Deut. 4:12)
- Peter: vision (Acts 10:10)
- Jesus: prayer (Luke 3:21)
- Ethiopian: a believer (Acts 8:37)
- Philip: Holy Spirit (Acts 8:29)
- Disciples: prayer with casting lots (Acts 1:24, 26)
- Ananias: vision (Acts 9:10)
- People: preachers (Acts 2:14; 1 Cor. 15:11)
- Paul: revelation (Gal. 2:2)
- Believers: Christ's words as recorded in the Bible (Heb. 1:2)
- Saul: audible voice (Acts 9:4)
- Believers: word of God (Heb. 4:12)
- Mankind: rainbow (Gen. 9:13–16)
- People: spoke through a cloud (Matt. 17:5)

God uses a diversity of means to communicate with people. He chooses to relate to us in a manner we can understand so we clearly know what He is telling us. This is the primary role of the Holy Spirit. Jesus said He would send the Spirit as a Counselor (John 14:16), Comforter, Helper, Teacher (John 14:26), Revealer of Truth (John 16:13), and a Guide. It is difficult for the Spirit to teach, comfort, guide, help, or reveal unless He communicates with you in some way or another that you clearly understand!

Listening and Obeying (An Example from Tom)

When I was finishing university, I needed a break from school, so I applied for a two-year international missions position overseas. As I had completed a degree in education, I felt I could best be used as a teacher for homeschooled missionary children whose parents were away for extended periods of time. And, as I had lived in the Canadian prairies most of my life, I felt I needed to go somewhere warm for a change (tropical rain forest, here I come!). So I applied to places like the French West Indies, Honduras, and Peru. I thought serving as a teacher while wearing shorts and sandals and being surrounded by palm trees and exotic fruit sounded pretty good! When my acceptance letter arrived, it read, "Congratulations for being accepted as a *youth pastor* in NORWAY!" I was stunned and upset. I had never even belonged to a church that had a youth pastor, and I didn't know where Norway was. My plans to serve God seemed to be thwarted by misguided bureaucracy! I put the letter down and went for a walk to decide whether or not I would pursue the program or not. As I walked, I prayed. I sensed God saying, "Tom, I will be waiting for you in Norway if you choose to follow Me." I decided God knew what was best. I was disappointed, but I also knew I had given my life to Him for His purposes many years earlier, so I submitted to His will for my life, even though it had not been my plan. As you might expect, I had an amazing two years. However, little did I know that fifteen years later I would take a wife and three children to that same church and become the longest serving pastor in its history. God knows our hearts, but He has the right to direct our footsteps.

Four Primary Ways the Holy Spirit Communicates with People

1. The Bible

When you open God's Word, you are walking directly into God's presence. The Bible is not just a book of quaint sayings and interesting stories; it is God's living Word and His expressed will. The most straightforward and reliable way to hear God speak is to read Scripture and to ask the Holy Spirit to help you understand its meaning as well as its application for your life. Notice what the Bible says:

- "For the word of God is *living and effective* and sharper than any double-edged sword, penetrating as far as the separation of soul and spirit, joints and marrow. It is able to judge the ideas and thoughts of the heart." (Heb. 4:12 HCSB, italics added)

- "My word that comes from My mouth will not return to Me empty, but *it will accomplish what I please* and will prosper in what I send it *to do.*" (Isa. 55:11 HCSB, italics added)

Reading the Bible presents God the opportunity to reveal truth to you, give you specific answers to your questions, bring comfort, point out shortcomings that need addressing, and much more. Those who open their Bibles in the morning for a hurried reading or devotional thought completely miss the primary purpose of God's Word, which is *to know Him*. Some people read the Bible in a manner akin to gulping down a daily dose of cod liver oil. It is done dutifully but unprofitably. Others study each word in the text for meaning and understanding. Some will read their full quota of chapters each day so they can make it through the entire Bible within the year. Others can't get past one verse without sincerely pleading with God to help them implement that truth in their life. We can read for information, application, and revelation. The key, however, is to read so our relationship with Christ is deepened as we receive what God reveals to us about His heart, ways, and truth.

2. Prayer

It is not commonly known that our mother has said, "God speaks to me through my vacuum cleaner." What she *means* is that she learned to multitask while she was a mother of five who needed to clean her house. Rather than mindlessly vacuuming the floor, she uses that time to talk with God about her five children and their families. She brings up concerns that her friends voiced that week. She intercedes on behalf of people God brings to mind while she works around the house. There are numerous mundane activities we perform each day—such as doing the laundry, mowing the lawn, gardening, cooking, and cleaning—that can be used more productively if we turn them into times of conversing with God. Many people find swimming laps to be a good time for reflection and dialogue with God. Others bring their Bible studies with them to their kids' ball practise, swimming lessons, and tournaments to redeem the hundreds of hours that would be otherwise wasted sitting in bleachers or waiting in the car. What could have been a tedious lesson and commute is transformed into a life-changing Bible study and prayer time. By doing this throughout the day, you come to the place where you understand that prayer is not something reserved for mealtimes and morning devotionals; it is an ongoing conversation we have with God throughout the day. This is what Paul meant when He challenged us to "pray without ceasing" (1 Thess. 5:17).

One of the great privileges we have as parents is helping our children learn to talk with God. Notice we didn't say talk *to* God. Many people "say their prayers," but they are not really talking to God. You know what we mean:

- "God is great, God is good, let us thank Him for our food. Amen"
- "Now I lay me down to sleep; I pray the Lord my soul to keep. Angels on my left and right, keep me safe throughout the night. Amen." (This version is less worrisome to small children than "If I should die before I wake, I pray Lord my soul to take!")
- "For all we are about to receive, let us be truly thankful. Amen."
- "Bless the giver and the gift as to thy service. Amen."

You could probably add a few more memorized prayers too. When children are very young, it is great to get them into the habit of saying prayers. But as they grow older, teaching them *how to pray* is important. There is a wonderful book written by Rick Osborne called *How to Teach Your Child to Pray* that offers great suggestions in this regard. (It is one of the best books for teaching parents to pray too!)

Prayer is a spiritual term for "talking with God." Letting God direct our prayers is important. That's because we can't imagine what God wants to do in and through us (Eph. 3:20). What a shame to keep voicing our puny prayers when God wants to do exceedingly, abundantly more! Prayer is not focused on convincing God to grant our requests. Rather, it is having God lay His heart over ours so we grasp His perspective on our situation and the amazing work He intends to do. When we align *our* will with *God's* will, great things happen!

Prayer allows us the opportunity to present our concerns to God. Perhaps we are having difficulty communicating with our teenage son or daughter. We may be concerned about the negative impact of our son's friends are having on him. Or we may feel it is critical that our daughter be assigned a "good" teacher in the upcoming school year. Once we have voiced our concern, we must keep our spiritual senses alert to how God chooses to respond. He is fully prepared to guide us and to provide practical solutions for every need. Nevertheless, our every prayer ought to be climaxed with the earnest plea: "Not my will, but Thy will be done" (Matt. 26:39).

As you teach your children to pray, help them learn to take their eyes off of themselves and to begin looking at the needs of others around them. Watch for opportunities to encourage people at school or in your neighborhood or among your friends and relatives. Ask God to work in their lives and situations and then watch to see how God includes you in His answer! God will guide you to pray for things He is about to do in people around you. It is exciting when your family participates in God's activity in the lives of others.

3. The Church

Christ dwells within every believer. That means that when you encounter another Christian, you also have the possibility of hearing from Christ, who dwells within them (John 13:20). We should never discount what God could say to us through even the most ordinary Christian. God may choose to reveal His will for you by what He says through another. That is what being a part of a body of believers, a church, is all about (1 Cor. 12:12–31). In fact, God created His people to be interdependent, not independent. If we are to have access to everything God wants to share with us, we will need to live our life in close relationship with other believers. Each member of the church has a unique perspective and role to play (Rom. 12:4).

God may choose to speak to you through what the pastor preaches on Sunday or through what the Bible study leader mentions during his lesson. God might save His most profound word for you until you are talking with a friend in the lobby after the worship service is over. Whether or not the preacher or speaker is lively, boring, clever, funny, or inspiring, it is the divine message they deliver that is important, not the messenger. God may give other people who have been praying for you a special Scripture verse that applies specifically to your situation. He may give them an insight into a problem you are facing that brings you direction, resolution, and comfort.

At times, church members may encourage you or endorse you for particular places of ministry, such as was the case with George W. Truett (1867–1944). A humble country boy, he had moved with his family to Texas from North Carolina. He intended to be a lawyer, but during a meeting at his church, a deacon made a motion to ordain Truett to the gospel ministry. Though he initially protested, he relented to the call of God on his life, feeling unworthy of the position. His fellow church members affirmed God's activity in his life, and Truett eventually served as pastor of First Baptist in Dallas for forty-seven years, growing it to be one of the most influential churches in America. Not everything people say is necessarily a "word from God" and should always be tested against what God's Word says. Nevertheless, we should trust God with both the method and the messenger. Our role is to discern what God is saying and then immediately respond in obedience.

The same is true for your home. When God has access to someone's heart, no matter what their age, God can use them for His purposes. In fact, many of the people our family has ministered to were introduced to us through one of our children. We have taught one friend's mother to drive, shown a new family where to shop for kid's clothes, helped repair the car of another family, put together a friend's IKEA furniture, and cared for many children when their parents needed child care. Being a part of a church means being a part of a family, where we all have a right and a responsibility to speak truth into the lives of one another.

This truth has enormous application for parents in terms of seeking counsel from others. Parenting is one of the most challenging leadership roles you will ever be given. It is impossible to experience success apart from receiving God's guidance. It behoves every parent to seek counsel from other believers. For example, your teenage son may be rebelling against your authority, and you may feel that the best thing is to ask him to move out of the house. But when you talk to your friend about it, she feels led to emphasize God's grace and long-suffering. As a result, you decide to hold off on the unpleasant confrontation and see what God is about to do in your child's life. Or you are frustrated with the negative influence a friend is exerting on your ten-year-old son. As you discuss this with your friend at church, she mentions a new family that just joined your church who also has a ten-year-old son. You decide to invite the family over for lunch after church where the two boys meet and ultimately become best friends. God will often use other believers to help address specific issues we are facing. It would be foolish for parents to assume their problems were no one else's business but their own and refuse to talk about them with others. If God has a word for you and your family, you want to receive it from any source, at any time, under any situation!

COLOMBIA CALLING

A Colombian family was struggling with the violence in their society and were worried about raising their family amid the gangs and corruption that was so prevalent. As relatively new Christians, they asked God for guidance. The husband was a structural engineer; the mother, a fashion designer. They thought they would be good candidates for immigrating to a safer country. They had read *Experiencing God* and noted that many of the stories were from Canada, so that became their destination of choice. After finding a place to live and joining a church, they began to make a life for themselves in their new country. But the plight of Colombian children was never far from their hearts. In 2008, Jorge and Tirza convinced their church that they should begin a food distribution ministry among the slums on Nativity Hill, on the edge of Medellin, Colombia. Through business connections as an engineer and with the help of his church family, funds were raised, building materials donated, teams sent, and a structure built on 2.2 acres of land near the slums. A pastor was hired, kitchen staff employed, and equipment given to make a secure facility to feed children and, through sponsors, give them needed school supplies, medical and dental care, school uniforms, and eventually sending graduated teenagers to the university. Seeds of Love and Hope International Ministry provided forty-five thousand meals last year. It also sponsors ninety-three children through families in their church and community. The congregation is ministering beyond the walls of their church, their town, and even their country, and lives are being transformed daily. All this because one family sought to follow through with what God was placing on their heart. Can you imagine what God might do through *your* family if you listened for His voice and then did what He said?

4. Circumstances

God is an expert at engineering circumstances to provide answers and direction for our questions. The job opportunity that comes out of the blue, the invitation to speak at a special gathering of people, the request for you to host a Bible study in your home, the coach who asks you to help him with your child's team, the unexpected check that arrives in the mail are not coincidences but God at work around you. Some people mistake an "open door" or a "closed door" as clear evidence of God's activity. God may indeed open a door for you to walk through, but not every open door is from God. Satan offered several "open doors" for Jesus to walk through that would have destroyed His ministry (Matt. 4). Likewise, some doors (Moses and the Red Sea, Joshua and Jericho, Christ and the cross) may appear closed when, in fact, God intends for you to walk right through them. The key is for you to seek God's interpretation of your situation. The various circumstances you face in life will appear confusing apart from God's explanation. Some have observed that the difference between coincidences and God-directed circumstances is in the timing. God loves to act *after* we pray and just in time. He is rarely early and never late.

FROM RUSSIA WITH LOVE (AN EXAMPLE FROM TOM)

My two older children had an opportunity to go with their youth group on a mission trip to St. Petersburg, Russia, while we were living in Europe. While there, they ministered to residents of an orphanage as well as to children with tuberculosis at a residential school. The mission team led children in games, Bible stories, and music, as well as doing minor repairs on the facilities. They came home with the usual souvenirs, big furry black hats, and changed personalities. We lived in a very well-to-do society at the time where families went to Paris to shop, London for a show, Prague for Christmas, and Austria to ski. Most children at their international school sported the latest stylish clothing, accessories, and electronics. But seeing the poverty, the living conditions, and the bleak future of many of those Russian children changed my kids. Suddenly they were thanking me for everything. Thanks for dinner, thanks for driving me to my practise, thanks for going to my game, thanks for helping me with my homework, thanks, thanks, thanks. When my son's birthday was approaching, I asked him what he wanted. He said, "Oh, nothing really. I have everything I need . . . maybe a shirt." What???!! No iPod, no Nintendo game, no $200 pair of jeans or $330 basketball shoes? I wanted to ask the youth pastor where my real kids were (though I didn't want to give up the ones he had brought back!). The circumstances God put them in truly spoke to their hearts, and they were never the same again.

One of the keys to parenting is to place your children in situations and circumstances where they can clearly hear from God. As we write this, Richard's twenty-one-year-old daughter is in Greece on a two-week mission trip. It has stretched her beyond anything she has done before. But it is amazing to hear what God is teaching her! At times, parents can get their priorities confused. For example, some parents believe their children need to learn to work so they encourage them to take a Wednesday evening job at a fast-food establishment, even though Wednesdays are when the church youth group has its weekly worship and teaching time. While it *is* good for children to learn good work ethics, it is even more crucial to learn to hear from God. These same youth may have to forego the summer mission trip to inner city New York next summer because of that same job. While these kids earn money for iPads and designer clothes, other kids are experiencing life-changing moments on mission trips and youth-oriented worship times. Parents ought to do everything possible to provide opportunities for their children to receive and process a word from God.

Are You Hearing from God?

The pastor of Friendship Community Church decided he would take seriously the truth that God was the Head of His church. And, as the Head, God could clearly guide His church if only His people would listen to Him. Every Sunday night the pastor allowed time for "God Watch" sharing time. During this time, people were invited to tell the congregation where they saw God working in their workplace, schools, business, and family. At first, the church members didn't know what to say. But after they began to watch for God working around them, they began to see His activity everywhere. For the first few weeks, the time was spent in awkward silence while people wracked their brains trying to recall anything they had witnessed God doing in their lives. But gradually the sharing time was transformed into a cacophony of enthusiastic reports from people of all ages. Often answers to prayer were shared and opportunities to witness reported. The Holy Spirit was drawing people to suddenly ask their Christian colleague questions about God. Other members were feeling led to begin a Bible study at work or at their child's school. New ministries were launched as church members responded to what God was initiating around them. The church exploded with growth as its members began watching throughout the day for what God might reveal to them next about His activity.

When you learn to identify God's activity, you will regularly see Him at work. When you listen for God, you will regularly hear Him speaking to you. What you see and hear could forever change your life.

QUESTIONS FOR REFLECTION/DISCUSSION

1. What has God been revealing to you during your personal Bible study lately?

2. What answers or instructions has God been directing you to during your prayer time?

3. What have people in your church been saying lately about what God is telling them?

4. Are there any circumstances that have arisen that you think God may be using to speak to you?

5. Can you think of a recent time when you ignored what God's Spirit was saying to you? What was the consequence?

6. When was the last time you spoke with your spouse about what you sensed God saying?

7. Has God been speaking to any of your children? If so, what has He been saying, and how have you been helping your children respond to God's Word?

8. What are some ways you could help teach your children to hear from God?

CHAPTER 12

God's Invitation for You to Work with Him Always Leads You to a Crisis of Belief That Requires Faith and Action

Growth through Bungee Jumping
(An Example from Richard)

As they were growing up, my two sons, Mike and Daniel, were all boys. They loved adventure and pushing the edge of the envelope. My daughter Carrie, on the other hand, was the undisputed family princess. For whatever reason, she was timid about certain things. For one, she was extremely close to her mother. For years it was difficult for Carrie to part from her for long. This resulted in numerous stints for Lisa as a parent volunteer on school field trips, outdoor education excursions, and children's camps! Carrie eventually grew independent enough to go to summer camp sans her mother, but it was always complicated.

Carrie knew she needed to gain more independence, and over the years, she had made various heroic attempts. However, her Waterloo came when she was fifteen. One day she overheard me mentioning a three-week lecture tour I would be taking that summer to Singapore, Malaysia, Australia, and New Zealand. Carrie was instantly interested.

The movie trilogy *The Lord of the Rings* was popular, and Carrie was intrigued with the idea of going to New Zealand and seeing Hobbits. However, even as Carrie suggested she should accompany me on the odyssey, everyone knew there was an "elephant" in the room. Carrie had struggled to remain at church camp for a week when it was only two hours from home. How could she manage to be away from home for three weeks while on the opposite side of the planet? Needless to say, I obtained a refundable airline ticket!

We dreaded the moment when Carrie would part from her mother at the airport. Good-byes were expressed. Hugs were dispensed. Tears were shed. Then we were off. The young people in Singapore seemed far more intrigued by Carrie than the adults were with me! In fact, a group of teenage girls took Carrie to the "Midnight Safari" at the zoo where a zookeeper wrapped a python around Carrie's neck! (She definitely was no longer in Kansas!) In Malaysia, the hosts seemed more concerned with outdoing the Singapore Zoo than with hearing my lectures on spiritual leadership. They took Carrie to see monkeys in the wild. In Australia, a grandfatherly figure skipped my lectures and took Carrie by train into the outback where they walked among a herd of wild kangaroos. Carrie was having the time of her life! Finally, we arrived in New Zealand. The hostess immediately placed a packet of brochures in Carrie's hand and told her to see if there was anything that interested her. There was. Bungee jumping. I have no idea what possessed my princess. She had been playing it safe all of her life. For goodness sake, she'd put on her seat belt to back down our driveway! But something inside my daughter told her that if she was ever going to break free from her fears, bungee jumping was the answer.

The final day of our three-week marathon brought us to a deep canyon that boasted New Zealand's second highest bungee jump. I was informed that New Zealand had invented bungee jumping, and they were pretty crazy about it. Now before you think the worst of me as a parent for letting my only daughter fling herself off a cliff into a canyon with nothing but a thin rope separating her from instant death, let me say in my defense that I was concerned about that too. But I also knew that my sweet daughter had lived her life thus far with timidity and a rather healthy dose of fear. I knew her life would never achieve what it could if she always yielded to her fears. She needed to face them head on and put them behind her. What better way than by jumping off a cliff?

For the two days preceding that fateful moment, Carrie would ask me every hour, "Do you think I can do it?" I would assure her I knew she *could* do it, but if when gaping down into the endless abyss she opted *not* to jump, I would respect her just as much. An hour later, "So, do you think I can do it?"

Finally, the time came. This canyon made the Grand Canyon look like a crack in a sidewalk! The bungee tower hung perilously over the precipice. The jumpmaster instructed Carrie in three details. First, no nonjumping parents were allowed on the tower (no matter how much they wanted to encourage their offspring). Apparently they did not want children to grasp their father (who had no rope tied around *his* ankle) at the last moment and bring him hurtling over the edge with them. Second, the instructor informed Carrie that she would not be pushing or pulling her. There were some things people had to do all on their own. If Carrie couldn't bring herself to take that last step, no one could do it for her. Finally, the jumpmaster informed Carrie that the longer she stood staring over the edge, the harder it would be to jump. "So I'm going to count 3-2-1, and when I say 1, go for it!"

As the jumpmaster began counting, there stood Carrie, shaking like a leaf. But right on 1, over she went. Carrie screamed so loud I think it caused a disturbance in the Force. But she did it. When Carrie made it back to the top of the cliff once more, I was there to celebrate. She was exhilarated at her accomplishment, but I could tell something troubled her. Finally she blurted out, "Dad, I was scared." She was embarrassed at how frightened she had obviously been. I responded, "But Carrie, you jumped on 1!" I went on to tell her that courage is not the *absence* of fear. It is being scared to death and still jumping on 1. She had reached a major new milestone in her life.

That event has provided a poignant picture for my family of what often happens in our Christian life. When the Creator of the universe invites us to join Him in His work, it is inevitably going to cause a crisis of belief. That's because God typically does things that are God-sized. That is not so bad for the archangel Michael, who is used to the goings on in heaven, but it will often force us out of our comfort zone!

What we have often discovered is that, for many Christians, the biggest challenge is not *knowing* what God's will is; it is *doing* it. Tragically, there are many Christians standing at the edge of their spiritual "bungee tower" trying to muster the courage to take one more step to obey what they know in their heart God wants them to do. Some remain where they are a long time. As Carrie's instructor informed us, it doesn't get any easier by waiting until later! The reality is that in every person's life there are those critical moments of decision where what we do *next* could have repercussions for the rest of our lives.

What a Crisis of Belief Is Not

Perhaps one of the most misunderstood concepts in *Experiencing God* is the truth that God's invitations often lead to a crisis of belief. We tend to think of the word *crisis* as something negative. But what this means is that every time God speaks, you face an enormous decision: Will you believe Him and obey Him, or not? Scripture instructs us that, "without faith it is impossible to please God" (Heb. 11:6 HCSB). That being the case, God will continually put your life into a position where you *must* have faith. We tend to nestle ourselves into a comfort zone where we never have to do anything that stretches us or is too difficult or painful. That's human nature. But the problem is that when we live a life where we never need for God to intervene on our behalf, then we also don't accomplish God's work or experience His power. We believe the reason America is presently in the spiritual and moral condition it is in is because too many Christians have been content to live "safely."

A crisis of belief occurs when God invites you to do something that is difficult or clearly beyond your ability. It might be to take an unpopular stand. It could be to change your views. It might be to forgive someone who harmed you. It could be to do something (like speak in public) that you are terrified of doing. Perhaps it is going on a mission trip you do not think you can afford. It could be to donate money at a level beyond what you feel you are capable. It might be to lead a Bible study at your work or school. It could be anything God asks you to do that pushes you beyond where you are comfortable. It is when you come to the end of yourself that you are forced to trust Him.

The Bible is filled with moments where God invited people to leave their comfort zone and to follow Him. Consider some of the following.

Josiah

Josiah had the dubious distinction of having a grandfather who was the wickedest king ever to lead the nation. Listen to what God said of Manasseh, king of Judah: "He has acted more wickedly than all the Amorites who were before him, and has also made Judah sin with his idols. . . . Moreover Manasseh shed very much innocent blood, till he had filled Jerusalem from one end to another" (2 Kings 21:11, 16). In response, God declared: "Behold, I am bringing such calamity upon Jerusalem and Judah, that whoever hears of it, both his ears will tingle. . . . I will wipe Jerusalem as one wipes a dish, wiping it and turning it upside down. So I will forsake the remnant of My inheritance and deliver them into the hand of their enemies; and they shall become victims of plunder to all their enemies" (2 Kings 21:12–14).

King Manasseh was so wicked that God declared His judgment would be as certain as it was fierce. Manasseh's son Amon ruled only two years before his own servants murdered him (2 Kings 21:23). The people then rose up and put all of the conspirators to death before making Amon's son Josiah king in his place. Imagine! Your grandfather was so wicked that God declared He would devastate the nation as a consequence. Your father was murdered by his own servants. In response, citizens rose up and executed your father's enemies. Then you are made the new king. *And you are only eight years old.* Talk about a crisis of belief! Josiah inherited a nation that was wicked, divided, and under judgment.

Jeremiah

Jeremiah grew up under the evil king Manasseh. It was truly an evil age. Then, as a teenager, God approached Jeremiah and told him he was to be a spokesman for God, delivering unpopular messages to the nation's leaders. Jeremiah knew how wicked his society was and how unlikely they were to heed his message. So he responded, "Ah, Lord GOD! Behold, I cannot speak, for I am a youth" (Jer. 1:6). Jeremiah was experiencing a crisis of belief! God needed an older, more experienced spokesperson! God needed to call someone who commanded more respect from the nation's leaders and who had more experience in preaching. Perhaps a PhD in revival would help. But God chose a teenager to undertake an extremely difficult assignment.

Rebekah

Rebekah was the dutiful daughter of Bethuel and sister to Laban, who lived in Mesopotamia. One day she was performing her chores, walking to the well to retrieve water. A foreigner approached her and asked for a drink. Not only did she minister to the weary traveler; she also offered to bring water for the man's *ten* thirsty camels! These camels had just walked a great distance. It has been estimated that camels can drink up to 25 gallons of water at one time. Offering to quench the thirst of ten parched camels was no casual offer! By the time she was finished, the man knew he had found the wife for his master Isaac, the future patriarch of God's people (Gen. 24:1–28). How would you have responded if a total stranger approached you and needed you to haul, with your lone water jar, 250 gallons of water to quench the thirst of his road-weary camels? When it was agreed that Rebekah should be Isaac's wife, her family pled with Isaac's servant to allow her to remain with them for ten days so they could give her a proper farewell. After all, she was leaving them forever to go to a distant land. Yet the servant was anxious to return to Abraham to present him his new daughter-in-law. So her parents asked their daughter if she was willing to immediately depart with this stranger to a land where she had never been and from which she was unlikely to return. Her response? "I will go" (Gen. 24:58). She would become the mother of Jacob and Esau, the grandmother of the tribes of Israel, and a woman of faith who would inspire God's people for thousands of years.

Daniel

Daniel was a teenager during some of the most discouraging periods in his nation's history. King Nebuchadnezzar of Babylon had subdued Jerusalem and would eventually level its walls and raze its holy temple. His army abducted the finest young men from the nation and took them to Babylon to be immersed in the Babylonian culture. The king's stewards changed Daniel's name to a pagan name. They insisted that he eat foods that violated his own standards. They dressed him as a Babylonian and promised that if he complied, he could become highly successful in the most powerful empire in the world. This was enormous pressure for a teenage boy to endure. Yet we are told, "Daniel purposed in his heart that he would not defile himself" (Dan. 1:8). This was a crisis of belief! Daniel probably knew of many of his countrymen who had already been killed by the Babylonians. They did not tolerate opposition or resistance. Yet God intended to use Daniel in a powerful way to impact two kingdoms. His rise to prominence began when he chose to believe and obey God.

John Mark

John Mark was a young man who grew up in a home dedicated to Jesus. By all accounts he was a sincere follower of Jesus himself. When Paul and Barnabas set out on their historic first missionary journey, they chose this young man to accompany them. It was quite an honor. Things began well enough as they ministered in Cyprus, the place where Barnabas was from. But when the team ventured on to Asia Minor, John Mark apparently decided that he wanted to go home (Acts 13:13). His reasons are lost to history. All we know is that the apostle Paul was so frustrated with him that he refused to let him come on their next trip (Acts 15:36–41). John Mark had received an amazing invitation: to accompany two of the greatest missionaries in Christian history on a journey that would later be chronicled in the Bible. But he suffered a crisis of belief! And because he could not trust God, he experienced a humiliating failure.

Crises of Belief That Our Children Face

Statistics indicate that the majority of children who grow up going to church each week will ultimately walk away from church, and perhaps God, when they reach their teen and college years. Often the reason young people abandon the faith is because they experience a crisis of belief, and they fail to trust God. That is why it's crucial for parents to walk with their children through these watershed moments. The following are some of the most common issues that could cause our children to experience a crisis of belief.

Friends' Approval

As children grow up in our home, we have the "power" to take them to church and to teach them our beliefs. Our children will generally be open and accepting of our beliefs and standards when they are young. But at some point, holding on to the beliefs and values they were taught at home is going to put our children crossways with some of their friends and classmates. For many, that proves to be a crisis! "I know I was taught not to smoke cigarettes, but my friends are all doing it. What will they think of me if I am the only one who doesn't?" "Everyone at school is going to that party; I don't want to be the social outcast of my school and stay home with my parents that night." Children may have been taught for years that they should honor God with their bodies, but one semester sharing a dorm room with an unbeliever who drinks, smokes, and sleeps around can bring years of parental instruction and Sunday school classes tumbling down. Every child knows that the answer to "What's more important, what God thinks or what your friends think?" is "What God thinks!" (The correct answer in Sunday school is *always* God!) Yet knowing the theologically correct answer is not preventing thousands of children raised in churches from forfeiting their faith every year.

When Richard's son Mike entered college, he loved a party! Mike is a social animal and is extremely loyal to his friends. There were two young men who had been close friends with him throughout high school. These boys came from great Christian families and attended church and youth meetings every week. But upon entering college, these teenagers became enamored with drinking alcohol. Having been told by their parents all their life that they should refrain from alcohol, they now became fixated on it. And, since they no longer lived at home, they could finally indulge themselves with abandon.

This created a crisis of belief for Mike. Mike enjoyed hanging out with these two friends. They were a lot of fun. But every time he was at their place, they would inevitably begin making a strong alcoholic drink and pull out a stash of cigarettes. They urged Mike to "just try it!" Mike didn't want to appear like a prude, and he didn't want to miss out on fun gatherings with his friends. But these encounters were providing a direct clash with everything Mike had been taught at home and at church. It was a crisis of belief. Did Mike stick with what he had been taught and risk losing his friends? Or, did he participate, in moderation, so he was accepted? Ultimately, Mike worked out his own ethical stance. He would not participate in activities he believed were wrong. But neither did he "blow the whistle" on his friends to their parents. Mike would visit his friends and hang out with them up until the moment the "contraband" was pulled out. Then everyone knew Mike would say his good-byes and head home. While this might not have been the best solution, it was how Mike coped with a major crisis of belief where he had to determine just how seriously he was going to take the faith he was taught as a child.

Trusting God for a Boyfriend/Girlfriend

In modern society, Hollywood idolizes romance and celebrity couples. Today's teenagers feel enormous pressure to have a boyfriend or girlfriend. At high school dances (or at times, *church youth group dances*), teens can feel intense pressure to not look like a "loser" by not having a "significant other" on their arm. Many teenagers become obsessed with whether or not a popular teen notices them or asks them out. Of course, it's natural for teenage boys and girls to be attracted to one another. But for some, it becomes a crisis when the desire for romance overrides their trust and loyalty to God.

Tragically, scores of Christian teenage girls have forfeited their modesty, and at times their virginity, in a desperate attempt to gain a boy's affection. Many of these girls were taught as children to live in a God-honoring manner. Yet they demean themselves, discarding their ethical standards, out of fear they might never find someone who cares for them. There are Christian girls who shamelessly pursue boys in an effort to gain a boyfriend. Unwilling to wait for God to bring someone into their life who shares their values and who treats them respectfully, they cast aside many of the values and standards they were taught as children in order to feel that they are not a "loser" without a boyfriend.

This issue is extremely pertinent to us, as we each have a beautiful daughter for whom we want God's best. We taught our daughters to trust God to meet all the needs of their life, such as providing them a husband one day. We taught them to respect themselves and to expect others to treat them with honor. We also instructed them to be godly and to dress and conduct themselves modestly. Yet the crisis of belief comes when your fourteen-year-old friends are dressing to attract boys' attention, and they all have boyfriends. Or your eighteen-year-old friends are all in serious relationships and preparing for marriage while you do not yet have a steady boyfriend. That is when girls must ask: Do I *really* trust God that, if I live my life to honor Him, He will provide what I need for my life?

Trusting God with Your Life

The world tells us we must "take the bull by the horns" and grasp all we can out of life. Whether it is finding a spouse or a job or an education, we must aggressively take matters into our own hands. Unfortunately, the world will also be quick to tell us how unskilled we are or how unlikely we are to earn a scholarship. The world is continually working to diminish your children's dreams.

That's why our children will face a crisis of belief when God reveals His will for their life. It will have dimensions to it that are larger than they may have anticipated.

GOD'S CALL (AN EXAMPLE FROM RICHARD)

When my son Daniel turned fifteen, I thought it a strategic time to check in with him to see what God was doing in his life. Sitting at a Chinese buffet, I asked, "So Daniel, do you have any sense what God might want you to do in the future?" He responded, "Not yet. But one thing I *do* know, and that is that I won't be a pastor." I asked him how he knew that. He replied, "Because I can't preach like you or grandpa Henry." I told Daniel that, for one thing, it wouldn't be fair if he *could* preach like us, since my dad and I each had three more earned degrees than he did and decades more preaching experience. But I asked him why he thought that God would not ask him to do something he did not feel he was good at. That led to an interesting discussion!

The fact was that Daniel knew what he was good at and areas where he struggled. He had never enjoyed public speaking (he had managed to get through several grades while strategically avoiding "Show and Tell"). Daniel could not imagine a worse fate than being a public speaker. I felt like my role as his father was not to convince him he *should* be a minister. I simply wanted to encourage him to be open to whatever God had in mind. Daniel needed to understand that God might ask him to do something far beyond what he was comfortable (or even good at) doing. If Daniel would accept God's will for his life, he would find, just as every other person throughout Scripture and church history had discovered, that with God *all things* are possible! Sure enough, once Daniel was prepared to submit to whatever God asked him to do, he *did* sense God was leading him into some form of Christian ministry. Since that time, he has gone to seminary and has spoken with his father and grandfather in various settings across the country and even internationally. And Daniel has discovered the joy of doing things in God's power that he could never have done in his own strength.

WITHOUT FAITH

Because it is impossible to please God unless we live our life with faith in Him (Heb. 11:6), God will regularly provide opportunities for us to trust Him. God has little need to ask us to do things we can do in our own strength and wisdom. That is what we naturally gravitate toward anyway. God invites us to join Him in activities that allow Him to demonstrate His power to a watching world. But that will stretch us! As parents, we must be ready to join God as He invites our children to join in His activity.

Navigating Crises of Belief

Parents face a dual role in the home. First they must help their children navigate the crises of belief they will inevitably face. Second, they must resolve their own crises of belief as they trust God for their family. Each involves its own unique challenges! The crisis of belief is a call to action, not reflection. James reminds us, "For just as the body without the spirit is dead, so also faith without works is dead" (James 2:26 HCSB). Jesus does not ask us to merely *believe* in Him; He commands us to *follow* Him (Matt. 16:24).

Helping Our Children

As we have seen, our children will face moments of decision when they must choose what they believe about God. Whether it is choosing to hold on to their faith in college, or refusing to attend the drunken parties that all of the "cool" people are attending in high school, or trusting God to bring someone special into their life, your children must decide what they truly believe about God. Those are critical moments for you as a parent to be walking closely with them.

Career Choices (An Example from Richard)

I had always taught my children that God had a will for their lives, and they could trust Him for their future. When they were five years old, that belief was relatively easy to embrace. My daughter, Carrie, always knew that the correct answer in Sunday school was "Trust God!" But as she grew older, and her challenges became more complex, her faith was tested. College provided numerous challenges! But last spring, upon graduation, she faced a major crisis of belief.

Carrie was an English major in college. Not surprising, since her father was an author and her grandfather, uncles and aunts, and even her two older brothers had all been published. Nevertheless, college English majors always face the same question: "Are you going to get a degree in education now so you can get a job one day?" or, "Which Starbucks will you be working at?" The world is not kind to starry-eyed English majors with visions of writing best-selling novels or books of poetry swirling in their heads.

Carrie felt she should go on to earn a master's degree. But in what? The head of her English department urged her to apply for an MFA degree in creative nonfiction writing. She did apply and was accepted. But then she panicked. The degree wasn't cheap. Its focus was on honing your writing skills, but then, what was she going to write? And how was she going to earn a living? Visions of scribbling verses of poetry during her coffee breaks while working the midnight shift as a security guard gripped her with trepidation. "Dad, maybe I should get a master's degree in education instead. After all, schools always need teachers. I'd have a better chance of getting a job that way," she moaned. "But what is it God has given you a passion for?" I asked. "Teaching is a noble profession. But is it what God wired *you* to do?" I asked. I knew she had never been interested in teaching school, but she could not imagine how her life would work out if her only training was as a writer.

I recognized that Carrie was experiencing a crisis of belief. She knew in her heart what God was calling her to do, but it didn't appear to make sense financially. Unable to see how her future would unfold, she was afraid to move forward. She began to search Online for education programs or even master's degrees in English at other schools that might be better suited for teaching school. But by then she had already missed the application deadlines for that fall. It appeared she was stuck in an expensive program that led nowhere.

I had Carrie review her life thus far. God had gifted her in English. She had won her university's top English award. She had graduated summa cum laud. The head of the English department had told us Carrie was one of the most naturally gifted students to come out of their program. And she was clearly an excellent writer. After all that God had put into her life, perhaps Carrie should trust Him to guide her step-by-step in the coming days.

Carrie did proceed with the MFA degree. Of course I was praying earnestly that Carrie would experience God's active guidance in her life throughout. Interestingly, after Carrie committed herself to the program, she connected with a journalist who asked her to write some articles for publication in a newspaper. A former professional athlete contacted Carrie about helping him write his memoir. Because her MFA was a low-residency program, Carrie had the flexibility to enroll in a second master's degree so she could also study Christian apologetics. And, most recently, Carrie signed a contract with a Christian publisher to write her first book. A large church has also indicated they'd like to make use of her writing skills to enhance their publications and communication with their members. It would seem that God has numerous ways He intends to use the writing abilities He placed in Carrie! And she hasn't even finished her first semester of her master's degree yet!

Unfortunately, many children face a crisis of belief, but their parents do not recognize it as such. Young adults become intimidated by what lies before them, and they downsize their dreams. They allow fear or doubts to guide them rather than the Holy Spirit. I knew that if Carrie didn't proceed with her call to write, she would wonder the rest of her life if she had made a mistake. I felt she owed it to herself, and to her Creator, to explore the divine calling He had placed upon her life.

Parental Crises of Belief

A second type of crisis of belief parents must deal with is their own. We have both faced numerous and diverse challenges over the course of our lives, but few undertakings equal the degree of difficulty and complexity of what we have faced as parents. For many Christian parents, one of the greatest crises of faith they will experience is the question of whether God can work a miracle in their child's life. We know numerous parents who could successfully lead a company or achieve success as a professional but who suffered continual failure in raising their child. We know many wonderful Christian couples whose child chose to rebel and reject the Christian faith and values that had been instilled into them for years. Parents grieved as they watched their precious child throwing away their future, their purity, and their health with reckless abandon. It seemed as if no amount of talks or curfews or incentives or threats would turn their child back to the Lord.

In times like these, we as parents face a crisis of belief. What do we believe about God? Do we trust that He hears our prayers? Are we confident He can turn our child's heart back to Him and to us? When our child struggles to find his way educationally or in a career, do we have confidence God will guide him? If we are filled with worry and despair, we clearly do not! It may be that our own spiritual "Waterloo" may come, not through what God is doing in our own life but through what is happening with our child. At times it is easier to believe God for our own problems than it is to trust Him to work in the life of our child.

In one of the most beloved stories in Scripture, Jesus told of a man who had a prodigal son (Luke 15:11–32). Despite all that had been done for him, this young man was unhappy and wanted to get as far from his family as he could. In demanding his inheritance, the ungrateful child was telling his father that he wished his father were dead. Yet despite the youth's insolence, the loving father generously granted the requested inheritance, even though it might well have placed his own financial security in jeopardy. The son wasted no time in turning his back on his family and foolishly squandering everything of value he had been given.

This young man's return was not easy. He did not consider his family until he had nothing left. Yet at last he did make his way home. And what was the father doing? He was watching the horizon for the wayward child he knew would return one day. Oh, the father would have dearly wished he had come home sooner. Nevertheless, we are given the strong impression that each day the father gazed out on the horizon for the familiar silhouette of his second child. Scripture tells us that "when he was still a great way off" (v. 20) the father spied the son. The father could only have seen his distant son if he had been looking intently and purposefully. The father believed God would eventually get through to his son, and he wanted to be at his post when He did.

Summary

When God does a work in our life or in the lives of our children, it will inevitably lead to a crisis of belief. That's because God's ways are not our ways (Isa. 55:8–9). His ways are higher than ours. He knows the future and how our lives will turn out. We will come to the end of our knowledge and power and be forced to trust in the Lord for what comes next. And when we do, we will be right where God wants us to be! But once we experience a crisis of belief, we'll have to make some major adjustments in our life, and that is what we'll address next.

QUESTIONS FOR REFLECTION/DISCUSSION

1. Is there an issue in your home right now that is causing you to have a crisis of belief? If so, what is it?

2. What does your family witness when they watch you having to trust God for something?

3. Of your children, which one of them are you presently struggling to fully trust God for?

4. Take some time to reflect on the promises of God. Pray them into your children's lives. If a particular promise seems impossible at this point due to how your child is behaving, take time before God to fully trust Him for what He promised.

CHAPTER 13

You Must Make Major Adjustments in Your Life to Join God in What He Is Doing

Embarrassing Myself on a Mountain
(An Example from Richard)

My job requires extensive travel. Several years ago, I went through a period where I had been out of town almost constantly. One night I called home, and my wife, Lisa, commenced our conversation by saying, "You're not going to like this. . . ." Now I have asked her *never* to begin a long-distance phone call that way, but she did. Apparently, the following week our boys' school was having its annual downhill ski lessons. Every day after school, parents would drive their children an hour west to the Rocky Mountains and let them take ski lessons. The school had requested parent volunteers. Lisa, realizing I would finally be home for a week and knowing I had not spent much time with our kids of late, concluded that a perfect way to make up some of that deficit was for me to serve as a chaperone. Apparently I had been one of the lucky parents the school had chosen. Now I certainly did not mind spending time with my kids, but I had a problem. A BIG problem. You see, I didn't know how to ski. I grew up on the Canadian prairies in the province of Saskatchewan. It is so flat there that they say your dog can run away from home and you can still see it three days later! I was sure I was going to break my neck during those lessons! In addition, I had been out of town all week. What I wanted more than anything was some time at home. I had visions of sitting in my La-Z-Boy recliner by the fireplace and resting each evening. But now I'd be endangering my life on a ski hill.

The next day things got worse. There was a family we knew called the Baileys. They had three children the same ages as ours. The father had died of cancer five years earlier. Lisa hated for Mrs. Bailey to have to drive her children to the mountains every afternoon and then try and keep tabs on them while they skied. So Lisa invited them to join us.

The first couple of days went well enough, until Thursday. I was in the ski lodge pulling food out of our cooler. The lesson was over, and dinner was soon to commence. Mrs. Bailey was helping. In walked my twelve-year-old son Mike and his friend Jason. Mike pointed an accusing finger at his buddy and demanded, "Dad, give Jason the leg!" *That* was embarrassing. I need to explain. The kids and I had a game we played when they were young. Wrestling! We would roughhouse for hours on the living room floor. Even my little daughter Carrie would join the tumult. The problem was that as the kids were getting older, they were also growing bigger and stronger. As I was getting older, I was becoming increasingly out of shape and in danger of a major heart attack. So, I did what any self-respecting father would do. I learned to cheat. I developed a technique I dubbed "the leg." I would put my hand on the leg of one of my children just above the knee and squeeze tightly. My fingers would pinch right to the tendons and produce an effect much like an electric shock. So, if the kids were getting the best of me and I could feel "the big one" coming, I'd grab the nearest child and give him "the leg." That would put one of my opponents out of commission. Well, it was this same, aforementioned "leg" that my twelve-year-old son was demanding I give to his friend.

Apparently on their last ski run before dinner, Jason had accidentally bumped into Mike and sent him hurtling down the slope, face first. Mike had been exasperated and declared that, for justice to be served, when they went for dinner in the ski lodge his dad would give Jason "the leg." Now, in front of a hundred skiers sitting about the lodge eating their dinner, as well as Jason's mother, Mike was demanding that Jason receive what was due him. Jason knew of "the leg." All of my children's friends did. "No, Mr. Blackaby. Please. NOT the leg! ANYTHING but that!" he begged. I feared that any moment Mrs. Bailey was going to summon a security guard to intervene and protect her son. I turned to Mrs. Bailey. "Have no fear. Your son's leg is perfectly safe with me!" She rose from her chair and placed her arms around her son. I expected her to threaten me with a lawsuit if I laid one hand upon her firstborn. Instead, she looked gravely at me and stated matter-of-factly, "I think he deserves the leg too!"

Things were going from bad to worse. I was humiliated! There were a hundred pairs of eyes that would see me manhandling this child. I was certain I had seen a policeman on the premises, and I could imagine seeing my face splashed across the front page of the newspaper the next day for having been arrested on a school field trip. But then something unusual happened. As I looked at Jason as he pled, "Please, Mr. Blackaby, NOT the leg!" I sensed the Holy Spirit gently speaking to me. "Look into this boy's eyes," He whispered. As I did, I saw a twelve-year-old boy who had not had a father to wrestle with him for more than five years. "I am the Father to the fatherless," I heard God say. At that moment I felt the freedom to give Jason the "mother" of all legs! He went down hard, squealing and thrashing about. I was certain I'd be arrested at any moment, but I didn't care anymore.

Unbeknownst to me at the time, that showdown in the mountains would have profound consequences. Mrs. Bailey was so touched at the playful attention I had given her son that she encouraged him to spend time with our family whenever he could. Jason began coming to church with Mike and one night at a youth rally gave his life to Christ. Two years later Jason was at our house one evening. He told us that he believed that if he had not become involved in our family, he might well be dead. Apparently, as his father was dying of cancer, Jason had pled with God to spare his life. When God had not, Jason became bitter and pronounced himself an atheist. The following years were filled with bitterness and disappointment. Kids at school teased Jason and made his life miserable. Upon returning home from school each day, he would retreat to his room and listen to dark, depressing music, trying to muster the courage to end his life. That was when he crossed paths with Mike and our family. Ultimately, he discovered a Father in heaven who loved him. Now his life had meaning, peace, and joy.

I came to see that there had been far more at stake during that week of ski lessons than I could possibly have imagined. I thought I was merely making up time with my children after having been away on business too much. But the reality was that a young man had desperately been seeking a reason for living. God had invited our family to join Him in His activity to set a young man free. At the time I had felt that I was a martyr for having to forego my La-Z-Boy recliner to accompany school-children on the ski slopes. I had even chafed at the thought of having another family join ours during the mealtimes. The "leg" incident had certainly taken a toll on my dignity.

But the truth is that that you cannot stay where you are and be on mission with God. My natural inclination was to relax in my living room by the fireplace each evening. God intended to be fully present on that mountain where a young man still wondered if there was a God. I learned I could not remain in my recliner and join God's activity on the mountain!

You Must Make Major Adjustments in Your Life to Go with God

God is continually at work in the world around us. He is unrelent-ing in His effort to redeem humanity and to restore His fallen creation. Scripture is filled with examples of God inviting people to join Him in His redemptive work. And, in each case, people had to make major adjustments to go with God.

Moses

Moses had been herding sheep for forty years when God revealed His plans to save the Israelites. God said, "I have surely seen the oppression of My people who are in Egypt, and have heard their cry. . . . So I have come down to deliver them out of the hand of the Egyptians. . . . Come now, therefore, and I will send you to Pharaoh that you may bring My people, the children of Israel, out of Egypt" (Exod. 3:7–8, 10). When God first began talking with Moses, it must have seemed like an interesting discussion. God had seen the Israelites' plight, and He was going to do something about it! Great! But then

God invited Moses to join Him in His activity. God wasn't asking Moses to merely believe He could bring salvation to His people. He was asking Moses to leave the security of the only job he had known for forty years, return to a land where he was a wanted man, and to deliver a highly unpopular message to one of the most powerful rulers in the world. That was quite an adjustment!

Mary the Mother of Jesus

Mary was a godly teenager. She must have been filled with excitement when an angelic messenger approached her, saying, "Rejoice, highly favored one, the Lord is with you; blessed are you among women!" (Luke 1:28). Who would not be delighted with that message? But then the angel explained how she would become pregnant by the Holy Spirit *before* she was married to Joseph. This had never happened before! Furthermore, it was scandalous for an unmarried woman to become pregnant. What would this do to her relationship with her fiancé? How could a lady who had always lived so righteously endure the shame and the reproachful glares of the village women who assumed she was an adulterer? How could she bear the suspicion of Joseph or her own family? Clearly, becoming involved with God's activity was going to change Mary's life forever!

The Twelve Disciples

Peter, Andrew, James, and John were fishermen on the scenic Sea of Galilee. It was a noble profession providing a steady income. Their fathers were fishermen and would one day hand down their businesses to their sons. They lived in an idyllic, peaceful town, far removed from the noisy commotion of Jerusalem or Caesarea. They could enjoy their families and retire in comfort one day. By all accounts, these men were destined to enjoy a peaceful, predictable, purposeless life.

Then one day, as they were in the midst of their mundane tasks, Jesus was suddenly standing beside their boat. "Follow Me," He had said, "and I will make you become fishers of men" (Mark 1:17). That seemingly innocuous invitation would forever change the lives of those men. They had been content to remain in that backwater location all their lives, but now they would be scattered across the known world. They had never spoken in public before; now they would stand before large crowds pointing people to the Messiah. They would have most likely been popular people in their small town; now they would face angry mobs that opposed them and intended to kill them. They certainly would not have entertained any notion of writing a book for posterity, but Peter and John would ultimately pen words that would be cherished for more than two thousand years. They had assumed their lives would impact few others besides their immediate families, but after they chose to join Jesus in His work, their lives would transform the world, impacting people on every continent for millenniums to come.

As Jesus stood beside their boat that day, these men had to make the most important decision of their lives. Clearly, they could not stay where they were and go with Jesus at the same time. They could not hold on to the certainty and safety of their current life and simultaneously embrace the new life Jesus was offering them. Each of these men would have to make enormous adjustments if they were to join Jesus in His work.

So it is with us. God is at work all around our family. He will inevitably invite us to join Him in what He is doing. But it will require us, and our family, to make significant adjustments. We cannot remain where we are, doing the same things we have always done, and go with Him! For many believers, this is a crucial decision. It is all well and good to believe God can change our world. It is quite another thing to make adjustments in our own personal life in order for God to change the world *through us.*

Adjustments Families Must Make

When it comes to our family, there are two primary forms of adjustment that must be made if God is to involve our family in His work. First are the adjustments our children will need to make. The second are the adjustments *we* must make as parents if we are to join God in His activity in our home.

1. Our Children Must Learn to Make Adjustments to Go with God

The world in which our children are growing up is continually teaching them to be self-centered. The media celebrities hungrily followed by tabloids take self-indulgence to record levels. The marketplace is saturated with cars, medications, clothes, holidays, homes, electronics, and much more—are all designed to make our lives more *comfortable*. It goes completely against our natural instincts to let go of our pampered lives so we can join God in His activity. That is why our role as parents is crucial. We must teach our children what truly matters in life and what does not. We don't want to raise children who greedily grasp temporal pleasures that are fleeting while missing out on God's will. Learning to embrace God's will is best learned in our home where we grow up. Of course not everyone experiences a Christian upbringing. However, as you raise your children, be continually watching for ways to help them make whatever adjustment is necessary to fully participate in God's activity around them.

There are innumerable ways to help your family adjust to God's activity. A simple effort to teach your preschooler to share his toys with a friend from a poor family can set your child on the path to walking with Jesus. We grew up in a home where visiting speakers to our church regularly shared a meal at our dinner table. While that might mean we had to carve our lone pie for dessert into a few more slices, it also meant that as children we got to meet some amazing men and women of God! Some families regularly host international exchange students in their home for several months at a time. This calls for the children to adjust to a long-term houseguest who may speak poor English, but it also introduces them to people from around the world. We know of one kindhearted family who invited an international college student to their home for Thanksgiving. The student was from a different religion. Before she could share a meal with her North American hosts, she had to go out into the garden and ceremonially sprinkle dust over her plate and utensils to purify them! To say this family was not stuck in "traditional" Thanksgivings every year is an understatement!

Many families today are adopting children from poor countries or children with disabilities. This, of course, involves enormous adjustments for the entire family. The children must sacrifice time with their parents for their adopted sibling. They may have to share a room or toys with their new family member. Yet the impact on birth children after embracing an AIDS orphan from Uganda or a disabled child from China as a new brother or sister can be enormous. Other families regularly go on mission trips together. Whether it is helping serve food at an addiction recovery center downtown or ministering to orphans in Africa, investing the family's resources in missions is life changing. Both of us have gone to great lengths to send our children on international trips. There is always a cost involved as well as much investment of time and energy putting the trips together; yet the impact on our children has been priceless.

ADJUSTING IN THE PHILIPPINES (AN EXAMPLE FROM RICHARD)

I was once scheduled to speak in the Philippines where, among other things, I would be meeting with President Gloria Arroyo at her presidential palace. At the time, my son Daniel was a university student who was struggling with a sense of purpose and divine calling for his life. Daniel had traveled the world the year after high school, but this was almost two years later. Bogged down in assignments, exams, and books to read, it seemed like he could use a "booster" to keep his life in perspective and to receive a fresh word from God.

I intentionally scheduled the trip over Daniel's spring break from university so he would not have to miss too much school. Still, the trip was for two weeks, which meant he'd have to miss one week of classes. I had Daniel approach all five of his professors to ask permission to miss, telling them he had a wonderful opportunity to speak to large crowds gathered in coliseums and to meet a world leader in her presidential palace. Four of the professors were excited for him and said he could make up any exam or assignment he missed upon his return. The fifth professor informed him he'd be missing a midterm, and if he was absent, he'd fail the class. Now Daniel has never been squeamish about skipping classes, but he did not want to lose credit for an entire semester because of one missed exam. Ultimately, however, we sensed that this was a divine invitation from God and that Daniel needed to make whatever adjustment was necessary in order to go. He dropped that class and went to the Philippines. (Daniel has also never been squeamish about dropping classes!)

Daniel had a life-changing experience. He met amazing people who were investing their lives to reach that great nation for Christ. It was his first experience of having a personal bodyguard! He spoke in large meetings. He addressed youth groups across Manila. He was enticed to eat the Philippine's infamous delicacy, balut (I don't recommend it). He shook hands with a national president. He spent quality time with his dad and grandfather. And, during our trip home, I spoke in a large church in South Korea where Daniel witnessed the powerful moving of God.

Making the adjustment necessary to go on the trip required a sacrifice for Daniel. He had to make up a lot of reading and classwork upon his return. He also had to pick up an additional class over the next two years if he was to graduate on time (he did). Of course, not every parent has the luxury (or air miles) to take a child to Asia. But the fundamental truth applies to every family: Are you prepared to make whatever adjustment God asks of you in order to go with Him?

2. Adjusting Our Life As Parents

One truth that ought to give parents pause is that children who grow up in selfish homes tend to become selfish themselves. If we are reluctant to make adjustments in our walk with God, then our children will be disinclined to do so also. However, if we continually make whatever adjustment is necessary to be a part of God's activity around us, then our children may be inspired to do so as well.

To be an outstanding parent, making adjustments is a prerequisite! That's partly because when we begin having children, we do not have all the wisdom or experience that is necessary. We have to learn on the job. And, if we are open to His leading, God will guide us to make whatever adjustments are required. The following are four areas of your life where you may need to make major adjustments if you are to join God in His activity in your home.

Devotional Life

If you want to be involved in what God is doing in your family, you may well need to take your walk with Him to a deeper level. We once had a friend named Lou who was inspired by the fact that our father, Henry, rose at 4:00 a.m. each morning to spend time with God. He decided that he would follow the same schedule. When his face kept wearily falling into his plate of food at dinnertime, his wife urged him to forego his early morning routine. The husband complained, "You can't have a Henry Blackaby for a husband who doesn't keep a Henry Blackaby schedule." (He eventually adjusted the starting time for his devotions to a time he could manage.)

When God places children in your home, it is an awesome responsibility. Jesus clearly understood this truth. Though Jesus was not a parent, His Father did entrust Him with twelve disciples. As a result, Jesus prayed, "And for their sakes I sanctify Myself, that they also may be sanctified by the truth" (John 17:19). Having been given the responsibility for twelve people, Jesus knew He could not be careless with His own walk with His heavenly Father. We, too, must recognize that we cannot take people to places spiritually where we have not gone ourselves. If we want to see our children go deep in their walk with God, then we must go there first.

This certainly is true of our devotional life. While having children at home can certainly be demanding, it is not the time to be careless with our prayer life. In fact, God may ask you to deepen your time spent in prayer while your kids are in school or when they become teenagers and face increased temptations and pressures. Tom and I well know the value of parents willing to make adjustments in prayer for their children! When we were in university, we both attended a weekend conference in a city seven hours away. On our return home, we were driving sixty miles per hour on an undivided, two-lane highway when our car struck a patch of black ice. The vehicle was spinning in circles down the middle of the highway. An eighteen-wheeler was heading straight for us from the opposite direction. At the last moment, our car tires caught dry pavement, and we were hurtled backwards into a snow-filled ditch.

When we finally pulled into the driveway of our home, our mother came running out to our car. "What happened?" she asked. Apparently that afternoon, while our dad was enjoying his Sunday afternoon nap, our mother was puttering in the kitchen when she was suddenly struck with grave concern for her three sons who were returning home on the highway. So burdened did she become that she woke our father from his slumber and knelt down by the bed with him and prayed for our safety. Upon our return, she asked what time our car had spun out of control. It was at 2:30 that afternoon, the exact time our parents were on their knees interceding for us. We have been thankful ever since that our parents were prepared to make adjustments in their prayer life when God summoned them to.

Could we offer one other challenge to you in this regard? If you are going to raise your children to know, love, and obey God's Word, then you must know it yourself. One of the games we played as a family when driving in the car on long trips was the "stump Dad on the Bible game." We would turn to an obscure passage in the Bible and read a verse or two and then see if our dad could tell us where the verse was to be found. He might not always know the *exact* reference in Leviticus where God gave instructions on making freewill offerings, but he could routinely identify the chapter of the Bible where it was located. We were always impressed. Yet there are parents who can tell their kids the batting average against left-handed pitchers that the winning third baseman had during the 1973 World Series, but they cannot give their children a verse that explains why they should remain a virgin until they are married. If we truly want godly children, we will pay the price to know God's Word ourselves and to share it regularly with our children.

SCHEDULE

A second area of adjustment God may ask us to make will be in our schedule. To say that having children is time-consuming is a huge understatement! Yet we know parents who insisted that having children was not going to cause them to dramatically alter their schedules! These parents continued to indulge in their golfing, hunting, and other recreational activities just as before. They spend weekends glued to the television or catching up on their work from the office. These adults fail to understand that when they became parents, they assumed the commitment to make whatever adjustments were necessary to be involved with God's activity in their children's lives.

Our uncle Will always understood that his schedule as a parent belonged to God. For many years, he and his wife, Margaret, were youth sponsors at their church. The teenagers of the church loved them and expected to see them at all of their activities. We have volunteered to coach our kid's sports teams. We often weren't the most experienced or skilled coaches, but we wanted to be a part of whatever God was doing in our children's lives. We found that participating in team sports provided a marvelous opportunity for our children to learn about teamwork and how to get along with other kids. Tom's son Matt excelled in basketball. Tom often volunteered to coach Matt's team and spent countless hours shooting hoops with him and talking about how to be a team player.

For several years Richard coached both of his sons on the same in-line hockey team. Richard's job as a seminary president required extensive travel, and so every year he would try and step down as his sons' coach. Each year the league director would call Richard and inform him that no other parent had volunteered, so Richard would take the helm of the team for another season. One Saturday, Richard had a game to coach, but the contest backed right up to his seminary's annual graduation ceremony. That Saturday, Richard arrived at the arena in a suit and tie. Everyone thought he was taking his coaching responsibilities a little too seriously! Even as the team was returning to the locker room after the game, Richard was frantically racing to the church where the commencement ceremony was being held. The Registrar had Richard's doctoral robe at the ready. He flung it on and seconds later was leading the procession of faculty members down the aisle to begin the ceremony!

As we've already shared, parents must be prepared to adjust their schedules at a moment's notice. One day you might sense one of your children needs your attention, so you schedule to have lunch with her. Or you take you son with you on a business trip. Or you adjust your schedule to attend a child's band concert. Allow God to show you what adjustments you might need to make in your schedule so you don't miss what God is doing in your home. One day Richard's teenage son Mike mentioned he didn't have to go to school that day. Seizing the opportunity, Richard suggested he take his son out for lunch. "Uh-oh," Mike moaned, "where are we going for lunch?" "It doesn't matter," replied Richard. "Wherever you want." Mike then confessed that his father had developed a pattern. Whenever he wanted a private place to talk to his son about awkward issues, such as the dangers of pornography, he would take Mike to a large Chinese buffet. When talking about drugs and peer pressure, Richard tended to take his son to Dairy Queen. Mike wanted to know which restaurant they were going to so he could prepare himself for the kind of talk they were going to have!

FINANCES

A third area that must be adjusted if you are to join in God's work is your finances. Where you put your money reveals what is most important to you. At times, parents make the mistake of donating money to their church and other charities without letting their children participate in the process. Your children need to learn that money is not something to be greedily hoarded but generously invested in God's kingdom. When appropriate, children should participate in decisions concerning how family finances are donated.

When Richard's son Mike graduated from college, Richard and Lisa gave him a unique graduation gift. It was an orphan from Bolivia. Richard and Lisa signed Mike up to sponsor the young girl through Compassion International. They paid the first couple of months while Mike got on his feet financially, then they left the monthly payments to him. Mike was thrilled!

There are innumerable ways in which you may need to adjust your finances in order to join God in His activity in your home. Some parents turn down promotions or lucrative transfers because they know their teenager is plugged in to his youth group. The parents realize God's activity in their child's life at that crucial stage of development is more important than the parent advancing another rung up the corporate ladder. Parents may decide to spend less on Christmas gifts so their family can go on a mission trip instead. Our parents wanted to invest in the spiritual condition of their children and grandchildren, so they paid to bring them all on a trip to Israel. Though it cost a lot of money, what a thrill it was for them to sail on the Sea of Galilee and to stand on the Temple Mount along with their grandchildren and talk about the significance of the Scripture with them! When we were both in college, our parents wanted to help us experience an international trip. They paid for us to go to Austria. We had an amazing trip seeing numerous tourist sites. We also got to participate in a worship service with Romanian refugees who had escaped from their oppressive Communist regime so they could practice religious liberty. Many escaped with nothing but the clothes on their backs. Some were shot at as they swam across the river to freedom. As we worshipped with these people, it was incredible. They were filled with joy! They would approach us and lovingly share Bible verses with us. They worshipped for hours, having four different sermons, Communion, and a foot washing! As two North American Christians, we had never witnessed anything like that! To this day we have no idea how our parents came up with the money to pay for that trip. They just knew it was important. But even they might have been surprised to know how many dozen countries we would minister to in the following years as a result of the seeds our parents planted in our hearts when we were college students.

The key is not the dollar amount you spend on your children. Some families have more income than others. The crucial factor is being willing to adjust your spending as the Lord directs you so you can join Him in what He is doing in your children's lives. We might also add one caution. Sometimes we get too obsessed with what it will cost us to do what God is telling us. The price may seem too steep. We may know it would be good to take our teenager on a mission trip or to forego a promotion to stay near home, but we may balk at the apparent cost involved. The problem is that at times we fail to consider the cost involved for *not* following through with what God is calling us to do. The price of disobedience to God is *always* far greater than the cost of obedience!

Family Time/Vacations

A final area of adjustment for parents is with family time. As we've shared, we grew up in a home that was always filled with guests around the dinner table. Our father had the world's *worst* puns! We'd sit around the dinner table and try and "one up" each other with a play on words. Guests would look on in bewilderment as we would laugh uproariously. We never had a large home, but we seemed to always have company. We learned that our home was an oasis of healing. On at least two occasions, high school or college students who were thrown out of their home by their parents ended up at our house when they had nowhere else to go. Latchkey kids often spent time after school at our house. Holidays were often an opportunity to share our joy with others. Both of our families have shared Christmas with people who had nowhere else to spend it. One year, Richard's family became aware of a single young woman in his church who worked with college students. She was unable to return home to spend Christmas with her family, so Richard invited her to share Christmas with his. Richard secretly asked people in the church to contribute Christmas presents for their guest. On Christmas morning, the young woman was overwhelmed when Richard's children kept pulling more and more presents out from under the Christmas tree with her name on them. It was a wonderful opportunity for Richard's children to experience what it was like to bring joy to someone else rather than merely indulging themselves.

There are times when you may feel that God is leading you to use your family vacation to go on a mission trip or to invest at least a portion of the time helping someone in need. Our uncle Will took his family to the same vacation spot every summer for years. Each year they would minister to the same small church near their campsite. The children would bring their instruments to play special music, and their family would seek to bless the small church each year. Their family still had lots of fun, but they also incorporated blessing a local church into their vacation plans.

Of course, there are times when God may lead you to focus specifically on ministering to your own family rather than to others. The important thing is being open to how God might lead you to use your family times for God to work in and through your home.

Summary

You cannot go with God *and* stay where you are! The reason more Christians are not experiencing God is that they are unwilling to make the adjustments required to join God in His work. Whether it is helping your children adjust to God's activity in their lives, or it is you making the adjustments, it is crucial to respond immediately to what God is doing. We hope that in the coming days you will be quick to respond to whatever it is God asks of you.

QUESTIONS FOR REFLECTION/DISCUSSION

1. What are some adjustments you sense God wants your children to make? How might you help them do that? Where do you think the greatest area of struggle might come in that process?

2. How might you need to make adjustments in your walk with God if you are to join Him in what He is doing in your children's lives?

3. How might you need to adjust your schedule to join God in His activity?

4. How might you need to make adjustments in your finances to join in God's activity?

5. How might you adjust your family times or vacations so God can work in fresh ways in your home?

CHAPTER 14

You Come to Know God by Experience as You Obey Him and He Accomplishes His Purposes through You

A Sad Car and a Happy Daughter
(A Story from Tom)

My daughter Erin called recently and informed me there was a loud noise emanating from her car engine and lots of liquid on the street. She was able to drive it safely to a parking lot where she was hoping I could magically solve her problem over the phone. It turned out her 1996 Neon was on its last legs. I had already changed the brakes, brake pump, radiator, gas intake pipe, lights, and tires. Now the water pump was gone. My mechanic friend and I fetched her car, and through a series of driving, stopping, refilling the coolant, driving, stopping, refilling the coolant, we eventually made it home. I intended to perform the four-hour ritual of installing a new water pump myself. Well the four-hour job mushroomed into eight, with no end in sight. In desperation, I called my mechanic friend to rescue me. No amount of phone calls was going to get that water pump replaced. He brought the right tool (which I didn't know existed) to dislodge the pump, and within minutes it and the timing belt were replaced with covers, bolts, and screws all tightened

172

fast. When the master mechanic works with you, things go a lot quicker! I received a nice "shout out" on Facebook from my daughter along with a photo of a dishevelled dad with greasy hands and a bemused look on my face.

Involving God through Obedience

"Tell me and I'll forget; show me and I may remember; involve me and I'll understand." This quote has been attributed to Confucius. It may be an elaboration on another quote attributed to him: "I hear and I forget. I see and I remember. I do and I understand" (circa 450 BC).

Many of us have heard Bible stories since childhood, but we could never identify with them, nor did they seem real to us or applicable to our daily lives. We may have listened to stories about God's amazing work through the great saints of the past or through missionaries in remote villages, but it always involved *other* people in *distant* places. There is a heart cry within many Christians today to experience in their life what they have heard about all of their life.

The Christian life was not meant to be *read about* but to be *experienced*. It is only as we step out in faith, as God prompts us, that we experience in our life what people in the Bible experienced in theirs. The quickest way to help young believers grow in their faith is not to have them read a book about it but to take them by the hand and guide them to obey God's instructions themselves, one step at a time.

There is an interesting story in the life of Joshua that, while truly spectacular, has great implications for our life and family:

> When the people broke camp to cross the Jordan, the priests carried the ark of the covenant ahead of the people. Now the Jordan overflows its banks throughout the harvest season. But as soon as the priests carrying the ark reached the Jordan, their feet touched the water at its edge and the water flowing downstream stood still, rising up in a mass that extended as far as Adam, a city next to Zarethan. The water flowing downstream into the Sea of the Arabah (the Dead Sea) was completely cut off, and the people crossed opposite Jericho. The priests carrying the ark of the LORD's covenant stood firmly on dry ground

in the middle of the Jordan, while all Israel crossed on dry
ground until the entire nation had finished crossing the Jordan.
(Josh. 3:14–17 HCSB)

Joshua had only recently been commissioned as the top general of
his nation. He didn't have a lot of experience at the helm, yet people
must have wondered what they were in for when he ordered the army to
begin marching straight for a fast-flowing river! That was not the most
strategic way of launching an invasion! If the army *did* get across, they'd
be trapped in a land brimming with enemies who wanted to kill them. It
appeared that the young general was marching his army headlong into a
disaster. Yet this was no random decision on Joshua's part. He wasn't trying to prove he could be just as daring as Moses had been. The Israelites
were stepping into the Jordan River in *obedience* to what God had *told*
them to do. When Moses parted the Red Sea, he had done so by raising
his staff *as God directed* (Exod. 14:16). Joshua might have been excused
if he had frantically scrambled to find Moses' staff as they approached
the edge of the river! This time, however, God did not make use of any
shepherding paraphernalia. Instead, He instructed the priests to take the
lead and march straight into the river.

How did the priests know the water would part as their feet touched
it? They didn't. For all we know, the priests at the front were taking deep
breaths and strapping on their life vests (water wings)! But forward they
went. The most significant truth of this story may be this: the water
didn't stop flowing until their feet touched it. Had the Israelites decided
to stop at the river's edge and wait for things to dry up, they might still
be waiting! Often God's power is not exercised until His people's feet
get wet. The priests and soldiers had all heard stories from their parents
of how, in an earlier era, God parted the Red Sea. Only that day, they
weren't hearing stories about what God had done through other people;
they were experiencing God's power *firsthand*. Our children don't need
to merely hear about what God did in the Bible, or through missionaries
in the 1900s, or even in our life. They need to experience God firsthand.

Stepping Out in Faith (An Example from Tom)

Every family should have its own "Jordan River" experiences where
God performs miracles as they obey God's will. A couple of years ago I

faced a crisis. I was trying to pass through the airport in Lagos, Nigeria, with my seventy-five-year-old father. Due to delays in previous flights, we arrived in Lagos after the check-in counter had closed. Though the plane did not leave for another hour, we were told it was too late to check in. With my father being diabetic, the next plane to Atlanta leaving two days later, and our plane still sitting at the gate, we had to find a way to get ourselves (and our luggage) aboard. My father is anything but a confrontational person (he would rather wander down the aisles of Walmart for hours before he would bother to ask an employee for directions to the laundry detergent aisle), so I knew that though he has flown roughly three million miles over the years, he was not exactly going to get "raucous" with the airline agents in order to get us checked in! We bowed our heads in the crowded airport and prayed for God's intervention. As we approached an agent, he firmly shook their head and said "no" to our plea, mumbling something about "airline policies." But then gradually, he relented and agreed to allow us to present our case to the person in authority over him. The process continued (slowly) while we watched our plane being loaded and preparing to depart (without us). My father remained remarkably calm (there are times he can look amazingly "Moses-like!"). I, on the other hand, was on the edge of panic, knowing how difficult it would be to be stranded for two days in that foreign city. I tried to summon all of my charm and problem-solving ability and, when that didn't work, attempted to look as pitiful and pathetic as possible! (That wasn't difficult!) Without going into all the details of what God did to get us on that plane, I can assure you that when we finally boarded our plane, we knew we had just witnessed God in action helping us arrive home safely. God didn't have to part a sea or a river, nor did I get to use a cool shepherd's staff. But God had miraculously parted a sea of red tape and had made a pathway through bribery-infested, corrupt, inefficient bureaucrats. When you repeatedly experience God intervening in your life in practical ways, you marvel at how amazing life can be when God walks with you throughout each day.

Christians are divinely intended to live by faith. But what does that mean? The writer of Hebrews says, "Now without faith it is impossible to please God, for the one who draws near to Him must believe that He exists and rewards those who seek Him" (Heb. 11:6 HCSB). James says it another way: "Foolish man! Are you willing to learn that faith without works is useless?" (James 2:20 HCSB). Scripture is clear: we can say we *believe* in God until we are blue in the face, but those are just words until we actually *live* like we believe God.

This is immensely important when it comes to passing on our faith to our kids. Today's younger generation is not content merely to *hear* about God from books or the pulpit; they want to *see* faith that is real and alive. They want to experience God doing miracles in their own home and through their family. This is what inspires our kids and what can prevent them from walking away from God one day.

This is what we often experienced in our childhood home. Over and over again, God would provide for our family right on time. Our parents never hesitated to obey what they sensed God telling our family to do, even when it appeared impossible. Sure enough, right when a bill was due that we could not afford to pay, a check would arrive in the mail. Or when we still had more week left than we had groceries, someone would happen to drop by with some meat and produce from their farm they thought we could use. Such experiences left a profound impression on each of us children as we watched the practical reality of walking with and obeying God daily.

A Family Learning to Trust God (An Example from Richard)

Growing up in a home where obeying God was nonnegotiable, I took that approach into my own family once I was married. Ten days after our wedding, Lisa and I packed our meager belongings and headed one thousand miles south to Texas to attend seminary. We knew God wanted us to go, but we had one small problem: we had no money! We had both graduated from university that summer, and we had no funds with which to pay for tuition or rent. I have known many people who would advise that we should wait a year and work so we could save up enough money to at least pay for tuition and a few months' rent. But I had been taught that when God tells you to do something, the time to obey is *now!*

We arrived in Fort Worth on a Thursday evening. School orientation began Monday. My aunt called and told us that their wedding gift to us was to pay our first month's rent (a gift they could not afford to give). My aunt worked at a law firm and had taken it upon herself to arrange for my wife, Lisa, to drop off an application on Friday. She did. The firm asked her to start work Monday. I went to orientation on Monday, knowing that by Thursday I had to pay for my semester. Right on schedule, I was informed that a rattletrap vehicle I had left in Canada had been purchased, and the proceeds were exactly enough to cover tuition . . . and so our journey of faith commenced. Two years later, we had a new son, Michael. We were barely eking a living for two; how could we going to afford a third mouth to feed? One day we discovered we were down to our last jar of baby food. It was a week before payday. We did not even have the eighteen cents required to purchase another jar. We had no credit card and no means of getting money from our relatives in Canada (if they could have afforded to send some). As a young couple, we felt overwhelmed. Here we were, far from home, trying to obey God. Why was life so impossible? Should I quit school and get a job so I could pay for baby food? Was it right to be putting my family through such hardship in order to obey God? Was I being selfish, pursuing an education when I couldn't afford to feed my baby? Lisa and I prayed over our meager meal that evening and humbly asked God for food for our baby. While we were still sitting at the table, the phone rang. It was a woman Lisa had met the day before. She sounded horribly embarrassed. "I am *so* sorry to bother you at dinnertime!" she began. "I hope you are not offended by this . . ." She proceeded to explain that her baby (a few months older than ours) had suddenly developed a disdain for baby food. The mother finally decided to throw away the remaining jars since they were no longer needed. Her husband happened to be passing by and said, "Honey, you shouldn't throw all that food away. Don't you know anyone with a baby who could use that stuff?" The woman thought for a moment and remembered meeting Lisa the day before. She looked up our number and called. She was afraid we might be offended at being treated like a "charity case!" The next day the woman brought *dozens* of supersized, top-of-the-line Gerber's baby food. It was the first nongeneric food our son had eaten in his life! He was thrilled! (Who knew Tutty Frutty could taste so good?) And we knew, once again, that God is so practical, He can part a sea if you need Him to, or He can move someone to donate baby food if that happens to be your need at the moment. God is simply looking for us to trust Him, and obey Him. The Bible is not simply a storybook about what God did thousands of years ago. It is the living Word of God that reveals what God can and will do through families *today*.

In Marriage

Our father has often stated that God's voice often sounds a lot like his wife's voice! While he is joking (sort of), he is also acknowledging a profound truth: Husbands and wives are designed to be one flesh (Matt. 19:4–5). It means that God doesn't just speak to the husband. Nor does it mean that the wife is responsible for all of the family's praying. It means that couples must discern God's will together. Typically, husbands will be sensitive to certain issues while wives may be more alert to others. It is only when they are both listening to God and sharing what they are hearing that couples can clearly understand how God is guiding them.

A Couple Hears from God

At church one Sunday, the pastor issues an impassioned plea for more homes to be opened for community Bible studies. Over lunch that day, the husband ventures to say that he was struck by what the pastor said, and he would like to let their home be used to reach their neighborhood. But, he adds, he knows it would put a lot more pressure on his wife to have guests coming over every Tuesday evening, so he does not want to add more work to her busy schedule. To his surprise, the wife replies that recently God has been speaking to her about their home. In her quiet times, God has been impressing upon her that He entrusted a beautiful home to them, and He expects them to invest it in His kingdom. She, too, had been struck by the pastor's words that day but had hesitated to mention it because she knew that Tuesdays were busy days for her husband. Together, the couple responds to the Holy Spirit's promptings and offers their home for a Bible study on Tuesday evenings. The family begins making adjustments. The children help to clean and vacuum the house after school on Tuesdays. The husband picks up pizza on the way home from work. The wife does some baking to serve that evening. God does a profound work in several of the attendee's lives through the study. Several people accept Christ as their Savior. Great new friendships are established. The parents regularly report to their children how God is working in the Bible study. The family celebrates how God is using their ordinary family to bless others and to expand His kingdom. And years later, when the children are grown with their own families, they, too, allow God to use their homes as outposts for God's work in their community.

It is crucial that parents understand God's agenda for their family. In which neighborhood should we live? Which company do I work for? What church do we join? What schools do the children attend? What causes do we donate money and time to? If you assume God does not care about details, read His instructions to Noah on how to build an ark or to Moses on how to make a tabernacle. God is a master of details. That being said, we are pretty sure He doesn't care what kind of toothpaste you use (and we have major questions on God's view on flossing!). But when it comes to building His kingdom and setting people free, God is extremely intentional about how He works through ordinary people's lives. We are seeing CEOs in corporate America, factory workers, business owners, and parents experiencing the amazing reality that almighty God intends to use their life, where they live and work, for His divine purposes. They are experiencing the truth that when they seek first God's kingdom purposes, everything else in their life comes together (Matt. 6:33).

Clear the Road! (An Example from Tom the Driving Instructor)

I have taught five people to drive a car, including my two oldest children. Many parents would cringe at the thought and frantically hire a driving instructor. I was a little bolder (or frugal) and embraced the challenge with gusto. I once took my son Matt to a deserted highway. As he drove, I instructed him to step hard on the gas pedal in order to feel the passing gear kick in. I wanted him to know how much extra power was available should he ever need to pass a car quickly (such a "need" I was certain he *would* feel!). I assured him it was OK, and I gave him a wink. He must have thought his dad was crazy, actually *telling* him to speed! The next thing that happened scared the life out of me. Rather than pressing the gas pedal while cruising at fifty miles per hour, Matt stomped on the brake pedal, sending the car screeching to a skidding, swerving stop. Needless to say, I was a little shaken and looked at him in disbelief. He said meekly, "I got the pedals mixed up."

Following the rules of driving allows you to enjoy the privilege of commuting on public roads in relative safety. Observing the signs, speed limits, traffic signals, and the rules of the road enables you to go from your home to your destination easily and safely. Once you get the hang of it, you can actually *enjoy* driving, listening to your music, and looking at the sights. If you choose not to follow the rules and you ignore the signage, you will most likely find flashing lights pulling up behind you and a nice man asking to see that great photo you took for your driver's license! My son learned the hard way what can happen when you fail to observe certain road signs. He later missed some signs and was rear-ended, totalling my car (guess I should have hired a professional instructor).

God's Guidelines for Success

There are many similarities between driving a car and functioning in the kingdom of God. There are laws of the kingdom that, if followed, lead to abundant life. From the commencement of human history, Adam and Eve were given rules to follow that led to an amazing life. There was only one restriction, but it was a major one. As long as they heeded God's word, they had complete freedom to explore and enjoy their world. They chose to break the one rule God gave them, and they and their family paid a horrific price. Obedience brings life. Disobedience (sin) brings death (Rom. 6:23). God wasn't being harsh. He was being true to His Word.

The Tragic Cost of Disobedience

The first funeral our father ever performed was under extremely tragic circumstances. A beautiful baby girl was born. She was the couple's first child. She was the first grandchild on either side of the family. Everyone adored her! And spoiled her. As she grew as a preschooler, she developed a playful game with her doting relatives. An adult would call and ask her to come to them. She would grant them a radiant smile and then turn and run in the opposite direction. The adults would howl with laughter. And so the game continued. One day the girl was playing in the front yard when her ball rolled into the street. Her mother was startled to see a car speeding down the street toward her child. Seeing her precious daughter making her way toward the street to collect her ball, the mother shouted frantically at her daughter to stop and come to her immediately. The preschooler stopped, gave her mother a playful smile, then darted right in front of the speeding vehicle. The child's parents had made a game of disobedience, and it had cost their child her life.

The Little Things Count Too

God is serious about guiding us and our children to experience abundant life. However, He will not force abundant life upon us. Many of the covenants God made in the Bible were conditional. The covenant God made with Abraham, Isaac, Jacob, and their descendants generally began with, "If you . . . then I will." If you obey my commands . . . if you serve Me . . . if you follow in My ways . . . if you keep My commandments. . . .Then I will give you the land as an inheritance . . . I will protect you from your enemies . . . I will give you peace . . . I will multiply your descendants . . . I will deliver you from your enemies . . . and so forth. Notice some of God's expectations for His people:

- "For if you carefully observe every one of these commands I am giving you to follow—to love the LORD your God, walk in all His ways, and remain faithful to Him. The LORD will drive out all these nations before you, and you will drive out nations greater and stronger than you are. Every place the sole of your foot treads will be yours. Your territory will extend from the wilderness to Lebanon and from the Euphrates River to the Mediterranean Sea." (Deut. 11:22 HCSB)

- "Love the LORD your God, obey Him, and remain faithful to Him. For He is your life, and He will prolong your life in the land the LORD swore to give to your fathers Abraham, Isaac, and Jacob." (Deut. 30:20 HCSB)

- "Only carefully obey the command and instruction that Moses the LORD's servant gave you: to love the LORD your God, walk in all His ways, keep His commands, remain faithful to Him, and serve Him with all your heart and all your soul." (Josh. 22:5 HCSB)

- "This is how we know that we love God's children when we love God and obey His commands." (1 John 5:2 HCSB)

- "Jesus answered, 'If anyone loves Me, he will keep My word. My Father will love him, and We will come to him and make Our home with him.'" (John 14:23 HCSB)

In American society today, the word *obedience* is not very popular. Try hosting an "Obedience" conference at your church for your community and see if you need overflow seating! (Better have a pretty snazzy billboard!) But hold a "God's Secrets to Wealth and Happiness" conference, and even unbelievers will come, just in case. Unfortunately, even in the church, many pastors avoid emphasizing the word *obedience* from the pulpit because it seems too demeaning, almost abusive. But the truth is that God declared that as we obeyed Him, we would experience Him. Too many Christians today are disobeying God and then wondering why He seems so distant! Recall what people in the Bible experienced when they obeyed God:

- Abraham obeyed and experienced God miraculously granting him a son at the age of 100 (Gen. 17).
- Moses obeyed and experienced God powerfully delivering an entire nation from bondage (Exod. 6:6–8; 12:31).
- Noah obeyed and experienced God's amazing deliverance from a cataclysmic destruction (Gen. 7).
- Joseph obeyed and experienced God's timely deliverance from King Herod's hit squad (Matt. 2:13).
- Gideon obeyed and experienced God using a mere 300 men to defeat an army of more than 135,000 (Judg. 7).

Whenever people obeyed what God told them, they experienced God in fresh new ways. Had Moses remained in the desert with his sheep, he would have known *about* God, but he would never have experienced God's incredible power himself. Gideon might have believed the stories he was told about God granting victory to Abraham's band of men over the armies of King Chedorlaomer and his allies (Gen. 14:1–17), but when Gideon obeyed what God told *him*, he experienced firsthand what God's deliverance was like! But there is something more important than experiencing God's power, or deliverance, or wisdom. When we obey God's voice, we experience *Him*. Nothing is better than that!

Obedience in the Street (An Example from Richard)

One Saturday afternoon I was at home brushing up on my sermon for Sunday. My wife had our two younger children with her doing errands. My six-year-old son Mike was playing at home. The doorbell rang. It was two boys Mike's age calling to see if he could hang out with them. One of the boys, named Will, lived across the street from our house and was always getting into trouble. Adjacent to Will's house was a busy street. We had a firm rule in our home that our children were forbidden to cross that road without their parents for *any* reason. Mike was mortified, however, when I recited that rule in front of his two callers. Will immediately piped up: "My parents let *me* cross that street!" I made it clear that Mike could not join them if they intended to cross that forbidden territory. Will promised they would remain in his front yard. I acquiesced. Mike left with them.

It didn't take long for me to begin to worry. I got up and walked over to the living room window. Pulling back the blinds, I could clearly see the boys playing on Will's front yard, just as they had promised. All seemed fine. Fifteen minutes later I thought I'd check just one more time. This time the situation had changed. As I gazed out the window, I saw Will standing beside the contraband street, beckoning his companions to follow. "I knew it!" That Will could *not* be trusted! I began to charge toward the front door. Those boys were going to get so *busted*! But then it dawned on me. What was Mike going to do? He hadn't crossed the street, *yet*.

I returned to the window and watched. Will was now standing *in* the street urging his friends to join him. Mike and the other boy were on the sidewalk, approaching the street. After additional urging by Will, the other boy meekly joined him in the street. Now they both prodded Mike to quit wasting time and come with them. Mike was hesitant. He knew what his dad had said. But his two friends were calling him a "chicken" and taunting him. Mike edged closer to the edge of the sidewalk. He stood so close to the street at this point that if his mother had not recently trimmed his toenails, he'd already be in a state of disobedience! My heart lurched within me. I feared I was about to witness my son blatantly disobeying me. I felt sick at the disappointment and the discipline I'd have to deal with at any moment.

But then something happened. Mike looked at his friends. Then he looked toward our house. Suddenly he waved good-bye to his wayward companions and trotted back to the house. I was overcome with emotion! My son had just rejected his two friends in order to honor his father! I wiped tears from my eyes and quickly sat back down in my chair. As Mike entered the house, I asked nonchalantly, "How come you're home, Mike?" He responded, "I just wanted to be here with you, Dad." I had never been so proud as a parent as at that moment! I immediately put my work aside and got up to spend time with my son. "Can I get you some ice cream, son? How about a sandwich? Would you like a pony?!" What a special time we had together that afternoon!

At times, talking about obeying God can seem sterile, stiff, and even a bit legalistic. But if you have ever spent time with a loving parent just after you honored them with your actions, you may have caught a glimpse of the joy that can be yours when you obey your Father in heaven.

How Can You Experience God in the Family?

As a parent, you are not only seeking to experience God yourself; you are simultaneously helping your family to experience Him too. Here are some ways to do that.

Seek God as a family.

Read God's Word together as a family. As you read, keep your ears and heart open for God to speak to you through the stories, verses, characters, and teachings. God's Word is "living and active" (Heb. 4:12 NASB) and will "accomplish what [He sends] it to do" (Isa. 55:11 HCSB). Share what God reveals to you. Be sure to listen to what God says to your family. Identify verses where God's will for people is spelled out. Then talk together about how you will obey what God said. Expect God to speak to your family through His Word.

Pray together as a family. Lift the various concerns of your children up to God and ask Him for direction and wisdom. Teach your children to talk to God conversationally. Take time to be silent as you listen to what the Holy Spirit is saying to you as a family. Ask God to show you to

whom He wants you to minister. Then later invite your family to discuss
how God answered your prayers.

Find places of service.

God has placed each member in the church body as it pleased Him
(1 Cor. 12:18). Encourage family members to find the place of service
God has for them. It might be helping to pass out bulletins at the
entrance to the auditorium. It might be serving in the nursery. It could
be singing on the praise team or greeting visitors, or joining someone
in the service who is sitting alone. It could be helping to teach ESL to
local immigrants, mowing the lawn of a widow, or going with a team
to minister in the local prison. Don't be satisfied until every member of
your family has found a meaningful way to serve Christ in your church.

If You Love Me

Jesus said, "You are My friends if you do whatever I command you"
(John 15:14). He did not say we were His friends if we worshipped Him,
loved Him, or believed in Him. The measure of whether or not we are
His friends is our obedience. But obeying God is not a chore or a prison
sentence! It is a pleasure! In fact, as we obey God, we truly experience
Him. God's will may at times appear confusing or even daunting. But
as you step put in faith, trusting Him in each step, an amazing world of
divine activity will open up to you. Immeasurable joy can be yours as
you walk in step with God throughout your life.

Transitions in Life (An Example from Tom)

For fifteen years I served as an associate pastor in various churches.
In those years I did everything from leading worship to working with
youth. I had developed expertise in those fields and had even been asked
to serve as a national consultant for our denomination. We were living
in the beautiful city of Vancouver near several of our relatives. Life was
quite comfortable.

Then a time came when Kim and I began to sense that God was
preparing us for a change. It became clear that God's next assignment
for me was as a senior pastor. That was a big stretch! I wasn't used to

preaching every week! I also liked having the senior pastor handle the disgruntled church members! I had not had to manage staff before. I wondered if I could handle the increase in responsibility. I knew I had to obey, and so I assembled a resume. At that time, however, there were not many available positions in my denomination. I was confused. Why would God ask me to be open to being a senior pastor if there were no such positions available? Kim and I continued to pray. One day I was asked if I would submit my resume for a senior pastor position . . . in Norway! And I thought I was already being stretched to the limit! Our children were ages six months, six years, and seven years at that time. It would be an enormous adjustment for my family, let alone my career. But the more we prayed, the clearer it became that this was what God had been preparing me for.

I spent seven incredible years at that church. The experience built many new dimensions into my family. We were able to travel throughout Europe and develop a love for diverse cultures. My children had the world opened up before them, and they met some amazing people. That experience also prepared me for my current job, directing the international ministry of Blackaby Ministries International (I put the "I" in "International!). God knew all along what I would experience if only I would trust Him and accept His invitation. God also knew that my family would be enormously blessed and changed by that step of obedience. I am so glad I made it! Will you?

QUESTIONS FOR REFLECTION/DISCUSSION

1. As you reflect honestly about your walk with God, does your knowledge of God come solely from reading books, or have you also experienced Him?

2. What characteristics (such as power, holiness, love) of God have you experienced? List them.

3. What is God presently asking you to do that you know you must obey?

4. How are you helping your children learn to obey what God tells them?

5. In what ways is your family presently serving God together? Who is your family ministering to?

6. When was the last time your family stepped out in faith?

CHAPTER 15

Getting Your Family on the Right Track

The Problem

Statistics indicate that many of the of children who grow up in Christian homes will eventually walk away from the church and from God, at least for a time. Some never return. We have heard hundreds of heartbreaking tales of children who grew up in godly homes yet succumbed to worldly enticements, peer pressure, or sinful rebellion. Numerous bewildered parents have told us of their child's drug addiction, teenage pregnancy, angry rebellion, or infatuation with sin. These children grew up being taught how to live God-honoring lives; yet they rejected that instruction and made choices that scarred them for the remainder of their lives.

The causes for prodigals are legion. Some parents assume that simply taking their children to church on Sundays and to youth group on Wednesdays is sufficient to ensure they will follow God as adults. Other parents tell their children how they should live but then negate their instruction by living as hypocrites. They instruct their children to behave one way while they act another—a sure means of short-circuiting God's work in children.

Still other parents fail to invest the long hours and hard work required to raise godly children. Their neglect eventually becomes evident. Some Christian parents struggle with sin—not in their children but in their own lives. Behavior such as adultery is devastating not merely because of the harm it causes a marriage. Divorce is a horrific experience for couples, but it can also impose life-altering effects on children. Children who were wholesome, happy young people may begin to act out sexually and rebelliously. Teenagers who were trying to live godly lives, and even talking about entering the Christian ministry, now don't even want to attend church. Finally, there are parents who seemingly do all the right things but whose children reject their faith and values nonetheless. Just as Adam and Eve rebelled against a loving Father, so some children choose to sin regardless of what they were taught.

The Wrong Response

Having a child reject your faith or your love is devastating. It can fill you with conflicting emotions. Yet if this happens, we must avoid several unhealthy responses.

1. Becoming Immobilized by Guilt and Remorse

One of the most common responses by Christian parents whose family falls short of what they hoped for is to become immobilized by feelings of guilt and remorse. We have talked with numerous parents who grieved deeply over the fact that they believed they had failed as parents. Their son who showed such promise as a child is now serving twenty years in prison. Their beautiful teenage daughter who brought sunshine to their world is now pregnant out of wedlock. Their son who used to fill their home with laughter now fills it with angry shouting. Their daughter who grew up regularly attending church now wants nothing to do with it. Children who grew up in a home that abstained from alcohol now can think of nothing else but how inebriated they will become over the weekend.

Parents whose children have rejected their faith and standards may continually rehearse in their minds what they did and said to their children that resulted in such disappointment. Some children may use their parents' past mistakes as a club to punish or manipulate them. The truth is: *no* parents are perfect (even if they claim to be!). We *all* make mistakes we would dearly love to take back. But while we ought to strive to learn from our shortcomings, it is impossible for even the most repentant parents to alter the past. You can rehearse those angry words you spoke to your daughter a thousand times, but you cannot retrieve them. You can wish with all your heart that you had been home more when your children were younger, but the past is now cast in granite.

The apostle Paul was no stranger to regret. He had participated in the brutally unjust murder of Stephen. Yet no amount of remorse or apologies could bring the godly deacon back from the dead. What Paul could do was "[forget] those things which are behind and [reach] forward to those things which are ahead" (Phil. 3:13). One of the great promises of Scripture is this: "As far as the east is from the west, so far has He removed our transgressions from us" (Ps. 103:12). God is not the author of perpetual guilt trips! His heart delights in setting people free (John 8:32)! You won't help your children by beating yourself up over the past! Seek God with all of your heart today, receive His forgiveness for every one of your shortcomings, then allow Him to guide you and your family into His perfect will tomorrow.

2. Giving Up

A second mistake many parents make is to give up. Parents can grow discouraged after all their effort leads to failure. Despite attending countless ball games and music recitals, as well as making innumerable trips to the school, church, and doctor, their child responds by rebelling. Some parents are so disappointed at how their children are behaving that they resign themselves to perpetual defeat, disappointment, and grief. Others grimly accept their fate and proclaim, "I guess they have to sow their wild oats," as if it were inevitable that their child would reject Christian values. Such parents batten down the hatches and prepare to ride out the domestic storm.

This, however, is not an acceptable response. Parents are often their child's last line of defense. They can't afford to give up. Our response to wayward children ought to be like that of our heavenly Father who declared: "How can I give you up, Ephraim? How can I hand you over, Israel? How can I make you like Admah? How can I set you like Zeboiim? My heart churns within me; My sympathy is stirred" (Hos. 11:8). God *never* gives up! Parents must continue to believe what the apostle Paul said when he claimed: "Being confident of this very thing, that He who has begun a good work in you will complete it" (Phil. 1:6). Parents must cling to the "good work" God began in their children at an earlier age and continue to believe He will one day bring that work to fruition. When your parents give up on you, you are in a miserable state indeed. Refuse to surrender hope that God can reclaim your children, regardless of how far away they appear to be at the moment.

3. Suffering in Silence

A third mistake parents make when their family gets off track is to treat the problem as strictly a private affair. Some parents are deeply ashamed of their children's behavior. As a result they refuse to inform their friends or fellow church members about what is happening in their home. Though their child is acting promiscuously, experimenting with drugs, or flunking classes at school, the parents grimly put on their "game face" at church and respond with "Great!" whenever friends ask how their family is doing. Consequently, these grieving parents suffer alone.

While it may be difficult for you to talk in public about something so painful, you cannot allow pride to hinder you from enlisting support for your wayward child. The apostle James instructed the early church, saying: "Confess your trespasses to one another, and pray for one another, that you may be healed" (James 5:16). James knew that people are reluctant to admit their mistakes or to confess their sins. Yet he understood that confession was the pathway to healing. At times, parents refuse to admit they have a problem. They worry people will think less of them if they learn they failed to raise their children to be godly. Yet by refusing to acknowledge their struggle, they prevent friends from walking with them and praying for them. In the remainder of James 5:16, the apostle makes the famous claim: "The effective, fervent prayer of a righteous man avails much." Scripture's promise for effective prayer follows a command to confess our shortcomings. By admitting our need, we open ourselves up to the effective prayers of righteous people. If you are allowing pride to rob your children of the intercession they could be receiving, ask God to relieve you of your concern for others' opinions and immediately enlist everyone you can to pray for your children.

We both went through seasons of parenting when we had a child who was struggling with life issues. When that happened, we weren't shy about asking people to pray for them. We were sensitive to our child's privacy; people didn't need to know every detail of their problems. But people did need to know our child was experiencing difficulty and needed prayer and encouragement. During one difficult season in his son's life, Richard was a seminary president. Richard asked some of the seminary students to pray for his son. It was humbling for a seminary president to admit to his students that his family had problems and his son needed prayer, but Richard didn't care. What mattered was not what people thought about him but that his son received help.

Refusing to suffer in silence also means we actively seek help and advice from others. It is astounding how many parents carry the burden of prodigal children in silence rather than seeking advice and counsel from others. Unfortunately, this often occurs in churches. Some families are being torn asunder by heartache, arguments, and rebellion. In the same congregation are other families that are seeing their children grow into godly young adults. You would think that the parents whose families were struggling would fervently seek counsel from the parents who were experiencing success, but rarely does that happen. Normally, struggling parents assume their situation is different from those whose children are doing well. (We have often been told that we are "lucky" our children turned out so well.) Or, they feel too humiliated to ask for parenting advice. So, they suffer in silence and never benefit from the advice or encouragement they might have received.

Can we encourage you at this point? Parenting is one of the most challenging of human endeavors. We will most certainly make mistakes. Yet, if God has entrusted you with children, He has granted you a high calling. You cannot give up. God is an expert in handling "impossible" situations! Let Him guide you, one day at a time, until He moves your family from where it is now, to where He wants it to be. Be willing to do whatever it takes in order to be the best parent possible. Trust Him. It's worth it.

Getting Your Family Back on Track

Every family is susceptible to getting off track. Even the healthiest of families can gradually succumb to bad habits or unhealthy relationships. While some issues only require minor tweaking in order for families to return to health, others necessitate a major overhaul. Whether your family is miles away from where it needs to be, or only a matter of inches, we'd suggest the following process.

1. Look in the Mirror

When our children begin to struggle, our first instinct may be to don our superhero costume and dash to the rescue. Yet, the most important response we can make is to retreat to our prayer closet and cry out to God. The truth is that if our own walk with God is unhealthy, we will be unable to extend to our children the help they need. Our challenge is that when our children experience difficulty, we tend to focus on their issues, not ours. If our child is using drugs or failing school, it can seem like an unnecessary diversion to invest prolonged sessions in our own prayer times and Bible study. But that is precisely when we need to care for our own walk with God more than ever. We must be able to clearly hear from God when our family is struggling. Likewise, if one of our children is stumbling in his walk with God, we can't afford to allow hypocrisy into our life. It would be horrific if carelessness in our walk with God were contributing to our children's apostasy. So, if we sense that one of our children is experiencing difficulty, we should immediately take time alone with God to ensure that our walk with Him is up to date and unhindered by sin (Ps. 17:1). That way our prayers, words, and example can be used by God to turn our child back to health and godliness.

2. Get on the Same Page As Your Spouse

The second place to check when our children are struggling is our marriage. "Divide and conquer" has traditionally been one of the fundamental stratagems for winning a battle. General George Custer gained notoriety not for winning but for being defeated. On June 25, 1876, he and his two hundred troopers were surrounded by more than four thousand Sioux warriors at Little Big Horn, and they were cut down to a man. Few generals have become so famous in defeat! Ever since, historians have questioned whether Custer's massacre was avoidable. When Custer and his Seventh Cavalry were dispatched from the main army on June 22 to search for the enemy, Custer declined the use of Gatling guns because he feared they would slow him down!

On the day of the battle, the commander divided his 655 men into three groups, taking only one-third himself. All 231 men died with Custer at his famous "last stand." While the size of the enemy was unprecedented, most military experts believe that had Custer kept his forces united, he would not have suffered catastrophe. A concentration of 655 troopers on the open plain was a formidable force in those days. Divided and cut off from each other, they became easy prey. Custer's last stand, while heroic, was largely unnecessary.

When your children experience difficulty in their lives, it is crucial that you and your spouse make a united stand. This is a time for parents to share the same goals for their children. Parents must agree on their expectations and standards. Most couples have one parent who is "softer" than the other. Every child who wants money from a parent knows which one to request it from! Children instinctively recognize which parent is more lenient or gullible or softhearted, and they will shamelessly use that knowledge to their advantage. Even couples who have experienced divorce can still agree on what approach is best for their children.

When children struggle in the home, it often causes intense pressure on marriages. Again, it can seem like a diversion for couples to work on their marriage while their children are floundering, but it is critical that parents have the most robust marriage relationship possible when dealing with struggling children. Rebellious children can bring great pain to parents and can create fissures that harm or even end marriages. Parents must close ranks and be of one heart and mind if they want to be a part of God's solution in their children's lives.

3. Evaluate the Condition of Your Family

This may appear self-evident, but it is surprising how many parents fail to properly diagnose the spiritual and emotional health of their family. This has been one of the downfalls of many of the Bible's greatest heroes. Perhaps Noah assumed that after having been saved from a cataclysmic flood, his sons would all walk closely with the Lord. Yet, his son Ham humiliated him and was estranged the remainder of Noah's life (Gen. 9:18–25). Isaac may have assumed his household was devoted to God's ways in light of their spiritual heritage. Yet, his family was torn asunder by plotting and intrigue (Gen. 27). Jacob might have believed each of his twelve sons embraced their spiritual calling, yet ten of them betrayed their brother and then lied to their father about what they had done (Gen. 37:12–36). Any physician knows that the proper treatment for any illness hinges on an accurate diagnosis. We cannot develop healthy families if we do not recognize when disease is present.

Here are some examples of improper diagnoses:

- A child is constantly experiencing conflict with his peers; yet his parents always blame the other children for instigating the problem.
- A child is extremely attention seeking; yet his parents think it is cute.
- A teenager is obsessed with people of the opposite sex; yet her parents assume this is normal adolescent behavior.
- A child throws tantrums every time he does not get his way so the parents inevitably yield to the little tyrant's demands.
- The youth minister alerts parents of concern he has over their child's behavior. The parents are offended and pull their child out of the youth group.
- A teenager refuses to attend church or talk about religious issues. The parents assume she'll eventually come around.
- The "good" kids at church become cautious of one of the teenagers. Rather than finding out what his problem is, the parents complain that the youth group is filled with cliques.

In each case, though the parents truly love their child, they do not recognize the fundamental problem. Certainly there may be a multiplicity of issues involved, but wise parents determine the root cause. For example, when Richard's sons were teenagers, they were betrayed by one of the other boys in their youth group. During a sleepover, the boys shared some confidential information with one another. At the first opportunity, this youth sought to ingratiate himself with the girls of the youth group by divulging every embarrassing tidbit he had heard. Needless to say, his companions were mortified and disinclined to extend their betrayer an invitation to the next sleepover. When the youth's parents discovered that their son was being left off people's guest list, they complained about the exclusivity of the youth group.

Certainly the youth should have forgiven him. But the boy's parents never encouraged their son to apologize. They didn't help him learn social skills in getting along with other boys or the importance of keeping a confidence. The parents assumed the primary problem was that there was an "in" group among the youth, and their cherubic son was being excluded.

Likewise, when children are intensely attention seeking, wise parents search for the reason. A parent could assume that because he goes to all of his son's ball games and plans fun family vacations, the problem cannot lie in his parenting. Yet, when children crave attention to an unhealthy extent, it could indicate that they have not received adequate healthy attention (and correction) from their parents. Astute parents are alert to any sign that unhealthy attitudes or behaviors have crept into their children, and then they relentlessly, and humbly, seek its cause.

Failing at Home

Scripture relates that Samuel was one of the godliest leaders in Israelite history. No one could fault him for his conduct as a leader of God's people (1 Sam. 12:3–5). Citizens could not recall one act of dishonesty or deceit on his part. Yet it was obvious to the people that Samuel's sons were dishonest and corrupt (1 Sam. 8:1–5). The people told it to their revered judge straight: "Look, you are old, and your sons do not walk in your ways" (1 Sam. 8:5). Yet, instead of listening to the people, Scripture indicates: "But the thing displeased Samuel" (1 Sam. 8:6). This is one of those puzzling accounts we find in the Bible. How could a man who was blameless in so many ways produce such disastrous sons?

Scripture offers a few clues that help to explain Samuel's domestic disaster. We are informed that while Samuel was judging, "He went from year to year on a circuit to Bethel, Gilgal, and Mizpah, and judged Israel in all those places. But he always returned to Ramah, for his home was there. There he judged Israel, and there he built an altar to the LORD" (1 Sam. 7:16–17). That is all fine and good. Everyone needs a hometown. But this is what we read of his two sons: "Now it came to pass when Samuel was old that he made his sons judges over Israel. The name of his firstborn was Joel, and the name of his second, Abijah; they were judges in Beersheba" (1 Sam. 8:1–2). When Samuel made his sons judges, he sent them to serve in the desert, far from him. Ramah is north of Jerusalem. Beersheba is to the southwest. There, unhampered by their father's supervision, the two prodigals indulged all of their sensual appetites.

Why didn't Samuel keep his sons closer to home? Perhaps he felt like they were men now and should be trusted. Maybe he chose to believe the best of his sons, regardless of the compelling evidence to the contrary. The truth is that the revered judge maintained his full ministry schedule while naively assuming his sons were up to the task of ministering to God's people in a community distant from his own. We are not told that Samuel included Beersheba in his travels. Perhaps he sent his sons to a remote location in which he himself did not want to minister. It is clear that people knew of his sons' degeneracy; yet Samuel apparently did nothing to address it. The signs were there, but the father chose not to pay any heed. There are times when parents are truly caught by surprise by the uncharacteristic or even bizarre behavior of their child, but most of the time there are telltale signs of what is coming, and why. Parents are wise to observe carefully, receive feedback humbly, and respond quickly.

4. Seek God's Activity in Your Child's Life

There is an interesting story recounted in the book of 2 Kings. The prophet Elisha had befriended a childless couple from Shunem (2 Kings 4:8–37). God chose to bless the couple and give them a child. Yet, one day their son began experiencing severe pains in his head, and he subsequently died. The mother knew at that moment she had only one place to turn if her son had any chance at life. She hurriedly made her way to the prophet Elisha. Even when the man of God sent his servant ahead of him to the boy's home, the woman refused to leave Elisha's side. She knew where God's power could be found. Ultimately, the child's life was restored.

There is much we can learn from this faithful Shunamite parent. The moment she realized her son was in danger, she hastily made her way to God. In fact, she remained as close as she could so as not to miss anything God might do. The woman also wisely understood there was nothing she and her husband could do to change the condition of their child. For the parents to have frantically applied their own remedies would have been supremely futile. Finally, the woman cooperated fully with God's method of healing. It may have sounded strange to the woman when Elisha told his servant to lay his staff over the dead boy's face, but the woman did not object. She knew her son's life depended on her cooperation with God and His ways. The key to saving her son was the promptness and thoroughness of her obedience to the divine command.

We have talked with many parents who recognized that all their efforts to "talk sense" into their wayward children were merely driving them farther away. One mother grieved that her son grew angry every time she brought up the subject of God, church, or his behavior. But as his mother, she desperately wanted to "get through" to him so he understood that his actions could lead to devastating consequences. One day as she was praying for her son, God seemed to say, "Leave your child to Me." The woman knew she could not change her son. On several occasions afterward, the youth made a provocative comment; and before the mother could respond, she sensed the Holy Spirit telling her to remain silent and not to engage in argument as she had done previously. Instead, she prayed and kept expressing love to her son. Gradually, God tore down the walls that had been erected and quenched the fires of anger that had been smouldering. God had always been prepared to work in the young man's life, but the mother first needed to surrender her agenda and to allow God to do things His way.

At times God is working far more extensively in children's lives than their parents realize. Only a few chapters later in the Bible, we read another marvelous story about the prophet Elisha and his servant. The king of Syria was extremely agitated at the fact that every time he attempted a hostile action against the Israelites, the Jewish prophet would alert his sovereign to the danger (2 Kings 6:8–13). Finally, in exasperation, the Syrian monarch dispatched a strong force with instructions to capture the annoying prophet. When the Syrian army surrounded the man of God in the city of Dothan, it appeared as if his career and his life were about to come to an abrupt end. Elisha's terrified servant cried out: "Alas, my master! What shall we do?" (2 Kings 6:15). To anyone observing the situation, it appeared that Israel would soon need to elect a "prophet search committee" to replace Elisha. Yet Elisha prayed, "LORD, I pray, open his eyes that he may see" (2 Kings 6:17). Suddenly, Elisha's distraught assistant clearly saw the reality of their situation. The Syrian army that had appeared so invincible was surrounded itself by angelic horses and chariots of fire. God had been at work all along, but the man had failed to recognize God's presence and activity. There may be times as a parent when we feel as hopeless as Elisha's assistant. It may appear to you as if your family is being besieged by an ominous enemy. Yet, that is the time you must be spiritually alert to God's activity in your home. He *is* at work! Don't miss Him!

5. Enlist Advocates

We have already referred to the account of Gideon in the book of Judges. This young man was facing a herculean task. The dreaded Midianites would invade his nation like a plague of locusts. Gideon could have been nominated for "least likely" to be anyone's deliverer. Though he knew God had called him to save his people from their oppression, the task appeared impossible. But Scripture tells us the reluctant deliverer put out a call for those willing to stand with him. The timid Ephraimite may have thought he had to undertake the task alone, but incredibly thirty-two thousand men arrived at his call. Where had all of these warriors been the previous seven years? Waiting for someone to summon them! In fact, there were so many who responded to Gideon's appeal for help that God used two different means of weeding out all but three hundred of them. With this select group of soldiers, Gideon routed the enemy and set his and every other family free.

One of the greatest deceptions parents succumb to is the lie that they must handle their family problems on their own. Raising a family was never meant to be a solitary affair! It requires a group effort! Sadly, parents often fail to enlist the help of those God makes available to them when they are confronting challenges in their family. Of course, we understand there are situations where no one seems interested in helping. We have known some desperate parents who asked for help from their church but who tragically received none. Yet at times, the primary problem is that we have not asked. Gideon might have continued threshing wheat in his father's winepress for years without anyone coming to his aid. But when he diligently sent out a plea for help, he was overwhelmed by the response.

Many parents have told us that they keep trying to reach out to a wayward child even though their efforts bear little or no fruit. At times parents exclaim, "I don't know what else I can do." Ironically, perhaps, parents may not always be the ones best suited to work directly with their children. Sometimes the role of parents is to enlist others who can better exert a positive impact.

ENLISTING HELP (AN EXAMPLE FROM RICHARD)

When my oldest child, Mike, was a teenager, he experienced a period of struggle. I tried to talk with him about some of the issues he was facing, but Mike was not very responsive. As the oldest child, he was trying to assert his independence. He didn't want to simply do everything his mother or father told him to do. But he still needed guidance. I tried adjusting my communication technique; I talked more loudly! But that didn't seem to help matters any. Ultimately, I took a different route. I knew there was a young couple in our church that Mike greatly admired. The husband was a talented hockey player and an excellent drummer. He had traveled the world and, according to Mike, had "coolness" oozing out of his every pore. The husband was in his twenties and did not yet have children of his own. My wife, Lisa, and I approached them and asked for help. We explained that our son needed some wise counsel, but he was at a stage of life where he would be more responsive if it came from someone other than his parents. This was a humbling experience for me. After all, I had three teenage children, and I was asking for help from childless newlyweds. I was a Christian speaker, author, as well as a leader in my church. It surprised the couple that we would ask them for assistance in raising our children, but they graciously agreed to do what they could. They were true to their word. They always sought Mike out at church and encouraged him. They invited him over to their house and provided a listening ear. They told Mike many things we had also been saying to him, only it seemed more palatable, somehow, coming from them. Mike ultimately navigated himself through that volatile period of his life. I could produce a long list of names of people who walked with our family as we were raising our children. I am extremely pleased with who my children have grown up to become, but I am not naïve enough to think my wife and I deserve all the credit. There were many people in

our church and among our friends and family who responded when we
sent out a call for help. We owe a great debt to them.

Augustine and His Mom

Monica did not have an easy life. Her husband, Patricus, was an
unbeliever. As such, he lived a dissolute life, indulging in carnal desires.
He also had a violent temper. Monica had three sons, but her greatest
concern was for her eldest child, named Augustine. He was lazy and
shamelessly lived an immoral lifestyle. In response, Monica earnestly
prayed and sought help from leaders in her church. For seventeen years
Augustine rejected the efforts of his saintly mother. At one point she
asked for help from a bishop. The cleric responded, "The child of those
tears shall never perish." When Augustine moved to Rome, Monica pur-
sued him. There she sought the assistance of Bishop Ambrose. Through
him, she ultimately saw her wayward son come to faith in Christ.
Augustine would become one of the most revered of the early Church
Fathers whose influence would impact countless people over the ensuing
centuries, including an Augustinian monk named Martin Luther.

6. Wait on the Lord

The final encouragement for restoring your family is this: don't
give up! We know parents such as Monica who spent many years, even
decades, seeking to bring their children into a close relationship with
themselves and with God. The key is to wait on the Lord and to be
responsive to how He intends to restore your family (Ps. 27:14). Some
children are responsive and quickly restored. Others take more time.
While it is not always profitable to debate or argue with your child, it is
always important to pray for them. Some of the greatest saints in history
were convinced to put their trust in Christ by the fervent intercession
of their mother.

As you pray, you'll become more sensitive to God's timing. You can
have confidence that the Spirit is constantly working in your children's
lives to convict and draw them to Himself. God knows when your children are open to hear the truth and when they are not. The Holy Spirit
will guide you to know when to pray, when to speak, when to remain
silent, and when to act (Rom. 8:26–28). Like the father of the prodigal
son, if you have been waiting on the Lord, you will be prepared when

a crisis or turning point occurs that draws your child back to God and to you.

Perhaps the most difficult thing parents must do is to wait upon the Lord. Notice what the psalmist said in this regard:

Rest in the LORD, and wait patiently for Him. (Ps. 37:7)

I waited patiently for the LORD; and He inclined to me, and heard my cry. He also brought me up out of a horrible pit, out of the miry clay, and set my feet upon a rock, and established my steps. He has put a new song in my mouth—praise to our God. (Ps. 40:1–3)

If you are presently bewildered about what to do to help your family get back on track, make sure you are waiting upon the Lord, patiently and expectantly. He knows what He is doing. You can trust Him! Fervently seek Him and be quick to respond to His promptings.

Conclusion

There is no simplistic or one-size-fits-all answer for what it takes to get your family back where God wants it to be. People are unique, with particular struggles, temptations, and issues. But God knows how to draw each person to Himself. Only He can bring forgiveness as well as heal any wound. He will take as long as necessary to draw your children to Himself. Watch to see where He is working in your family. Adjust yourself to His activity and join Him in His work. One day your family will thank you that you did!

QUESTIONS FOR REFLECTION/DISCUSSION

1. If you are currently concerned about one of your family members, take a moment to ask, "Am I in a place personally in my walk with God that I can be of help with my struggling family member? What is the condition of my personal life? My walk with God? My relationships? What might I need to adjust before I am in a position to be of maximum help to my family?

2. If you are married, is your spouse in unity with you in trying to help your children experience God's best? If not, is there anything you could do to draw closer to your spouse?

3. If your child is presently experiencing difficulty, take time to pray and ask God to help you understand what the underlying issues are. Talk with people who know your family, and ask them what they see. Don't argue. Just listen.

4. Do you need to release your control or agenda over your family in order to allow God to do things His way? Have you been getting in the way of what God is trying to do? How might you better cooperate with God's activity in your family?

5. Are you willing to wait on the Lord for as long as it takes for your family to experience healing and restoration? Daily ask God for patience and faith to trust Him with your problems.

CHAPTER 16

Developing a Godly Legacy

Leaving a Legacy

Our younger brother Mel is the senior pastor of First Baptist Church, Jonesboro, Georgia. One of his longtime members is Truett Cathy. Truett was born in Eatonton, Georgia, in 1921. A born entrepreneur, he launched his stellar business career as a youth by purchasing six bottles of Coca-Cola for twenty-five cents and reselling them for a nickel a piece. In 1949, he started his first restaurant in Hapeville, Georgia. Famed for inventing the chicken sandwich and the iconic advertisements "Eat Mor Chikin," Cathy leveraged his business acumen into legendary success with the national chain of Chick-fil-A restaurants. In 2007, *Forbes* listed Cathy as the 380th richest person in the United States and the 799th wealthiest person in the world.

Perhaps Chick-fil-A is best known for following Cathy's conviction of closing on Sundays so employees can spend time with their families and go to church. But Cathy will leave a larger legacy than merely the chicken sandwich. He also established a Winshape Foundation that has poured millions of dollars into developing young leaders and strengthening families. Chick-fil-A also provides scholarships to help its employees go to college. When you visit First Baptist Church in Jonesboro, you learn something else. Cathy taught a fifth-grade boys' Sunday school class for more than fifty years. Today there are middle-aged men all over the church who will proudly tell you they are one of "Truett's Boys." We know numerous young adults in Atlanta who got their first job at Chick-fil-A. There they obtained leadership training and skills that launched them into successful careers. The Cathy family is legendary for its generosity in helping children go to camp, teenagers go to college, and widows receive financial assistance.

Not only are Truett's children actively involved in the business, but a number of his grandchildren are as well. Cathy has won numerous awards, honorary degrees, and even recognition by the president of the United States. But perhaps his greatest honor will be the legacy of Christian charity and integrity he will pass on to the generations that follow.

> **Legacy:** 1. A gift given through a will, usually money or personal property.
> 2. Something of value handed down or received from an ancestor or predecessor such as an antique, a title, or a privilege.

We had a great uncle named Stu. He was a lifelong bachelor who was notorious for giving all the ladies a kiss at family gatherings! When he died, he dispersed his estate among his relatives. We each received a small legacy. Richard bought a pool table for his family with it. Every time thereafter, whenever we looked at the pool table, we thought of Uncle Stu. Certainly not the noblest of memories, but at least he was remembered!

Legal wills provide the opportunity for people to pass on a blessing to others after they have died. It indicates how your estate will be divided between your loved ones or the institutions of your choice. Some people without dependents establish a foundation, a scholarship, or donate the proceeds from the sale of their property to a cause, an organization, or a school. Often organizations will place the donor's name on a plaque and place it somewhere prominent so that years later the deceased person will continue to be remembered.

Most parents are too busy trying to pay bills, changing diapers, coaching Little League, and going to work to think about the legacy they will one day bequeath to their children. Some parents are proactive enough to plan for the inheritance they will eventually pass on to their children. They purchase life insurance, make shrewd investments, and establish trust funds. However, there is much more to leaving a legacy than leaving money in your will for your relatives. Recall the stories your parents told you about your relatives over the years. As we tell stories about our parents or grandparents, or eccentric uncles and aunts, we are highlighting character traits, values, and beliefs that they passed down to us. Such tales may reflect their sterling character, strong work ethic, or indomitable spirit. Our family stories may poke fun at our family's foibles and idiosyncrasies, or they might describe character traits we admire and want our children to emulate.

Sober Drunk

Our grandfather always acted like a proper British gentleman. He was a voracious reader who loved poetry but loved God more. As a bank manager, he maintained a high degree of decorum, and as a lay pastor and church planter, he upheld the highest standards of godliness (no playing cards, movies, or other tools of the devil in *his* home!). One day the superintendant of his denomination came to town for a visit. He had heard of our godly grandfather and wanted to meet him. Upon spying the superintendent walking down the street with a colleague, our grandfather ducked into the entrance of the nearest bar. He cocked his hat sideways, loosened his tie, and, just as the two men were passing by, he stumbled out of the doorway deliberately bumping into them. Wiping his arm across his mouth, he said (with his best slurred speech), "Gentlemen! What a *ssssurprize!*" There was always a twinkle in his eye and a joke to be played on unsuspecting people.

Mr. G .R. S. Blackaby: Banker, Soldier, Father, Legacy Builder

Stories about our grandfather G. R. S. Blackaby (including the one above) were legendary to us grandchildren, particularly because only one of us ever met him. When he died, his first grandson, Richard, was only a few months old (some say the sight of Richard as a baby was too much for the old man!). G. Richard Blackaby was named after G. Richard Sanders Blackaby and carries his name proudly.

G. R. S. Blackaby immigrated to Canada in the early 1900s and found work at the Bank of Montreal. He worked as a branch manager in various small towns in the interior of British Columbia, Canada. As children, we were told fascinating stories about how "Blackie" served as a machine gunner with the Canadian army during WWI. He survived many of the war's major battles, though he suffered from a mustard gas attack and from shrapnel wounds he carried in his body for the remainder of his life. As a father of three young children, he started a church in the isolated town of Prince Rupert. That church is still going strong to this day. We came across a book that included three of his published poems[1] and discovered a gold mine of his sermon notes from which he preached before the church he started could call a full-time pastor.

The many stories about our grandfather's character were retold to inspire and challenge us. For example, when he fought in WWI, there were Sundays when the troops were allowed to attend a local church in the area. On one occasion the commanding officer assembled his troops in formation. Those soldiers wishing to attend a Protestant service were to march to a nearby Anglican church. Catholic soldiers would break rank and march to the Catholic Church. As the soldiers advanced, our grandfather remained standing, alone. "Are you a Catholic?" asked the officer. "No sir," replied Grandpa. "Are you a Protestant then?" "No, sir. I'm a Baptist," replied Grandpa. "Then go with the Protestants," said the officer. "No, sir. There is a Baptist church in town, and as we are permitted to attend the church of our choice, that's where I would like to go, sir." "Very well," replied the officer. Our grandfather then marched in a parade of one to the Baptist church, dismissed himself to attend the little Baptist service, and then formed back into rank and marched himself back to camp.

The legacy G. R. S. Blackaby left was one of faithfulness to God, to his church, and to his family. He was a man of principle and conviction and upheld extremely high personal standards. Perhaps that is why his commanding officer gave him inventory duty for the alcohol during the war. With Grandpa in charge, nothing ever went missing!

Follow the Leader

The apostle Peter urges us to follow the example Christ set for us in 1 Peter 2:21: "For you were called to this, because Christ also suffered for you, leaving you an example, so that you should follow in His steps" (HCSB). The writer of Hebrews also urges us to look to godly examples to follow: "Remember your leaders who have spoken God's word to you. As you carefully observe the outcome of their lives, imitate their faith" (Heb. 13:7 HCSB). The reason you leave a godly legacy is to set an example for those who will follow in your steps.

Each time we were told a story about a godly relative, the implication was that we should follow their example. Our mother's quiet, saintly Grandmother Rooker tithed every Sunday even though she often did not have money remaining for food. God always provided something for her family to eat. Occasionally God would send a local farmer to leave groceries on her doorstep. The lesson for us: If Great-Grandma Rooker could trust in God during the Great Depression, we can trust God to provide for us too.

After retiring from their jobs as a store manager at Sears and as a surgical assistant at a local hospital, our mother's parents, Melvin and Carrie Wells, went as missionary associates to Lusaka, Zambia. Our grandfather put his carpentry skills to use building a home for missionary children (and attempting to build "snake-resistant" fences!), and our grandmother spoiled them with her legendary cooking. Their example taught us that we were never too old for God to use us.

A godly legacy is a wonderful treasure to leave behind you, but it is only beneficial to those who are willing to receive it. Two of Grandpa Blackaby's three sons, Henry and William, chose to follow their godly parents' example. They married devout Christian women and wholeheartedly followed in their father's footsteps. The third son did not. Henry and William had a total of nine children: six boys and three girls, and twenty-one grandchildren. Of those nine children, two have been seminary presidents, six served as pastors, two served as missionaries, several have been worship leaders, and all serve in leadership positions in their local churches. As of this writing, all twenty-one of Henry and William's grandchildren are following their Great-Grandpa Blackaby's legacy of faith. Three of them are currently enrolled in seminary, and one is already a pastor.

A person's spiritual legacy can extend well beyond their immediate family, as is the case of our father. If you visit Dallas Baptist University in Texas, you will see a stately red-brick building housing the bookstore, music rooms, and offices. It is called "Henry Blackaby Hall" in honor of the impact his life has exerted on God's kingdom. (Our father breathed a sigh of relief when they did not place his name on the school's sewage treatment plant!)

Legacy of Character

A sterling character is a quality that money cannot buy. In fact, exemplary character and a good name can be far more valuable and powerful than money or investments. I (Tom) live in a small town where some families trace their relatives back more than one hundred years. This town has grown from a tiny logging village along the Fraser River to a city of more than seventy thousand people. Loyalty runs deep among the established families, and even though there are large chain grocery stores and quick oil-change shops littering the roadways, long-term residents still shop at the same little mom-and-pop grocery stores and get their car serviced by their longtime mechanic's shop. They tell me, "They're good folk. I've known them for years." Long-term residents trust people they know and respect and will go out of their way to frequent their shops out of loyalty and friendship.

Character determines who we are. It guides how we act in response to situations we face in life. Character also determines what our reputation will be.

Mahatma Gandhi is reported to have said,

Seven Deadly Sins . . .
Wealth without work
Pleasure without conscience
Science without humanity
Knowledge without character
Politics without principle
Commerce without morality
Worship without sacrifice.[2]

Harry S. Truman stated: "Fame is a vapor, popularity is an accident, riches take wings, those who cheer today may curse tomorrow and only one thing endures—character."[3]

King Solomon observed: "A good name is to be chosen over great wealth; favor is better than silver and gold."[4]

A godly legacy is not something you can earn or acquire. You either had one passed down to you or you did not. Some people are born into a rich family heritage. Others are birthed into spiritual poverty. G. R. S. Blackaby passed down a wonderful legacy to his children, grandchildren, and great-grandchildren. But much of what he bequeathed to us was first handed down to him. Grandpa's father and two uncles attended Spurgeon's college in London, England. The college founder, Charles H. Spurgeon, was known as the "prince of preachers." People had to obtain a ticket to gain admittance into his church on Sundays to hear the famed expositor. Grandpa Blackaby's uncle, Frederick E. Blackaby (1855–1929) pastored six churches in England and was noted to be "a popular platform speaker, an acceptable preacher, and an ideal pastor. He had a gracious personality, was a successful winner of souls, and was in the active ministry for forty-two years."[5] His uncle Samuel followed in his brother Frederick's footsteps. After giving his life to Christ and being baptized by his brother Frederick, he also attended Spurgeon's College for pastors. Unfortunately, his ministry was brief as his life was cut short by an illness, and he died at thirty-four years old. G. R. S. Blackaby's father, Joseph Blackaby, also attended the same college as his brothers, but instead of becoming a pastor, he became a baker, with a sweet shop on High Street in Stanstead Abbotts. He became well known for his Christian character and generosity. Not often do three brothers attend the same pastor's training college, but this was the spiritual atmosphere in which our grandfather was raised. In addition, G. R. S. Blackaby's brother-in-law and his wife were missionaries to China during the great Manchurian Revival. Much spiritual treasure was given to our grandfather. Those living three generations later are still being enriched by it.

How to Leave a Spiritual Legacy

First, you don't have to write a best-selling book or return home safely from a war to leave a legacy. You don't have to start a church or have all your kids go to seminary either. You can be in any walk of life, any culture, and any country. The key to leaving a spiritual legacy is faithfulness to God, a desire to know Him, and honoring Christ with your life.

1. Spiritual Assessment

Regardless of your age, make it your aim to pass on a vast spiritual treasure to your children. Consider what you have accumulated thus far: House? Cars? Money? Property? Jewelery? Ask yourself: When I die, what are the most valuable assets I will pass on? Will any of them honor God? Will any of them encourage my family to trust and serve God? Then invest the necessary effort to collect spiritual assets for the remainder of your life.

Survey where you are spending your time. How much of your time is spent on having an impact on other people's lives versus spending time on yourself (Matt. 6:33)? How many of your personal/financial goals are meant to impact eternity, and how many are designed to give you a comfortable retirement? When you stand before Christ one day, will you be able to confidently say, "I have completed everything you gave me to do" (see John 17:4)?

2. Determination

As a mother or a father, determine to be faithful to God and to honor Him in your home. Maintain high personal moral standards, serve your church faithfully, and help your children understand the benefits and blessings that come from obeying God. Jesus urged His followers to be mindful of the example they were setting, saying, "In the same way, let your light shine before men, so that they may see your good works and give glory to your Father in heaven" (Matt. 5:16 HCSB). Your most constant and perceptive audience are your family members. If you make concessions in your character or compromise your morals, you risk forfeiting your spiritual legacy.

3. Prayer

A good place to begin developing your spiritual legacy is your prayer life. Begin a prayer journal where you keep track of what you pray and how and when God answers. One day one of your grandchildren may inherit your prayer journal and discover that much of what occurred in his life was initiated in your prayer times on his behalf. When you pray:

- Look to the future; don't just focus solely on the present. For example, while your children and grandchildren are still young, pray for God to provide them with godly spouses so their homes will be committed to honoring Him. Pray for their education and career choices so their lives achieve all God intends for them.

- Ask God to keep each member of your family faithful to the values and the spiritual legacy handed to them. Pray for God to protect them from temptations, compromise, and distraction that would divert them from God's path.

- Ask God to protect your children's marriages from dissension and divorce. One of the reasons God "hates" divorce is because of the adverse affect it exerts on children for generations to come. God wants to produce "godly offspring" from parents who reflect God's faithfulness in their relationship to one another (Mal. 2:15).

- Ask God to give your family members discernment to know His will in every situation.

4. Regular Review

Regularly reflect on your life and ask God if you should adjust the way you are currently spending your time. Allow God's Spirit to deepen your walk with Him and continue to conform you into Christ's image (Rom. 8:29). When you file your taxes, review how much money you spent on your kingdom and how much you spent on God's. When you look at your monthly calendar, review what percentage of time you gave to ministry and service to others and how much you spent on pleasure. At the end of each year, you may want to conduct a year-end review with your family (perhaps at Christmas). During that time, you can review the past year and discuss what God accomplished through your family over the course of the year. Reflecting on stories of God working through your family is a great way to build a spiritual tradition and a legacy of faithfulness in your home.

5. Service

Scripture indicates that God has a unique role for each Christian: "Now as we have many parts in one body, and all the parts do not have the same function, in the same way we who are many are one body in Christ and individually members of one another. According to the grace

given to us, we have different gifts" (Rom. 12:4-6 HCSB). The Bible also
tells us that "we are His creation, created in Christ Jesus for good works,
which God prepared ahead of time so that we should walk in them"
(Eph. 2:10 HCSB). There are thousands of ways God can use your family members to bless others. Take time to review the various ministries
and volunteer positions you and your family held last year. Ask God if
He wants you to continue with each one or if it is time to release one of
those responsibilities so you have room in your life for a new ministry
God is giving you. Continually ask: Is my life presently serving Christ
at its maximum potential? Don't be satisfied until it is!

A Legacy of Valor

Second Samuel 23 is a peculiar chapter in the Bible. Here the writer
lists each of David's thirty-seven *mighty men of valor* by name. The
mightiest of the warriors come first, and the writer describes some of
their heroic feats:

- Josheb-Basshebeth the Tachmonite, chief of the three; killed
  eight hundred at one time.
- Eleazar arose and struck the Philistines until his hand was
  weary and until his hand clung to the sword.
- Abishai, the brother of Joab, was chief among three. And he
  lifted up his spear against three hundred and killed them.
- Benaiah, the son of Jehoiada from Kabzeel, a son of a mighty
  man, was great in deeds. He killed two lion-like men of Moab.
  He also killed a lion in the middle of a pit.

The list of these thirty-seven men will forever be known as David's
Mighty Men—or the *Gibborim* in Hebrew. They left their mark on his-
tory and have inspired millions of people ever since. Here's the point.
First, God knows people by name (even if they are unpronounceable!).
People are important to God, and He knows each one of their deeds.
Second, God can use our faithfulness to Him as an inspiration for oth-
ers. Third, we can set a high standard for others to follow by how we live.
We don't have to simply try and meet the bar; we can raise it.

In many cases, people are known primarily for one significant contribution during their lifetime. A few are more prolific. Tragically, many others have little to show for the expenditure of their life.

- Moses led the people out of Egypt.
- Noah built an ark.
- Billy Graham preached to millions.
- Marie Curie was awarded two Nobel Prizes in chemistry and physics for her work with radium and radioactivity.
- James Naismith invented basketball.
- Nelson Mandela was the first president of South Africa to be elected by a fully representative, democratic election.
- George Herman (Babe) Ruth Jr. is known as the greatest baseball player of all time.
- William and Catherine Booth founded the Salvation Army.
- Thomas Alva Edison invented the phonograph, motion picture camera, and lightbulb.
- Abraham Lincoln emancipated American slaves.

While you will have your entire life to serve God, there may be a handful of achievements God intends to accomplish through you that will particularly mark your legacy. Perhaps it is to write a book, start a company, or lead someone to faith in Christ (such as Mr. Kimball, whose only known contribution to history was leading a young D. L. Moody to become a Christian!). Perhaps it is to make a contribution to science or to teach a generation of leaders who will one day impact their nation and world. Have you ever asked God why He placed you on the earth at the time, in the place, and with the skills that He did? If you haven't, you ought to. It might prove quite enlightening!

A Historic Ring (A Story from Tom)

Last year my oldest son, Matthew, graduated from high school in British Columbia, Canada, just like his grandpa Henry. He was captain of his senior high basketball team, just like his grandpa. He is smart, musical, and athletic, like his grandpa. He was also offered basketball scholarships at college, like his grandpa. So when I came across my father's high school graduation ring, with *HTB* engraved on the top, I

handed it to my son to wear as an inspiration when he gave his valedic-
torian speech at the graduation ceremony. I mentioned that when his
grandpa Henry Thomas Blackaby was finishing high school, he had
no idea what his future held, but God did. I wanted Matthew Thomas
Blackaby to realize he not only carried his grandpa's name with him but
his ring—a symbol of God's work and faithfulness in the past and a
promise of God's work and faithfulness in the future.

Our father, Henry, is known for many things (like raising amazing children!), but his greatest life contribution may well be authoring
the book *Experiencing God*. He was fifty-five years old when he wrote
that book. He had already spent a significant portion of his life serving
God and raising a family before penning that volume. By the time he
had entered his sixth decade, he might have thought his best days were
behind him. But in fact, they were just beginning. God is like that. He
knows all the days He has allotted to us, and He understands how best
to spend them (Ps. 139:14–16). That's why it is crucial for parents to
teach their children how to walk with God. Henry Blackaby has often
said he wanted to live his life in such a way that his children would want
to serve the God he served (he did). Today, children are being inundated
with enticements to take alternative pathways that lead away from God.
They need parents who will confidently teach them those pathways that
lead to life and away from destruction.

Restorative Justice (A Story from Tom)

I volunteer with a community youth service that works with local
police to help young offenders straighten out their lives before they get
into serious trouble. In this program, the teenagers come to us after having committed minor offences such as shoplifting, theft, defacing public
property, carrying a knife to school, or fighting. They are each assigned
a mentor to guide them through the completion of their assigned number of community service hours, any restitution that is needed, letters of
apology, and a variety of other assignments designed to help them focus
their energy on accomplishing their life goals. One day I met a fourteen-
year-old youth who, at first meeting, seemed like an ordinary teenager.
But then I learned that in a three-day span of time, he had been: (1)
suspended from school for carrying a knife; (2) placed on the police
watch list for drugs purchased with intent to sell; (3) been in a serious

fistfight; and (4) in jeopardy of being kicked out of the Youth Diversion program for breaking behavioral contracts. I was stunned at how many destructive choices this youth had made in such a brief amount of time. Three days of bad decisions could haunt him the remainder of his life.

Most of the kids in this youth rehabilitation program come from broken homes. Some are in foster care, and others are in protective custody safe houses. My heart breaks when I meet these teenagers and see how their future hangs precariously in the balance between success and youth detention centers. As a mentor, I talk about values, integrity, good character, making wise choices, seeking knowledge, and determining not to allow others to distract them from accomplishing their goals. These are all principles their parents failed to teach them. In some cases where parents have failed, grandparents, uncles, aunts, teachers, coaches, youth pastors, people at church, and foster parents can step in and be the godly examples children need. We all have a vested interest in providing a godly legacy to the youth of today whether they are our children or not.

Overcoming the Obstacles

Family names such as Ford, Kennedy, Vanderbilt, Bush, Gambino, Morgan, and Rockefeller are instantly recognizable. Some have influence in the arts or in politics. Others are leaders in organized crime, industry, the stock market, or in technology. Often multiple generations have worked together to build credibility, assets, and a well-respected (or feared) name.

If you are someone who inherited a legacy of disappointment or worse, there is still hope. You have the opportunity to commence a fresh new legacy with God's help. Sadly, you may have come from a home characterized by abuse, alcoholism, neglect, abandonment, anger, pride, divorce, and a host of issues that left you with emotional and physical scars. Take time to read through 1 and 2 Kings sometime. Pay close attention to King Asa (1 Kings 15:9–24), King Hezekiah (2 Kings 18–20), and King Josiah (2 Kings 22:1–20; 23:1–30) who were all raised by ungodly parents. Yet despite their terrible parental role models, they determined to live righteously themselves and help God's people return to a proper relationship with Him. They threw out the foreign gods, tore down the high places of pagan worship, and helped God's people focus on true worship in the temple once again. They met with varying degrees of success and often faced opposition. Doing what is right is not always easy. It often calls for determination and sacrifice, but then so do most efforts that leave a lasting legacy.

You can decide to create a God-centered home. The Bible commands us to "trust in the LORD with all your heart, and do not rely on your own understanding; think about Him in all your ways, and He will guide you on the right paths" (Prov. 3:5–6 HCSB). Another great verse comes from Psalm 25:4–5: "Make Your ways known to me, LORD; teach me Your paths. Guide me in Your truth and teach me, for You are the God of my salvation; I wait for You all day long" (HCSB). Although your parents may not have provided you with a godly example, God Himself as the only perfect Father will help you raise your children.

Passing on Your Valuables

Much to the delight of my (Tom's) wife and daughter, my mother-in-law has begun passing on some of her expensive jewelry to her daughters and granddaughters so she can watch them enjoying them while she is still alive. There were two sentimental heirlooms my father intentionally gave to each of his five children. One was a poem (below) written by Edgar Guest, and one was a book. The poem was first given to him by his father. His father explained that while he did not have a large sum of money to pass down to him, he did have one item of immense worth: his reputation. Our grandfather spent a lifetime investing value in his name. The poem summed up his father's gift. Our father always treasured it. He had received it from his beloved father when he was a young man, and when we were old enough, he passed it on to us.

> Your Name
> You got it from your father,
> t'was the best he had to give,
> And right gladly he bestowed it
> It's yours, the while you live.

You may lose the watch he gave you
and another you may claim,
But remember, when you're tempted,
to be careful of his name.

It was fair the day you got it,
and a worthy name to bear,
When he took it from his father
there was no dishonor there.

Through the years he proudly wore it,
to his father he was true,
And that name was clean and spotless
when he passed it on to you.

Oh there's much that he has given
that he values not at all,
He has watched you break your playthings
in the days when you were small.

You have lost the knife he gave you
and you've scattered many a game,
But you'll never hurt your father
if you're careful with his name.

It is yours to wear forever,
yours to wear the while you live,
Yours, perhaps some distant morn,
another boy to give.

And you'll smile as did your father,
with a smile that all can share,
If a clean name and a good name
you are giving him to wear.

Edgar A. Guest

The book our father gave each of us is even more meaningful. Each
child received a well-worn (often tattered) Bible that our father used for
his own personal Bible study and that he preached from. The margins

are filled with notes and insights from what God taught him during that period of his life. Numerous passages are highlighted in yellow and underlined in various colors. In those Bibles he recorded his relationship with God for his children. As his personal study Bible became worn and tattered, he would purchase a new one and then begin recording the fresh revelations God granted him. He would once again fill up the margins with a record of that portion of his spiritual journey. Perhaps one day we will gather all the Bibles and record his notes into one book! The Bible our father carried with him during the early days of Saskatoon was so worn that someone felt sorry for him and made a book cover out of moose hide. It now sits proudly on his eldest son's bookshelf as a treasured possession (though, admittedly, it lacks aesthetic appeal). Oh that our children would prize above any other heirloom the tattered Bible they used to see their mother or father using daily!

Conclusion

We have been extremely fortunate to have a godly legacy to build upon in our family. But what each of us does with what we have been given is a choice we will have to make. We have the opportunity to turn our backs on our legacy, selectively accept it by keeping the good and rejecting the bad, or embrace it outright. We have not incorporated everything into our own families that were passed down to us by our parents. We have added some dimensions that each of us children feel better suits our particular family for the times in which we live. Each set of parents does the best they can (faith, flaws, and all) to build a home they believe honors God. May the home you build be one that withstands life's storms and temptations and gives your children the strong foundation they need to thrive in the future.

My people, hear my instruction; listen to what I say. I will declare wise sayings; I will speak mysteries from the past— things we have heard and known and that our fathers have passed down to us. We must not hide them from their children, but must tell a future generation the praises of the LORD, His might, and the wonderful works He has performed. He established a testimony in Jacob and set up a law in Israel, which

He commanded our fathers to teach to their children so that a future generation—children yet to be born—might know. They were to rise and tell their children so that they might put their confidence in God and not forget God's works, but keep His commands. (Ps. 78:1–7 HCSB)

QUESTIONS FOR REFLECTION/DISCUSSION

1. What is the legacy you inherited from your family or the reputation of your family name?

2. What God-honoring legacy do you want to leave your children?

3. What do you want your family name to be known for?

4. What are you doing to pass on to your children what they will need to know and do to have a successful relationship with God?

5. Are there any aspects of the legacy you inherited that you need to remove from your family life?

Notes

1. *From Overseas: An Anthology of Contemporary Dominions and United States Poetry* (London; Fowler Write, LTD MDCCCCXXVII), 22–24.

2. Young India, October 22, 1925, see http://www.goodreads.com /quotes/32234-seven-deadly-sins-wealth-without-work-pleasure-without-conscience -science.

3. See http://www.goodreads.com/author/show/203941.Harry_S_Truman.

4. See Proverbs 22:1.

5. *Memoirs of Ministers and Missionaries: Memoirs of Deceased Ministers and Missionaries to 1st November, 1929,* 311.

CHAPTER 17

Blessing Other Families

Touching the World (An Example from Richard)

In 2002, I was invited to travel to the nation of Qatar in the Middle East to minister to a community of Westerners who were working in the country. I had never been to the Middle East before, and I decided to bring my oldest son, Mike, to share the experience with me. I knew that many of the international workers had children living there with them, and I was sure Mike (who is pretty cool) would be a hit with them. The international church held its Christian services on Fridays, in conjunction with the Islamic day of worship. I had been asked to speak in both of their overflowing services.

After the first service, a Canadian couple quickly made their way over to me. Their first comment was: "We became Christians in the church your grandfather started in Prince Rupert!" Now as we have already related in this book, our paternal grandfather was a bank manager for the Bank of Montreal (known today as BMO). He was transferred in the 1930s to a remote branch in Prince Rupert, a city on the west coast of Canada, roughly ninety miles south of the Alaska border. Ultimately he started a church that grew to become the largest evangelical congregation in that city. The couple standing before me in Qatar had become Christians in that church. There in the Middle East, sixty-five years later, a couple was telling my grandfather's grandson and great-grandson how grateful they were for his faithfulness. It left my son and me with goose bumps.

That same year I was asked to speak at a mission conference in Florida. The host church had enlisted numerous missionaries from all over the world to participate, and they had asked me to deliver the Sunday message. At the close of my morning sermon, three missionary couples lined up to speak with me. The first couple was serving in Africa. They related how one evening a band of guerrilla terrorists had scaled the fence of their compound and forced their way into the house. They bound the family and were speaking ominously of killing them. Suddenly a light flashed into the house. It appeared that police or soldiers were surrounding the compound. The intruders frantically escaped without harming anyone. When the family finally freed themselves, they could see no one. God had miraculously saved them.

Shaken by the experience, the couple concluded they should return to the safety of the United States. But their mission organization was holding a conference for missionaries in their region, and their director urged them to attend before resigning their post. My father was the speaker, and my mother had come to encourage the women. One afternoon the couple spent time with my parents, relating their experience and sharing their fears and concerns. My parents prayed with them, encouraged them, and urged them to tell their story in a book. As the couple introduced themselves to me several years later, they held up a book for me to give to my parents. "Tell them we stayed, and we wrote this book. Their encouragement made all the difference!"

The next couple held up a photograph of themselves in a canoe with my parents. They were missionaries in Central America. Two years earlier, they had grown so discouraged from the difficulty of their work that they decided to resign as missionaries and return home. But their region was holding a conference, and my parents were coming to minister to the missionaries. One afternoon during some free time, the couple took my parents out on the river in a canoe. There the couple poured out their hearts to their new friends. The couple asked me to relate to my parents that as a consequence of that afternoon canoe trip, they had gained fresh resolve and had remained on the field.

Then a third couple approached. They explained that after the husband retired from his job, they had gone as missionaries into northern

Russia. They found themselves caught between two feuding Christian groups, and when the couple refused to choose sides, they were ostracized by both. This couple suffered the cruel and petty indifference of people for whom they had traveled across the world to encourage. They grieved over being so far away from their grandchildren and friends while being ignored by the people they had come to help. They decided to abandon the ungrateful people and return to their comfortable retirement home. As they grimly told my parents how difficult it was to minister to an ungrateful people, my father gently mentioned that they must now have a small sense of what Christ experienced after He forsook the comforts of heaven to save a people who demonstrated their appreciation by denying, forsaking, criticizing, and crucifying Him. As the couple related this story to me, they grew emotional and choked out, "We stayed."

At the close of that one Sunday service, I had met people who were faithfully serving Christ in Africa, Central America, and Russia as a result of a seemingly chance encounter with my parents.

Now we realize that not everyone has the opportunity to travel the world and speak to gatherings of missionaries. But the truth is that our parents sought to encourage people whether it was to the widow living next door or the discouraged pastor serving in Australia. As a result, we learned as children that God intends to use families to be a dispenser of blessing to the people around them.

The Families of the Earth

Genesis 12:1–3 describes the formation of one of history's most famous families. Abram was a seventy-five-year-old, childless businessman who might have concluded, quite naturally, that he and his wife, Sarah, would always live in an empty nest. But one day he had a life-changing encounter. God revealed that He intended to develop a great nation from Abram's descendants. Before Abram would become a father, however, he needed to make some major life adjustments. God commanded him to "get out of your country, from your family and from your father's house, to a land that I will show you" (v. 1). God was asking the elderly Bedouin to trust Him with his family and his future. However, God also promised: "I will make you a great nation; I will bless you and make your name great. . . . I will bless those who bless you, and I will curse him who curses you" (vv. 2–3). Clearly this was going to be an outstanding deal for Abram! But then God concluded by announcing: "And in you all the families of the earth shall be blessed" (v. 3). God intended to make Abram's family a blessing to all the families of the earth. And, God was true to His word. Abram's family has profoundly blessed our families, and, we suspect, it has blessed yours too.

A Fruitful Tree

Being a blessing is a recurrent theme throughout the Bible. God doesn't bestow His favor merely for us to hoard it for ourselves. It is dispensed so we can pass the divine favor on to others. For example, the psalmist declared: "Blessed is the man who walks not in the counsel of the ungodly, nor stands in the path of sinners, nor sits in the seat of the scornful; but his delight is in the law of the LORD, and in His law he meditates day and night" (Ps. 1:1–2). God promised to bless those who shun wicked company and behavior and who, instead, immerse themselves in God's Word. The psalmist added: "He shall be like a tree planted by the rivers of water, that brings forth its fruit in its season, whose leaf also shall not whither; and whatever he does shall prosper" (Ps. 1:3). God intends for the righteous to be like fruit trees! Of course, a shady tree laden with fruit does not primarily benefit itself but others. A fruit tree doesn't eat its own fruit, but others sure do! Fruit provides refreshment and nourishment to those who are hungry. People as well as animals find relief from the oppressive heat in its shade. The psalmist was writing to a people living in a hot, dry, desert climate. To them, a shady fruit tree provided a marvelous oasis! That is what godly families are intended to be: an oasis of comfort and encouragement.

Blessing a Community

One final example of being a blessing is found in Luke 7:1–10. While Jesus was in Capernaum, a centurion sent a delegation to plead with Jesus to come and heal his terminally ill servant. The centurion was a Gentile. His role would have been to enforce Roman law and taxation over the occupied people of Israel. Yet this man apparently loved the people he worked with. He built a synagogue for the local citizens. When one of his servants became gravely ill, the military officer dispatched a delegation of Jewish elders to ask Jesus to come and heal the man. These elders explained to Jesus: "For he loves our nation, and has built us a synagogue" (v. 5). This man was a foreigner, living among people generally disposed to hate him. Yet, he had chosen to bless the city in which he lived, and the people had responded enthusiastically to his obvious love. As Proverbs declares, "When it goes well with the righteous, the city rejoices" (Prov. 11:10).

Living Lives of Blessing

So what does this mean for you? God wants to help you lead your family to bless others. The church or neighborhood or state or nation in which you live ought to be a better place because you belong to it. How do you do this? Here are four simple steps:

1. Bless Your Children

This seems obvious, but it is extremely difficult for your children to bless others if they have never received a blessing themselves. This need has become particularly prevalent in a society in which a high percentage of children are growing up in families where they have no contact with one of their parents. Many boys are growing up with little or no contact with their father. And, if they see their father, they are not receiving a blessing. If you have never received a blessing yourself, then it will be difficult for you to impart one to others, even if you want to.

Tom and I have both ministered to the inmates in the Louisiana State Maximum Security Prison at Angola. We've been told that 70 percent of the inmates' children will end up in prison just like their fathers. Part of the reason is modeling. Criminal behavior and attitudes are all many of those children have known. But second, many of the inmates' offspring have never received a blessing. No one has ever expressed belief that they could amount to anything or rise above the lifestyle of their parents. So, they resign themselves to functioning in the same antisocial and criminal manner in which they were raised. And the cycle continues.

Biblically, the patriarchs of God's people established a pattern of blessing the next generation. Abraham, the founding father of God's people, chose to obey God regardless of the cost or difficulty. As a result, God promised him: "By Myself I have sworn, says the LORD, because you have done this thing, and have not withheld your son, your only son—blessing I will bless you, and multiplying I will multiply your descendants as the stars of the heaven and as the sand which is on the seashore; and your descendants shall possess the gate of their enemies. In your seed all the nations of the earth shall be blessed, because you have obeyed My voice" (Gen. 22:16–18). Can you imagine being Isaac and growing up in a home that God was using to bless all the nations and families of the earth?

Isaac grew up understanding and experiencing blessing. In fact, his own blessing was so coveted by his offspring that his son Jacob connived against his older brother in order to cheat him of his (Gen. 27). Likewise, Jacob spent extensive time blessing his children and grandchildren (Gen. 48–49). One of the reasons God used the patriarchs of God's people so mightily is because they understood and dispensed blessing to their descendants.

We have been struck by the difference it makes in peoples' lives when they have, or have not, received a parental blessing. Richard was with two different pastors who had planted strong churches. Both were good men doing outstanding work. But the longer Richard spoke with them, the more apparent it became that something in these men was missing. Both expressed insecurities and doubts. Both seemed to need Richard to affirm what they were doing, even though they had only just met him. At last Richard asked each pastor about his father. In both cases, their fathers were not Christians and had openly rejected Christian values. When each man's father had visited his son's church, his comment had been, "Why are you wasting your time in a church?" Both of these men knew their father was not a believer, and neither was surprised at the negative response they received over their call to Christian ministry. Nevertheless, each man continued to long in his heart for some token of blessing and affirmation from his father. This is not saying that we must psychoanalyse everyone we meet to determine if they have an unmet childhood need that we can meet! But it does suggest that more so than ever before society is filled with people who long for a blessing.

2. Model Thoughtful Behavior to Your Children

Your children will tend to imitate the behavior they see in their parents. If you behave in a self-centered manner, expect to find that same attitude in your children. If you never go out of your way to bless others, don't expect your children to do so. However, if you demonstrate thoughtfulness toward others, your children will most likely develop kindness and consideration into their own social DNA. There are many ways you can do this. For example, parents who regularly open their homes to entertain friends and family are teaching their children how to be hospitable and good hosts. Parents who model gratitude by sending thank-you notes to people who have done something for them are teaching their children an important social skill. Families who serve in their church or who go on mission trips together will tend to have children who are also considerate of others.

BLESSING ORPHANS IN AFRICA

Our brother Mel and his wife, Gina, took their daughter Christa on a mission trip with their church to Mozambique. As a young teen, Christa felt God wanted her to join her church's effort, so she had raised her own money to go. The mission team was ministering to poor people and to orphans. One day the team planned to serve a meal to the many children in that area. Christa was assigned to spoon out rice onto each person's plate. To the team's dismay, however, they were informed that it was a practice of the local culture that all of the adults who were present should eat before any of the children. A long line of adults began to form, and the mission team feared there would not be enough food for the children who were hungrily watching the adults being served. It became clear that the mission team had not brought enough food for the rapidly growing crowd. Instructions were hastily dispatched to team members to refrain from eating any food, as there was not enough for the children. Finally, a long line of children began to be served. The mission volunteers felt sick that they might have to turn some of the hungry waifs away. The team members were fervently praying as they served the children. Christa kept scooping out one spoonful of rice after the next, praying for a miracle. Incredibly, each time Christa lowered her spoon into the large pot, another serving of rice emerged. To everyone's amazement, as she finally scraped the bottom of the kettle, the last child was served. Christa and the team believed they had experienced a miracle. When children are able to share such experiences with their parents, they are left with a permanent impression (and they want to experience God working through their lives that way again and again!). The key is to help our children experience the joy and satisfaction that results when we allow God to use our lives to impart a blessing to others.

3. Be Practical

There are many Christian families who would help others if they could, but they have no idea what to do. We have both had sincere people exclaim to us: "I just wish there was something I could do to help!" Such people then typically beat a hasty retreat out of earshot before you can offer any suggestions! Our advice is: Don't *say* you want to help. *Do something!* Here are some practical ways you might bless others:

- During the holidays, invite a single parent and her children to join you for your holiday meal.
- Help your children to regularly weed out good clothes they no longer wear, box them up, and deliver them to Goodwill or to a needy family that could use them.
- Go as a family and volunteer to do yard work at a widow's house.
- Watch for new children who are attending your church. Intentionally invite them to your home and encourage your children to make them feel welcome.
- When going on a fun family outing, consider inviting other children from broken homes to join you.
- As a parent, look for ways to volunteer time as a Little League coach or a chaperone of one of your children's clubs or teams.
- As a family, sponsor a child through an organization such as Compassion International.
- Save your money as a family and go on a mission trip together. Perhaps use the money you would have spent at Christmas and, instead, jointly invest it in God's kingdom.

- As a family, come up with a creative way to encourage the staff at your church.
- Sponsor an international exchange student in your home.
- During your children's birthday parties, intentionally invite some less-popular children who are not normally invited to parties.
- As a family, go to a nursing home and spend time with the residents. Perhaps you can paint the ladies' nails or play a board game with some of the men. The elderly always enjoy having young children in the vicinity!
- As a family, pay to send some frazzled parents on a date while you watch their children.

There are innumerable ways for your family to bring joy to others. (For a helpful resource, see Tom and Kim Blackaby *The Family God Uses: Leaving a Legacy of Influence* [Birmingham, AL: New Hope Publishers, 2009].) Ask yourself: What could someone do for me that would be an enormous help and bring me joy? Then go do it for someone else! The key is to be others focused rather than self-focused. If you are on the lookout for someone you can help, it won't take you long to find them!

4. Teach Your Children to Be a Blessing

Unfortunately, people are born in a self- centered condition! We aren't naturally considerate of others. The best parents are those who teach their children to be thoughtful of others. The apostle Paul instructed us to "let no corrupt word proceed out of your mouth, but what is good for necessary edification, that it may impart grace to the hearers" (Eph. 4:29). You bless others when you learn to season your words with grace. (A helpful resource in this regard is Richard Blackaby, *Putting a Face on Grace: Living a Life Worth Passing On* [Colorado Springs: Multnomah Books, 2006].) Wise parents monitor their children's speech and instruct them in how to use their words to edify others.

Astute parents work hard to teach their children social skills so they are a delight to have around. Sadly, many parents neglect to instill people skills into their children, and so rather than leaving a blessing, these children leave a bad taste in people's mouths! We have both suffered the adverse effects of a poorly raised child. Richard once invited a family over to his house for dinner. The guest's four-year-old child systematically went around the house taking everything off the shelves and placing it on the floor. Rather than stopping her, the parents laughed merrily! We have both hosted families where the children were continually asking for more candy or sodas or toys. Instead of intervening so their children were not underfoot while we tried to get dinner ready, the parents relaxed in the living room, oblivious to what their urchins were doing in the kitchen. Of course, the reason many parents do not teach proper people skills to their children is because no one ever taught them. We know of one family who stopped by a pastor's home to say hello and then proceeded to stay for three days!

In Training

When their children were young, Richard and Lisa were determined to teach them how to properly conduct themselves when visiting in people's homes. An extensive list of Do's and Don'ts was established and rehearsed on every outing. The list included:

- Do not run, roughhouse, or throw objects in the house.
- Do not tell the hostess that you do not like the food she is serving.
- Do not tell the host/hostess that you want something. Tell your parents, and they will (tactfully) work it out.
- If you make a mess while playing, clean everything up before we leave.
- Do not complain that you are bored and want to go home.
- Do not touch anything that is breakable.
- Do not be loud.
- Do not interrupt when adults are talking.
- Be sure to say thank you if the host/hostess gives you anything.
- Do not set anything on fire.

There were additional rules, but you get the idea. Infractions of these commandments were punishable by dire and unmentionable torments. As Richard's family was driving to someone's house for dinner, Richard would rehearse the rules with his children. It became a game. "OK kids, give me one of the rules," Richard would bellow. "Be sure

NOT to pick up any toys at the end of the night!" one cherub would shout from the backseat of the car. "Shout a lot and run through the house!" another would chime in. "And what will happen if you do NOT follow all the rules?" Richard would always ask. "We'll be slowly lowered into molten lava!" a child would shout. "Exactly!" Richard would conclude. The kids would laugh and have fun, but the rules stuck, and they *were* followed. (Richard never did get to use that molten lava.) Over the years, Richard and his children were invited to numerous social settings. The children were generally a delight to have around. At one point, a prominent couple in Richard's church (who owned a very nice house) made a confession to him. They admitted that they generally did not invite families with small children to their home because it was too stressful. But they had learned they could trust Richard's tribe, and so they made an exception in their case. In teaching your children social skills, you will be opening doors for them for years to come. And by teaching them to be thoughtful of others, you are enabling them to be a blessing to the people who enter into the orbit of their lives.

5. Allow Your Children to Take the Lead

Your goal as parents is to teach your children to be thoughtful of others. The key is not to simply force them to do nice things for others but to help them become thoughtful people. If guests you invited to your house for dinner have allowed their children to trash out your play room, break your children's toys, terrorize your pet, and draw pictures on your living room wall with permanent markers, then it is small consolation when their Tasmanian devils are forced to say "Thank you" as they vacate the premises. You want to teach your children to truly be considerate of others.

Teaching your children to be thoughtful people entails allowing them to take the lead in ministering to others. Ask your children how they think your family could encourage children in your church who do not have a father in their life. Or perhaps brainstorm around the dinner table one day about how your family might bless the staff at your church. Mention a widow or immigrant family and ask for your children's suggestions on how your family could encourage them. Then let your children take the lead in making it happen. If your children are still young, some of their ideas may not be feasible or necessarily helpful. But if you teach them to think about others when they are young, they will accomplish an enormous amount of good over the course of their lifetime.

Tom's family regularly invited other families to join them for the holidays. Often these were single-parent families. Tom and Kim would invite their kids to suggest ways their family could bless their guests. As a result, Tom's children developed great people skills, and each of them became thoughtful of others.

As Richard's children grew older, they loved to hold parties at their home. They particularly loved to hold costume parties, even as teenagers. They'd not only invite their friends but also adults in their church with whom they felt close. The kids would spend days decorating and rearranging the house until it was prepared for the grand event. The kids took the lead in preparing the house and constructing costumes. It was a family project that brought much laughter and great memories to their church family. And having learned how to throw a party and bring joy to others, Richard's young adult children are still throwing parties and spreading joy today. Encourage your kids to think of ways to bless others. The people around them will be glad you did!

Conclusion

God intends for families to pass on a blessing to others. Never has the need for this been greater than it is today. Society is saturated with brokenness and dysfunction. Families are desperate for hope and laughter. We must help our children to experience blessing and to overcome their natural self-centeredness. If we do, then we will launch young adults into the world who make people and situations better wherever they go. That is God's intention for the family. God is prepared to help your family be a dispenser of blessing today.

Questions for Reflection/Discussion

1. What are some ways you have blessed your children? Do they *feel* blessed? What are some actions you could take in the future to truly bless each of your children? List the names of each child, and then ask God to give you specific actions and words to use for each one.

2. Are you presently modeling thoughtfulness and concern for others to your children? Do you want them to grow up to act just like you? What adjustments might you need to make in your own behavior toward others so your children receive a more godly, encouraging model?

3. Make a list of people in your church, neighborhood, or family to whom your family could minister in a practical way. Make plans to involve your family in reaching out to others in the immediate future.

4. Take time to evaluate your children's current social skills. Are there some areas you need to address? Pray and ask God to show you how to gently help your children learn how to relate to others in a godly, caring manner. It will be worth the effort!

5. Hold a family meeting and brainstorm about people your family could bless. Let your children express their thoughts and, as is appropriate for their age, let them take the lead in organizing your efforts. Let them make calls, check websites, wrap gifts, or be as hands-on as they can. Be sure to affirm them for investing their time in helping someone else.

CONCLUSION

Helping Your Family Experience God Today

Thank you for taking this journey together with us! We hope that by reading this book, you have discovered fresh, new ways your family can experience God. We suspect many of you already have amazing families from which we could learn much. Our prayer, however, is that as you worked through this material, God gave you a clear vision of how you could help your family enjoy a deeper walk with Him. We trust that you love your family far too much to leave them where they are when you know there is still more of God for them to experience!

For others, this book may have brought to the surface certain issues you know you must address in your parenting style or in the family dynamics of your home. The good news is that God's solution for your problems is not a guilt trip! He always focuses on how to make your life and family better, if only you will trust Him and do what He says. So if you are finishing this book and feeling like a schmuck because you are a "bad" parent, then you have missed the point! God may make you *dissatisfied*, but that is only so He can then make you *better*.

One practice we make use of when we read books or attend conferences is to look for "takeaways." Ask yourself, "What is it I will take away from having read this book?" If your attitudes and actions remain the same after reading this book, then it did you no good (Regardless of

233

how much you might *believe* or *agree with* what was in it!). Before you close this book and put it on a shelf, grab a pen and paper. Hopefully you marked up the book (whether it was a paper book or electronic), as you read it. It is always good to underline key truths and quotes. (Don't worry, your copy will still be a "collector's item" one day even if you mark it up!) Now go back through the book and jot down on a piece of paper the key insights and quotes you marked as you read. When you have written them on a separate piece of paper, scan the notes to see if there are specific actions God told you to take. List those and put dates beside them when you intend to follow through. Identify questions raised that you do not feel you have adequate answers for yet. List those items on another page and keep those handy to ponder and pray over until God gives you the answers you need. When you are done, take the paper with the summary of the book highlights and put it in the inside cover of the book. *Now* you can put it on the shelf (or give it to a friend). The next time you are working through these issues, you can pull the sheet of paper out of the book for handy reference. If you will "mine" each book you read for its truths, your life can be greatly enriched over time.

If you have not been studying this book with your spouse, consider giving it to your spouse to read. Plan a time to meet with your spouse (even if you have been working through this book in a small-group setting) to discuss what God impressed upon you as you read, and ask God to help you implement the changes He wants you to make. Parenting is a team effort, and it is always most successful when parents work together.

Consider conducting a family discussion time to talk about what God has shown you. Perhaps your home has not been God centered, but you want that to change. Be open with your children and let them hold you to your word.

In order to help you glean helpful insights from this book, let's review one last time the seven realities of how God works in your family:

Reality 1: God is always at work around your family.

Reality 2: God pursues a continuing love relationship with each family member that is real and personal.

Reality 3: God invites you and your family to become involved in His work.

Reality 4: God speaks by the Holy Spirit through the Bible, prayer, circumstances, and the church to reveal Himself, His purposes, and His ways.

Reality 5: God's invitation for you to join Him always leads you to a crisis of belief that requires faith and action.

Reality 6: You and your family must make major adjustments in your lives to join God in what He is doing.

Reality 7: You and your family come to know God by experience as you obey Him and He accomplishes His work through you.

Take a moment to reflect on each reality. God *is* at work in your family *right now*. What are you seeing? How are you improving your ability to recognize God's activity around you? Second, God is pursuing a love relationship with you and your children that is fresh, personal, and dynamic. Is that what your children witness when they watch you relate to God? How are you helping your children enjoy that quality of a relationship with Christ? Third, God will speak to you. The question is: do you recognize His voice? If you are uncomfortable with hearing from God, you might want to read *Hearing God's Voice* by Henry and Richard Blackaby. This is one area of your life you can't afford to miss! Fifth, God will invite you, as well as your family, to join Him in His work. Have you sensed lately that God is leading you to join Him in something He is doing in the life of one of your family members? If you have, how are you responding? Could it be that what looks like a problem or difficulty in your family might, in fact, be a divine invitation? Fourth, when almighty God invites you to join Him in His work, it will inevitably lead to a crisis of belief. Are you there right now? Are you presently facing a situation in your family that is calling for every ounce of faith you have? Trust God with your circumstances and *don't give up!* Sixth, joining God's work will inevitably require you to make adjustments in your life. Your present walk with God or your prayer life may need some adjusting. You may need to do things that make you uncomfortable. This is often the watershed moment for families. Are we prepared to do whatever it takes to join God in His work? God will not adjust to *us!* We must adjust to *Him!* Finally, we, and our family, will experience God, just as He intended, when we have obeyed Him. That is the goal: to experience God at home.

If you are going to truly have the family God intends for you, you will need to do two more things. First, you'll need to invite others to walk with you in your journey. The first person who must be on side with you is your spouse. Take time to pray together and to commit together to help your family experience God. Resolve to model in your own lives everything you want to see in your children. Strive together, to live a Christian life before your children that is so dynamic and attractive that they feel drawn to relate to Christ in the same way.

Be sure to ask others to pray for you and your family. Never allow pride to rob your family of the prayers and encouragement they could receive! Seek advice from others. Read books. Attend conferences. Meet with a prayer partner or another couple and regularly pray for your families. Gather as many friends and allies as you can to ensure that you experience victory in your home!

Finally, build accountability into your home life. If there was ever a road paved with good intentions, it is the one leading up to our house. We have all made numerous commitments to spend more time with our children, to be more patient, to pray more, to be less angry, to listen more, to encourage more, to focus on important matters. But inevitably life gets in the way! We get busy. We have a bad day (or month), and before we know it, we never followed through with what God invited us to do.

The best way to address this chronic dilemma is to surround our life and home with accountability. Begin by putting a date beside every commitment you make. Don't say, "I will try and spend more time with my family." Rather, say, "This Saturday, instead of watching the game on TV, I am taking my daughter on a date to the zoo." Accountability can also be established with a group of friends. If you are a father, meet with some men and share with them what God is calling you to do with your family. The next time you meet, be ready for them to ask you how it went. It is amazing how a little accountability can radically impact our follow-through with what God tells us to do!

As we come to the end of this book, we hope you feel encouraged, inspired, and motivated. God dearly loves your family, and He is working night and day to help it to become everything He intended when He created it. You can trust Him. So roll up your sleeves, ask God for strength and wisdom, and never, ever settle for less than having each member of your family experience God at home.

Final Blessing

May you, as parents, so live your lives before your children that they will desire to serve the God they see their parents serving.

May your home be a lighthouse in your neighborhood and community that reflects God's love, peace, hope, and righteousness for every person who enters its doors.

May your family be bonded together with God's love for one another, and may it support and encourage one another to wholeheartedly serve the Lord. May the hallways of your house resound with laughter.

May God's peace, blessings, and presence rest on your home so that all who encounter your family recognize His activity working in and through you and may it be evident that your family belongs, unquestionably to Him.

About the Authors

Richard Blackaby is the president of Blackaby Ministries International (www.blackaby.org) and lives in Atlanta, Georgia. He travels internationally speaking on spiritual leadership in the home, church, and marketplace as well as on spiritual awakening, experiencing God, and the Christian life. Richard regularly ministers to Christian CEOs and business leaders.

Richard has been married to Lisa for thirty years and has three amazing kids: Mike (college minister at First Baptist Church, Jonesboro in Atlanta and currently working on his PhD in Apologetics), Daniel (married and a MDiv student at Golden Gate Baptist Seminary), and Carrie (master's level student in writing and apologetics).

Richard earned a BA; MDiv; and PhD, as well as an honorary doctorate from Dallas Baptist University. He served as a senior pastor at Friendship Baptist Church in Winnipeg and as president of the Canadian Southern Baptist Seminary.

Richard's books include:

- *The Seasons of God: How the Shifting Patterns of Your Life Reveal His Purposes for You*
- *The Inspired Leader: 101 Biblical Reflections for Becoming a Person of Influence*
- *Unlimiting God: Increasing Your Capacity to Experience the Divine*
- *Putting a Face on Grace: Living a Life Worth Passing On*
- *Experiencing God: Revised Edition*
- *Spiritual Leadership: Moving People on to God's Agenda*
- *Experiencing God: Day by Day*

- *Hearing God's Voice*
- *Called to Be God's Leader: Lessons from the Life of Joshua*
- *Discovering God's Daily Agenda*
- *Fresh Encounter: God's Pattern for Spiritual Awakening*
- *God in the Marketplace: 45 Questions Fortune 500 Executives Ask about Faith, Life, and Business*
- *The Blackaby Study Bible*

You can follow Richard on: Twitter: @richardblackaby, Facebook: DrRichardBlackaby, or his blog at www.richardblackaby.com.

Tom Blackaby holds a BEd, MDiv, and DMin and has served as an associate pastor of music/youth/education in four churches in three countries and as senior pastor of North Sea Baptist Church in Stavanger, Norway, for seven years. He was the National Worship Consultant for the Canadian National Baptist Convention and currently serves as International Director for Blackaby Ministries International. Tom leads conferences/seminars and speaks in the areas of men's ministry, worship, prayer, experiencing God, revival, the God-centered family, and spiritual leadership. Tom has authored or coauthored:

- *The Man God Uses* (and *The Student God Uses* version)
- *Anointed to Be God's Servants: Lessons from the Life of Paul and His Companions*
- *The Blackaby Study Bible*
- *Encounters with God Daily Bible*
- *The Family God Uses* (trade book and workbook)
- *Experiencing God's Love in the Church*
- *The Commands of Christ*
- *Sammy Experiences God* (children's book)
- *7 Steps to Knowing and Doing the Will of God for Teens*
- *Experiencing God at Home*
- *Experiencing God at Home Family Devotional*

Tom and Kim have three great kids: Erin and Matt (currently attending college), and Conor (still at home near Vancouver, Canada).

EXPERIENCING GOD AT HOME

For the Whole Family!

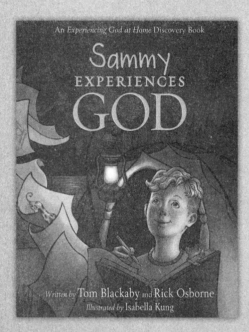

An *Experiencing God at Home* Discovery Book

Sammy EXPERIENCES GOD

Written by Tom Blackaby *and* Rick Osborne
Illustrated by Isabella Kung

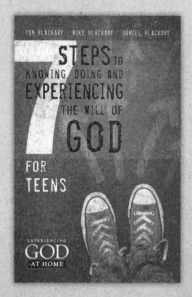

TOM BLACKABY   MIKE BLACKABY   DANIEL BLACKABY

7 STEPS TO KNOWING, DOING AND EXPERIENCING THE WILL OF GOD FOR TEENS

EXPERIENCING GOD AT HOME

A classically illustrated children's book about a little boy whose openhearted search for God is based on the world-renowned *Experiencing God* lessons from Henry Blackaby.

Based on the *Experiencing God* teachings of Henry Blackaby, *Seven Steps to Knowing and Doing the Will of God for Teens* provides students with relevant spiritual direction as they move toward adulthood.

Truly a modern classic, *Experiencing God* helps readers know and do God's will and is now revised and updated with seventy percent of its material newly written

Henry Blackaby's #1 selling book, the enduring classic *Experiencing God*, is presented here as a 365-day devotional reader featuring a new cover design, interior, and format.

The Story of Millions of Lives Touched

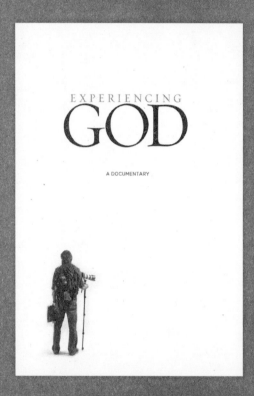

A documentary film team tracks one man's spiritual struggles and victories as he goes through the popular *Experiencing God* study; also includes interview with author Henry Blackaby about the teaching's worldwide influence.